MORE SPEECH

Dialogue Rights and Modern Liberty

MORE SPEECH
Dialogue Rights
and
Modern Liberty

PAUL CHEVIGNY

TEMPLE UNIVERSITY PRESS

PHILADELPHIA

Library of Congress Cataloging-in-Publication Data

Chevigny, Paul, 1935–
  More speech.

  Includes index.
  1. Freedom of speech.   2. Freedom of the press.
3. Human rights. I. Title.
K3253.C47 1988   342'.0853   87-10075
ISBN 0-87722-514-1 (alk. paper) 342.2853

Temple University Press, Philadelphia 19122
Copyright © 1988 by Temple University. All rights reserved
Published 1988
Printed in the United States of America

The paper used in this publication meets the minimum requirements of
American National Standard for Information Sciences—Permanence of
Paper for Printed Library Materials, ANSI Z39.48-1984

This book is
for
Katy and Blue—
between
thought and commission

If there be time to expose through discussion the falsehood and fallacies, to avert the evil by the processes of education, the remedy to be applied is more speech, not enforced silence. —Louis Brandeis

CONTENTS

Preface   xi

INTRODUCTION: Why Dialogue Rights?   1

PART I: The Framework for Freedom   21
Interlude: Language and Psychology 23

Chapter I: Interpretation and Freedom   27

Chapter II: Cognition and Rationality   53

PART II: Free Expression and the Obligation of the
    Government   73
*Interlude: Sketch of a Dialogical Freedom
    of Expression* 75

Chapter III: Three Irrational Government Decisions   81

Chapter IV: Political Protection for Free Expression   99

Chapter V: Access to the Dialogue   123

PART III: Procedural Rights and Individual Rights   149

   Interlude: Dialogues and Disputes 151

Chapter VI: Procedures for Disputes   155

CONCLUSION: The Place of Rights   173

Appendices   185

Notes   205

Index   241

PREFACE

Do rights really matter? Much of the time over the last twenty years, as I have worked on cases concerning freedom of expression and procedural due process, the rights have seemed mostly to matter to the lawyers. Clients on the left, especially, have been bemused by the seriousness with which we lawyers took the issues of principle in their cases.

They certainly never supposed that the judges would view the cases with the same solemnity as we did. I recall especially the astonishment of some members of a film company, whose footage of Vietnam had been seized by customs, when the court not only restored the film but criticized the customs officials as well.

Their amazement was only momentary. Rights of procedure and expression, they had found, might have some vitality, might not be mere rhetoric in this society. To people like the filmmakers, who, despite their calling, had little access to the mass media, those rights might even seem important as a way for them to remain in opposition. It was fortunate, they thought, that the judge accepted the lawyers' arguments, but that was no reason that they themselves ought to accept them.

I tried from time to time to persuade them and others like them of the independent importance of those rights. I

never got very far. The arguments for free expression traditional in Anglo-American politics, especially those rooted in individualism and free trade in ideas, were too easily dismissed as
peculiar to the society in which they have flourished. They
carry little or no weight with many socialists, for example.
The argument, identified with Alexander Meiklejohn, that
free discussion is essential for making decisions in a democracy,
does carry some weight with socialists, and I fell back on it
from time to time. But that argument did not work very well,
either. The usual answer given to it was that expression, like
democratic government itself, was bound to be skewed, to be
ineffective as an instrument for change, in a society where the
mass media are largely in the hands of the managers. Making
the Meiklejohn argument ran the risk that democracy would
be tossed out of the pantheon along with free expression.

If my clients were never persuaded by me, I was half-
persuaded by them. I certainly had no difficulty believing that
a society might reject the liberty of expression that is part of
my own tradition; it happens every day and is often justified
precisely in the way my friends justified it. What I was not
persuaded of, what I could not believe, was that society was
the better for it.

For years the problem remained at the back of my mind,
vexing but not pressing. It was not until the enforcement of
"human rights" became a major issue of international politics
that the questions in those old arguments seemed to demand a
rigorous solution, for reasons that will appear in the Introduction. This book, then, is an alternative explanation for the
right of free expression and some allied procedural rights. In
this preface, I set forth just a few words about the shape of that
explanation, about the problems the argument is designed to
answer.

A basic argument for liberty of expression is to be found
in the nature of language and of social problem-solving through
language and similar symbolic structures. Because meanings
are indeterminate, except in the context in which we understand them—and perhaps even there—we find our bearings in
the world of interpretation through a dialogue that is essential
to understanding. Contemporary critical theorists have used

the indeterminacy of language as one weapon to attack the received bases for rights; the next and more interesting question, it seems to me, is whether that indeterminacy does not itself imply a position favoring rights of expression and procedure (see the Interlude in Part II).

The indeterminacy gives rise to social limitations upon interpretation. We begin to understand a human situation through the schemas and stereotypes that we bring to it. We have disciplines, professions, areas of knowledge, through which we make decisions about the world; it is a great point of this book that we cannot make the decisions without those disciplines. While they are essential for action, they do not change the surrounding fact that interpretations may shift. The result of the tension of action and understanding is that we establish, we have no alternative to establishing, frameworks for decision, while we know that those decisions are never entirely closed to a different understanding. It is this tension that is at the cutting edge of the political argument for a right of free inquiry and free expression, as it is developed in Part II.

The argument has turned out to have some special characteristics. It is not "universalist" in the sense that it does not pretend to be applicable to every society. A society that does not understand "interpretation" in the modern sense used in this book might reject the arguments I have made here. The argument thus does not lock us into the embarrassing position of saying that it has to be applicable to a pre-modern society that does not view language in the way we now view it. The strength of the argument, on the other hand, is that it is applicable generally to modern societies, whether they purport to be liberal-capitalist or socialist, devoted more to the individual or to the collective good.

The argument has also linked procedural and free-expression rights in a way that is perhaps not as clear under other theories. All such rights are viewed as allied methods of problem solving. Procedure is a special, disciplined mode designed for disputes, while freedom of expression is a more generalized mode by which all the disciplines, including those of procedure, are criticized and "kept honest" by a constant test of their boundaries. The approach I have taken, using modern philosophy of language and psychology, thus ties them together as "dialogue rights" with a common origin.

My thanks are due to the New York University Law Center and the Filomen D'Agostino and Max E. Greenberg Research Fund of the New York University School of Law for generous support during the long period I have been writing this book. I thank also the Law and Philosophy Colloquium of NYU and the Law and Society Association for permitting me to present portions of the book and rigorously criticizing them. I thank the editors of the *New York University Law Review,* volumes 55 and 57, for giving me an opportunity to present early versions of some of these ideas as articles, and I thank Michael Martin for being interested enough to write a reply to one of them.

I thank the Cummington Community of the Arts for supplying me a place, many years ago, in which to start thinking about the issues in the book. I thank Helsinki Watch for giving me an opportunity to visit Poland and Ventana for the opportunity to visit Nicaragua.

Many people read all or part of the manuscript, and I have used their suggestions. Among them are Bruce Ackerman, Isaac Balbus, John Brigham, John Broughton, Bell Chevigny, Norman Dorsen, Thomas M. Franck, Judith Friedlander, Daniel Kaiser, Lewis Kornhauser, Bonnie Leadbeater, David Lichtenstein, Donald Moss, David Richards, Norman Rush, Marta Zahaykevich, and several anonymous readers. Many people pointed me toward research I might otherwise have missed, among them Max Azicri, Steven Brams, Mirjan Damaska, John Dore, Bernard Groffman, and Dennis Jennings. Robert Deyling and Eric Schwarz supplied invaluable research help in the later sections. Finally, I must particularly thank my editor, Jane Cullen, for her continuing faith in the book.

Introduction

WHY DIALOGUE

RIGHTS?

The institutional sources for human rights are many and obvious; they can be found, for example, in the U.N. Declaration of Human Rights and the Helsinki Accords of 1975, which encompass "economic and social" as well as "civil and political" rights. The civil-political rights, in turn, may be broadly divided into rights against intrusion on the person by the state, through arrest, torture or murder, and the freedoms of speech and conscience with which this book is chiefly concerned. Human rights nevertheless continue to be rights in search of a theory. It is notorious that there is, as Louis Henkin has put it, "no single, comprehensive theory of the relation of the individual to society"[1] underlying the documents and shared by the signatories.

After the Helsinki Accords, the United States tried to make compliance with the standards of human rights into an instrument of foreign policy. Although the Carter Doctrine included in its list of rights the "fulfillment of basic needs"[2] such as food and shelter, violations of these rights seldom form the basis of U.S. complaints. Accusations are more commonly made by United States administrations against governments, especially socialist governments, for their failures to honor the civil and political rights of individuals. Criticisms contained

3

in the State Department's *Country Reports on Human Rights Practices*, for example, are frequently based on notions of political rights rooted in the Anglo-American tradition.[3] The socialist governments, by the same token, tend to slant their arguments the opposite way, emphasizing the economic and social rights. While accusations of violations of human rights are viewed smugly, as a successful tool in the ideological war between east and west, such charges fail to be effective in part because there is no common ground of understanding. As the rhetoric of "human rights" has become an increasingly explosive part of world politics, their underlying rationale remains elusive and ambiguous.

The very concept of a universal right flies in the face of the cultural relativism that infuses the social sciences. When the U.N. Declaration on Human Rights was in draft almost forty years ago, the American Anthropological Association cautioned the drafting commission that "standards and values are relative to the culture from which they derive so that any attempt to formulate postulates that grow out of the beliefs or moral codes of one culture must to that extent detract from the applicability of any Declaration of Human Rights to mankind as a whole."[4] But even for those who believe that some generalizable basis for civil rights might exist, contemporary political practice offers little more than partisan biases. One western critic has said that "the current U.S.-sponsored drive for human rights necessarily reveals itself as a moralistic ideology that satisfies extra-moral needs." Another has accused the Freedom House reports, one of the chief sources for the State Department's *Country Reports on Human Rights Practices,* of "overbearing ethnocentrism."[5] For the freedoms of expression and conscience, at least, the reason for such criticisms is not far to seek.

The chief justifications for freedom of expression in modern political philosophy are perhaps four: an argument from the self-fulfillment of the individual, an argument from the autonomy of the individual, an argument based on "free trade in ideas," and an argument from the requirements of democracy.[6] Each of these is bound up with values precious to, if not actually peculiar to, Anglo-American liberalism.

The argument from the fulfillment of the individual

found its most notable expression in *On Liberty,* where J. S.
Mill argued that "individuality is the same thing with development, and that it is only the cultivation of individuality
which produces, or can produce, well-developed human beings." On this theory, freedom of conscience and expression is
but a special case of a broader liberty that in contemporary
parlance we might call a right of privacy; it is a right to use
one's talents, one's body, one's mind as one pleases. Such a
right depends upon another premise, that a mature individual
is the only appropriate agent to decide what is good for him,
because "he is the person most interested in his own well-
being. . . . The interest which society has in him individually
(except as to his conduct to others) is fractional, and altogether
indirect." Freedom of expression was thus loosely linked to
Mill's utilitarianism, although, as he said, "it must be utility
in the largest sense, grounded on the permanent interests of a
man as a progressive being."[7]

While the romantic notion of the individual constantly
developing his powers toward "originality,"[8] upon which Mill's
essay largely depends, still has its supporters,[9] Thomas Scanlon has shown that a political argument for freedom of expression may be rooted in a more spare notion of individualism.
He argued that a government conceived of as a contract among
"equal, autonomous and rational agents" must recognize the
right of freedom of expression; limitations on the dissemina-
tion of ideas would be equivalent to a decision by the state that
citizens are unable to make certain choices for themselves and
would thus be in conflict with the assumptions of autonomy
and rationality.[10] Scanlon's argument is a powerful one: Not
only does it rest upon fewer assumptions than Mill's theory,
but it reaches out beyond the self-regarding character of that
argument. The Scanlon view looks not merely within, to the
needs of the individual, but also outward, to the interests of an
aggregate of individuals as members of an audience as well as
persons who express themselves.

Liberal theory has sometimes expressed the interests of
the people as a whole in freedom of expression by a more vague
notion, that of "free trade in ideas." It received its classic formulation in a dissenting opinion of Justice Holmes to the effect that "the best test of truth is the power of thought to get

itself accepted in the competition of the market."[11] Without using the market metaphor in so many words, Mill made a similar argument about the advancement of "truth," concerning by turns what is putatively true, what is false, and what is partly true and false. If an opinion is true, Mill said, we will of course fall into error if we censor that opinion. If it is partly true and partly false, open discussion provides an opportunity to specify what part of it is true.

In the most original part of the argument, Mill finally said that expression of a false opinion should be permitted, because without discussion the reason for the truth of the contrary true opinion will be lost. "The fact . . . is," Mill wrote, "that not only the grounds of the opinion are forgotten in the absence of discussion, but too often the meaning of the opinion itself. The words which convey it cease to suggest ideas, or suggest only a small portion of those they were originally employed to communicate."[12] Those phrases are prophetic for this book, to which the elucidation and application of "meanings," in the sense of interpretations, is above all the key. The resources of language philosophy available to Mill did not, as we shall see, lead him to develop the implications of the phrase but instead to fall back upon the search for "truth." In fact, truth in any but a very special subjective sense matters not at all to most of Mill's argument. Quite the contrary. It is precisely because an individual understands better than anyone else what is good for her that she ought to be let alone to express herself and develop as she pleases. For the sake of argument, Mill set aside for the moment his view that there is for the most part no objective "truth" for matters of opinion, but only a truth that contributes to the development of the individual.

In making his three-step argument, Mill sidestepped a chief problem with the theory of the "marketplace of ideas." Markets, after all, are not usually expected to trade things except upon the basis of preferences; no one supposes that the market relations between the prices of different commodities represents or could represent anything "true" except (perhaps) a true price relationship. The notion of a "marketplace" test for truth, then, is a misnomer: If the exchange of ideas is expected to lead to some objective "truth," then it is not a marketplace, and if in fact it is a marketplace, then it does not test for truth but rather for acceptability. The marketplace of ideas is a popularity contest, in which the choices are made easier because ideas do not actually cost anything (except sometimes the effort of understanding); the most popular idea is just as cheap (or just as expensive) as the most unpopular.

Any argument for free expression that depends upon the ascertainment of truth has become increasingly suspect since the time of Mill, or even Holmes, for that matter.[13] That same cultural relativism that has led us to doubt the existence of such a thing as a "universal right" has made us doubt the existence of a universal test of truth for policy decisions. Even in the natural sciences, which have lasted a little longer than values as a touchstone of what is "objective," facts and theories are no longer clearly distinguishable, and what is fact may depend upon the theory in which it is cast.

Yet the metaphor of the market as a test of truth retains its ideological power, perhaps just because it conceals the painful question of how there can be "truth," for values or for anything else, in a society of individuals of the sort imagined by Mill. At the same time, the metaphor expresses the link, historical and emotional, if not logical, between economic and political individualism. Just as in the liberal economic world, it is thought that choices made by an individual will in the long run suit the general interest if he makes his decisions to suit his selfish interest, so also in the liberal world of belief, independent choice is viewed as necessary to social progress.[14]

Some liberals in search of a generalizable theory for freedom of expression have been offended by the bald ideology of "free trade in ideas." In *Free Speech and Its Relation to Self-Government*, Alexander Meiklejohn attacked the famous formulation in Holmes' dissent as an example of the "competitive individualism" that for him was the bane of American government and education. He proposed to replace it with a theory in which free expression was justified as essential to the decision-making process of a democratic government, conceived along the lines of a participatory town meeting. Meiklejohn said:

> The welfare of the community requires that those who decide issues shall understand them. . . . And this, in

turn, requires that so far as time allows, all facts and interests relevant to the problem shall be fully and fairly presented to the meeting. Both facts and interests must be given in such a way that all the alternative lines of action can be wisely measured in relation to one another. As the self-governing community seeks, by the method of voting, to gain wisdom in action, it can find it only in the minds of its individual citizens. If they fail, it fails. That is why freedom of discussion for those minds may not be abridged.[15]

This simple formulation has been enormously influential because it accounts for the needs of listeners as well as of speakers and avoids the obscurities of "free trade in ideas." Yet it is curiously narrow in application, being limited, as Meiklejohn thought, to societies run by "self-government by universal suffrage" and to overtly "political" opinions upon public issues as distinguished from private opinions about private interests.[16]

Critics who subscribe to justifications rooted in individualism for freedom of expression have not failed to point out the shortcomings of the Meiklejohn theory. Scanlon, for example, branded Meiklejohn's ideas "artificial," because they are linked to "particular political institutions." At the same time he saw nothing artificial in the individualism underlying his own theory. He said, for example, that Mill's theory "relies only on general moral grounds and is independent of the features of any particular laws or institutions." For Scanlon, "a legitimate government is one whose authority citizens can recognize while still regarding themselves as equal, autonomous, rational agents,"[17] even if that government is not of the precise sort envisioned by Meiklejohn. Scanlon, like most of us in the Anglo-American tradition of political thought, swims in individualism as a fish swims in water.

The assumptions of political individualism are, nevertheless, viewed by many as "artificial." It is sometimes argued, for example, that they are not consistent. Michael Sandel has pointed out that arguments concerning the social contract among individuals, similar to those that Scanlon relies upon, are in fact incoherent unless some assumptions are made about social aims common to all the individuals.[18] As a practical matter, moreover, and apart from its own theoretical difficulties, individualism, together with free trade in ideas and town-meeting democracy, is foreign to much of the world.

The anthropologists who issued their cautionary words to the United Nations in 1947 no doubt meant to speak for the multitudes of tribal and pre-modern peoples for whom the values underlying western freedom of expression must be exotic if not incomprehensible. More important for our purposes, many modern socialist states, although they have not found those values incomprehensible, have nevertheless rejected them. Theoreticians of the Soviet state have subscribed to a radical cultural relativism; for them, values "reflect the moral consciousness and material living conditions of a particular society in a specific historical context."[19] Values and the laws that embody them serve the interests of the dominant class. Thus the values of individualism, free trade, and town-meeting democracy serve the interests of the dominant class in bourgeois society just as the collective values of economic equality and freedom from exploitation are said to serve the interests of the dominant class in a proletarian society. In either case, it is the collective needs of the class that are served; although "individualism" makes a pretense of serving the interests of the individual, in a society of very unequal economic powers it must serve the interests of the powerful. In socialist society, the pretense is abandoned, and values must openly serve the collective interests of the class. All rights are derived from collective needs and cannot conflict with them, because there is no source of morality except the general good; rights are not conceived as rights as against the state and the rest of society, but rather as rights protected by and emanating from the state and society.[20]

These are no "underground" arguments; they are perfectly explicit both in statute and bureaucratic practice. Constitutions in authoritarian socialist states restrict individual rights, including the right to freedom of expression, to actions that are supposed to be in harmony with the collective good. The Cuban Constitution of 1977, for example, provides that "none of the freedoms which are recognised for citizens can be exercised contrary . . . to the existence and objectives of the socialist state, or contrary to the decision of the Cuban people to build socialism and communism," and other socialist constitutions commonly read to a similar effect.[21] Yuri Andropov, while he was still head of the KGB, was quoted in *Isvestia*:

> Any citizen of the Soviet Union whose interests coincide with the interests of society feels the entire scope of our democratic freedoms. It is another matter if these interests in certain instances do not coincide in some particular cases. Here we say straightforwardly that priority must be given to the interests of all of society.[22]

Lesser officials in socialist states both within and outside the Soviet camp rely on such values as justification for administrative actions; to pick just one of perhaps hundreds of examples, in 1983 a party official in Yugoslavia attacked the local press for their reporting on economic problems, saying, "If some alleged Marxists, in interpreting freedom of creativity, stoop to the bourgeois concept of false individual freedom, then good riddance to them."[23]

Western Marxists often attack this "sovietized" view of the status of the legal system, and of the place of rights within it, as a "vulgar Marxism" that draws an excessively mechanistic relation between culture and the world of production, failing to take account of the dialectical relation by which each influences the other.[24] After all that criticism, however, many western Marxists reach conclusions about questions of legal rights that are not widely different from those of the "official" Marxist-Leninist governments. They agree that legal rights are relative to the society in which they are found, that they are largely ideological instruments of legitimation for a system of domination, and that the entire category of "individual rights" as against the state is an expression of the alienated relation between mankind and the world.[25] Some socialists argue vigorously for the importance of individual rights,[26] of course, as they have always done, but the fact is that they do not have very strong theoretical support for their arguments, at least in the Marxist tradition. When the late Edward Sparer, a democratic socialist, pleaded with a group of radical legal scholars at the Conference on Critical Legal Studies to share his faith that the right to dissent is not merely part of the bourgeois tradition, but is really "inalienable," he was not able to persuade many, I believe, who were not already with him. His sad account of the repression of rights by governments and parties of the left could not take the place of a theoretical account of the right to individual dissent outside the liberal tradition. His listeners found only a vague aspiration in Sparer's brave claim "that individual autonomy and community are not contradictions at all; rather, they shape and give meaning and richness to each other."[27]

Authoritarian Marxist ideas about the place of rights in a socialist world, so far from being "vulgar," are consistent with at least one strain in the Marxist tradition. I think it is tolerably clear that Marx himself believed that, in a society without class conflicts, political rights would be meaningless nuisances, that people would agree "on all subjects which could possibly come before a parliament." While in some of his writings he was concerned with the development of the autonomous individual, he contrived also to believe in a future society of "total harmony."[28] It is this vein of communitarian romanticism, combined with the conviction that individual rights are peculiar to the bourgeois tradition, that has shaped the Marxist view of law, both in its official, governmental version and in its theoretical version. It has, of course, colored the official view that individual rights must always be subordinated to collective needs; more than that, it has colored the view of critical Marxists that while it is necessary as a matter of tactics to fight for rights in a liberal society, or in a failed or fraudulent socialist society like the Soviet Union, it is nevertheless not clear that the same sort of rights would be necessary in a truly socialist or communitarian society.

There is a fundamental disagreement, then, between the Anglo-American liberal tradition and the Marxist-Leninist tradition concerning the importance of freedom of expression. If there is in fact a theory for the right to dissent that is generalizable between governments rooted in each of those traditions, it is not easy to state what it is; in its absence, accusations made by one side against the other are like ships that pass in the night. The political philosophies that infuse and render legitimate the acts of officials toward individuals who dissent are so totally different that accusations of violations of human rights made by one society against the other often seem merely hypocritical.

Underdeveloped nations, whether or not they subscribe to the ideology of Marxism-Leninism, frequently make a similar judgment that the collective good is prior to individual needs. The task of nation-building, it is said, must come before the individual. African leaders such as Julius Nyerere of Tanzania and Kenneth Kaunda of Zambia have made the point repeatedly; Nyerere, at the opening of the university campus, said:

> Freedom of speech, freedom of movement and association, are valuable things which we want to secure for all our people. But at the same time we must secure, urgently, freedom from hunger, and from ignorance and disease, for everyone. Can we allow the abuse of one freedom to sabotage our national search for another freedom?[29]

It is for reasons such as these that some critics of the United States' approach to human rights have been able to conclude, in the words of Adamantia Pollis and Peter Schwab, that "the Western conception of human rights is not only inapplicable to Third World countries or to socialist states, but also to some states that profess to adhere to democratic precepts and to states that are considered part of the West."[30]

But not quite. The Soviet Union and similar socialist countries show more respect for individual liberties than their philosophy and traditions would seem to require. They did sign the U.N. Declaration and the Helsinki Accords; they are ill at ease in their philosophy that, in a conflict between collective needs and individual rights, collective needs must prevail. Is there something missing, or are the individual rights written into socialist constitutions and international human rights agreements simply concessions to political expediency? If there is something missing, it must be an argument for liberty of dissent that is different from the arguments from individualism, free trade in ideas, or the needs of town-meeting democracy. The question for this book is whether a more nearly generalizable argument for freedom of expression and allied rights can be made than the arguments that prevail in the Anglo-American legal tradition.

I shall argue that there can be no understanding, no rational decision-making, without open discussion. Society needs the discussion for the same reasons the individual does, and needs to devise means to pull people into the discussion in order to find new contexts and new answers for problems. While we do ordinarily adopt limited conceptual frameworks for our thinking to ensure that we will be able to reach a decision, nevertheless the notion that the collective good can be understood without argument that has no predictable limits, made in forums open to society, seems to me to make no sense either as philosophy or psychology, While these views can be squared with much of Marxism, there will remain a residual conflict. The romantic-utopian hope, in whatever guise, however attenuated or watered down, that decisions can be made without major dissension that must be settled by argument, fails to grasp the reality of language and thought. Thus it seems to me that the unease of authoritarian socialist bureaucrats shows a good instinct. Even if their recognition of the scope of individual rights is a result only of political expediency, it is a wise expediency, rooted in real needs.

Views such as mine are not entirely foreign to the liberal tradition. Thomas Emerson, for example, offered as one of several summary justifications for freedom of expression that "suppression of discussion makes a rational judgment impossible."[31] And more recently, Bruce Ackerman has adopted a carefully circumscribed discussion that he calls "neutral dialogue" as a basic tenet of his *Social Justice in the Liberal State*.[32] Our individualist tradition in political rights, nevertheless, has largely slighted the social nature of thinking and knowledge. Any strong individualism, even if it is only "methodological"—assumed for the purpose of deciding questions of social choice—tends to ignore the fact that all our understandings, all our decisions, are rooted in a dialogue and even a personal history shared with others in society.

At the root of my conclusions is an inquiry into the nature of communication by language and related methods of solving problems. The first two chapters, and thus the first section of the book, are consumed by that investigation, pursued first through philosophy of language and then through cognitive psychology.

Modern philosophy of language, as I see it, shows that sentences can be interpreted only in context and through use. Knowledge, of both the physical and social worlds, is bound up with and can be understood and shared only through language. Understanding, even when it is most in dissent from the views of others, is anchored in the common consciousness established by language. It can be found only through a dialogue, a term I use in this book in its most general sense to include face-to-face discussions and interpretations of texts and other artifacts, extending even to one's own personal work as it is recorded from past action and subjected to criticism.

The second chapter shows that contemporary cognitive and allied psychology has reached similar conclusions concerning the way people think and solve problems. We search for the understanding of problems through language and through means that are organized on the analogy of language. We attempt to apply to new situations familiar schemas, altering them as we find that they do not fit. As in the case of language, the search for the "fit" of proposed solutions, and for alternative solutions, is made through a dialogue, sometimes between people, and sometimes between the thinker himself, his past verbal proposals, and his perceptions of the problem.

Language, then, under both the philosophical and cognitive-psychological views, cannot be trusted to fit the world; there is no way to predict what "best" solutions to problems will be found, or how to find them, or how to decide that they are going to be appropriate. Although we do, of course, find interpretations of language and other social actions, as well as solutions to problems, that seem to us adequate in the light of arguments, we have no reliable "method"—even though we often act as though we have one—for finding them. The rational approach to interpretation, I shall argue, is the one that supplies us with new arguments. Accordingly, in Chapter II I introduce a concept of the "modern rational" approach to problems, which I define not as the "formally rational," in the familiar sense of the ability to draw logical conclusions from premises, but rather as the ability to entertain alternatives, to take a fresh point of view. Although this concept does exclude a magical approach to language, I do not believe that it prescribes any economic or political framework for a society that accepts it.

Part I, then, is dedicated to the personal and social need for free expression and inquiry. Part II will be chiefly devoted to demonstrating the government's obligation, using the theories of the first part, to recognize such freedoms. Here I argue that a modern government that fails to encourage discussion will fail to take a "rational" approach to problems and will systematically tend to overlook optimum solutions. Those failures will undermine the government's authority among citizens who understand, even in a vague way, the nature of a rational approach to problems. In Chapter III I describe three case studies of irrational government decisions made in Poland, Cuba, and the United States, together with their consequences for those governments. With these I seek to illustrate, as concretely as possible, the practical operation of the philosophical and psychological theories described in the first section by showing the effects on policy and in turn on the authority of the government of the failure or refusal to take a modern rational approach to decision-making through the open consideration of alternatives. In the following chapter, which sets forth the central theoretical argument of the second section, I draw upon those and other examples to explain the theory of the government's obligation, as well as elements of the legal structure of freedom of expression when it is based on dialogue. Chapter V grapples with what I see as the most difficult practical problem of the dialogical theory of freedom, namely access to such means of expression as the media. The chapter discusses access to information controlled by the government, as well as the much more complex issues surrounding affirmative state aid to expression.

As I was engaged in developing the dialogical approach to freedom of expression, I saw that the same philosophical and psychological views could be used to illuminate some procedural rights commonly recognized in systems of dispute resolution. In Chapter VI I show that a disputant's right to notice of the nature of a claim against him, together with his right to answer the claim through a hearing, and his rights, at least under Anglo-American law, to question the witnesses against him are all linked, by the theory used in this book, to the right of free expression. These are all "rights of method," rooted in the need to solve problems. In the final chapter, I confront the issue of the relation between the sort of "rights" described in this book, with their social orientation, and the more traditional individual rights. Because the human individual is the only language-user, the only real problem-solver, I show that dialogically based rights must value the individual, invest her with rights, quite as much as conventional liberal theories, but for different reasons and with a different emphasis.

Although this book argues that dialogue rights are "human" rights, in the sense that they grow out of characteristics that are peculiarly human, I have not tried to construct an all-encompassing theory of human rights. The argument here does not concern other human rights set forth in international agreements, such as the right to be free of torture or the broad "economic" rights, except indirectly, insofar as a false conflict is suggested between economic and dialogical rights, or insofar as torture may be become politically impossible in a society with open discussion. And of course the argument concerns only what are usually called "civil" rights—rights of the individual as against the state—as distinguished from rights such as property rights that may be enforced against other private persons.

The use of the term "human rights" raises the question whether the dialogical theory of rights should properly be classed as a theory of natural rights. While I do think that acceptance of these rights is very nearly inescapable for a system that accepts the underlying premises of modern rationality (as I use the term), I find the natural rights characterization misleading. Although the dialogic rights are held by individuals as well as groups, they grow out of social relations; they are instrumental, in the very broad sense that they are necessary to rational decision-making under modern conditions. Most important, I do not argue that these rights are "universal," in the sense that every society, however primitive it may be, is obliged to recognize them. It is possible for a government to refuse these rights, if for some reason it is willing to pay the price; some societies may be governed by magic, for example, and may not accept modern ideas about language. For them, the philosophy underlying these rights has no validity. More commonly, a government may be so lacking in legitimacy that it cannot withstand any rational decision-making; then it will simply pay the price—and will be in constant danger of a coup or revolution. Finally, a government freshly created by revolution, and still in need of consolidating its legitimacy, may make a judgment that it has to limit dissent in order to begin a minimal program against its enemies, and it may make that judgment the more readily when it has powerful outside powers trying to undermine it. While we may find that understandable, in a few cases, it does not change the fact that the trade-off in errors of judgment and lost legitimacy is enormous, and becomes bigger as the government gets better established. These issues will be more fully explored in Part II.

It may seem that the argument from the nature of language and thinking does not create a very strong obligation on governments to accept the right of free expression and other dialogic rights. An argument from individualism may appear more "natural" to us, in the sense that, once the sovereignty of the individual is accepted, the right of self-expression has a familiar ground; but as the history of the ideological conflict with the socialist world has shown, the rejection of individual sovereignty sweeps the argument away. The power of any political argument depends on the persuasiveness of the premise; the premises of this argument are not made less persuasive merely by the fact that they are less familiar.

The arguments made in this book are broadly "consequentialist" in the sense that they are intended to show that systematic limits on dialogue have effects on understanding, on problem-solving, and on the legitimacy of the government. They bear a family resemblance, then, to the arguments of Meiklejohn, which draw a connection between democracy and individual political expression, and the arguments of J. S. Mill, which draw a connection between individual expression and the development of the person as well as the elaboration of "truth." The arguments here, however, are conceived along different lines even when they are compatible with Meiklejohn or Mill. They are concerned not with truth but with problem-solving and the social action that goes with it;[33] they are concerned less with individual development than with understanding as an action both social and idiosyncratic; they are concerned less with democracy as a particular form of government than with the general sources of legitimacy for modern governments. Freedom, as conceived here, serves social as well as individual needs because it is rooted in the social nature of language.

This point suggests a further question: To whom is the argument in this book directed? Those who accept individualism as a premise for government have a ready-made basis for freedom of expression and do not need another. Surely I do not expect, on the other hand, to persuade the repressive official to dismiss the censor and write a writ of habeas corpus for the prisoners of conscience? I have no such hope, of course; I want to persuade those who are doubtful that there is any really strong ground, outside the accepted arguments of our political system, for criticizing the repressive official; those who think that limiting dissent can contribute to economic or cultural development; those who think that rights are peculiar to alienated, bourgeois society, or are not useful where there is a strong sense of community. I think it is essential, in short, to answer the question whether the right to dissent has any more generalizable basis than the warrant of Anglo-American tradition. Finally, it seems to me that the philosophical and psychological bases for the arguments I make are often at work, in a half-conscious way, affecting decisions concerning the applications of rights under the First Amendment even though they are not relied on explicitly. For lawyers familiar with the Anglo-American tradition of political rights, my arguments should suggest some fresh solutions and approaches to old problems.

That last sentence describes, among other people, the author. This book is, in a way, written for the author as he was—when I first asked the question whether an argument for free expression could be made independent of the Anglo-American legal tradition. It is the book that I would have hoped to find if this book had existed before I started to think about writing it. The arguments are built from the ground up; they assume no prior knowledge, except, of course, of the language itself.* From time to time throughout the book I have introduced Interludes to elaborate or orient the argument. Although I hope that philosophers and psychologists will be persuaded by the book, it is written in a manner and style intended to be able to persuade the general reader. I hope that lawyers and others who fancy themselves impatient with speculation will not find it impenetrable, or in fact anything other than convincing.

*The argument in Chapter II depends in part on the conclusions of Chapter I; the connection is expanded in Appendix II.

PART I

The
Framework
for
Freedom

Interlude

Language and Psychology

When we think about the practical effects of free discussion, we typically imagine some grand question of policy. We might recall, for example, the decision early in the administration of John F. Kennedy to invade Cuba (as I shall do at some length in Chapter III), and ask whether less secrecy and more open inquiry might have led to a different outcome. I shall be concerned in this book with that sort of question; in the second section, in fact, I show how open criticism is essential to rational policy decisions. But it is a central theme of this book that "policy" knowledge cannot be separated from other sorts of knowledge, that rational decision-making of a basically similar sort is needed for any sort of understanding, whether linguistic, scientific, political, or artistic.

Since the two chapters that follow this interlude are concerned with that theme, they may seem at first somewhat far afield from the central discussion, given in later chapters, concerning liberty of expression. They do not make a fully developed political argument, but rather lay the groundwork, in as basic a way as I can envision it, for such an argument. They show the need for free inquiry, the space where free expression fits, through philosophy of language and then through psychology, particularly through the aspects of cognitive psychology that try to explain how humans solve problems.

23

The first chapter, concerned with philosophy of language and its relation to knowledge in the social and natural sciences, ultimately implies one central conclusion. In its most tendentious form, the conclusion is that there is no speech worthy of the name that is not free speech. That proposition depends upon the view, widely accepted in modern philosophy, that the understanding of sentences in a language springs from the understanding of other parts of the language, which point round to still other meanings and groups of meanings in the language. Such a view is commonplace; it acquires a cutting edge again only when we say, as I do in the next chapter, that the interdependency of interpretations is unavoidable and endless except insofar as we choose to set an end to it in order, for example, to reach a particular sort of decision. I shall argue on the one hand that we have to make such choices in order to say that we have understood, while on the other hand we have to leave them open to further interpretation.

In showing why this is so, I draw upon the Anglo-American tradition of ordinary language philosophy and the continental tradition of critical hermeneutics. I am not mining these traditions for any sort of "authority," in the way that a lawyer relies on precedents; I don't expect anyone to be persuaded merely by the presence of venerable names and doctrines. These are simply the tools by which I make an argument that is, I hope, acceptable on its own terms; the traditions supply us with guideposts of the familiar along the way. The point, in short, is not to invoke philosophy but to demonstrate persuasively that inquiry by dialogic means is indispensable to whatever understanding we think we have. "Speech" presupposes discussion such that the speaker may have to explain his meaning or that others may explain it for him.

This approach to understanding language implies that there should be a psychology, a view of the mind, consistent with the indeterminacy of linguistic interpretation. And indeed a large body of research in cognitive psychology and allied fields implies a habit of mind, not only for language but for the solution of problems generally, that depends on a dialogue with other minds. It is a habit of joint communicative action acquired during infancy and continued in later life. (The reasons I have relied on cognitive psychology rather than on some more positivist school are explained in Appendix II.)

Yet there continues to run even through cognitive psychological research the thread of a longing for an invariant "rational method" for the solution of problems. It appears notably in Jean Piaget's program of levels of cognitive development, culminating in the "formally rational" and in Lawrence Kohlberg's similar scheme of levels of moral development. I have spent a good part of the second chapter picking out that thread, because in the failure of that search for the "formally rational" lies one of the keys to the need for free expression and inquiry.

In that search the psychologists have shared a general human longing for a method, a longing rooted in the recognition that, without some reliable way into the problems of the social and linguistic world, it is difficult to imagine being able to think at all. Thus we fall back on habitual heuristics at least for the beginning of understanding, treating them as though they were reliable. Because the knowledge we draw on for the solution of problems, as well as the methods of solution themselves, are dependent on language and symbolic structures similar to language, however, it is essential that we recognize that our methods, like our interpretations of language, are interdependent and uncertain. In this is the source of the concept of "modern rationality" mentioned in the Introduction, defined loosely as the ability to entertain alternatives, to take a fresh point of view.

The attitude toward language and the psychology of problem-solving that emerges from the first two chapters is one that refuses to make a choice between the individual and the collective, the private and the public. Dialogue is inevitable for understanding because the act of interpretation is both idiosyncratic and at the same time rooted in public artifacts such as language. One of the purposes of the book is to show that this tension, like the tension between choosing a method and recognizing that the method is open to criticism, supplies some of the energy with which we govern our lives and hope to govern our societies.

Chapter I

INTERPRETATION AND FREEDOM

Language is public, a social creation. Wittgenstein hammered home the impossibility of a private language when he wrote:

> It is not possible that there should have been only one occasion on which a report was made, an order given, or understood; and so on.—To obey a rule, to make a report, to play a game of chess are *customs* (uses, institutions). . . .
>
> And hence also "obeying a rule" is a practice. And to *think* one is obeying a rule is not to obey a rule. Hence it is not possible to obey a rule "privately": otherwise thinking one was obeying a rule would be the same thing as obeying it.[1]

There are, of course, occasions when we want to speak in code, to restrict entry to our discourse. But such codes are parasitic on natural language; there is always a way, more or less arbitrary, for translating back into the natural language. It is just because the language is public that the need for the code can arise.

Even if it were possible to conceive of a private language, such a thing would have no place in our discussion in this book of freedom of expression because it is just the public aspects of expression with which rights are concerned. Only utterances "expressed"—"pushed out"—into the world, however idiosyncratic or obscure their form, can give rise to an issue of rights. There is no dispute with the government, no censorship, no desire to suppress, except in the case of public language. A private diary, written in a natural language or translated from a private code, if it is seized by the government and charged with a seditious purpose, raises a question of rights only because it is the putative public aspect of the diary, its effect on others, that provokes the charge of sedition. Even the notion "freedom of conscience" is concerned with the purely private conscience only insofar as it is betrayed to the world by speech or action.

The question of the right to speak, furthermore, emphasizes the division between our knowledge insofar as it is social, shared with others, and such private knowledge as we think we have by direct observation of the world. We may think we are certain that our perceptions are true, and the certainty may serve to anchor some meanings for us; we may be sure, for example, that we never say "shiny" except of something that is seen to be shiny. But that certainty of private perception (if that is what it is) is not at the center of gravity of the problem of language and its philosophical implications, which cluster instead around the communication of meanings in sentences to others or to ourselves at a later time.

Although I shall talk from time to time, as I have in the previous sentence, about the philosophical problem of "meaning," that little word is too opaque for our purposes in most cases. "Meaning" has too many meanings (or senses, if you prefer); some think it refers only to the unvarying denotations of a word, while others use it, as I do, to include the notion of an interpretation of a phrase or a sentence in context. The important meanings for the present project are intersubjective, called variously by such names as interpretation, translation or understanding. The question for this book is: Is there something special about the understanding of language, and other forms of symbolic expression that resemble language, that gives rise to the need for rights to protect the free expression of that understanding?

This chapter asks what light the philosophy of language can shed on that question. I shall begin by describing a "common sense" notion of understanding—a theory that sentences copy or correspond to the world—for the purpose of showing that such a notion leads to indeterminacies and incoherences from which philosophy has found no escape.

Correspondence Theories and Their Problems

The notion that words stand for things, and that sentences describe the relations of things, seems, at first glance, to be a simple approach to meaning. Locke remarked that speakers commonly act "as if the name carried with it the knowledge of the species or the essence of it." Locke thought that we could have clear ideas of things, independent of our words for them, and that an accurate language ought to have a "double conformity," both to things and to our ideas of them. It was the failure of the conformity, the "cheat of words," that interfered with the clarity of our ideas.[2] The cheat of words is a perennial difficulty in every copy or correspondence theory; much of language appears designed at least to distract from, if not actually to mislead about, reality.

The common sense theory, nevertheless, seems to offer a glimpse of what we feel language "ought" to do, even if it does not do it. At the beginning of this century, language philosophers were pursuing that intuition, trying to define a logical language, a clarified version of natural language, that could be used to describe the physical world. Logic, it was thought, would trace the design of the world, and the form of sentences would be the same as the form of events in the world. Bertrand Russell expressed with his usual elegance the faith he shared at the time with Wittgenstein: "Logic, I should maintain, must no more admit a unicorn than zoology can; for logic is concerned with the real world just as truly as zoology, though with its more abstract and general features."[3] As events turned out, it was only the effort to make the copy theory thoroughly formal, as Russell and Wittgenstein attempted to do, that forced its problems to the surface.

In his *Tractatus Logico-Philosophicus* Wittgenstein sketched a version of the logical language implied by a copy theory limited to sentences that described the observable world. A statement in that language contained components that were testable by the senses, assertions about facts in the world. It might read "a man is walking down the stairs." That statement has a "sense" in the parlance used by Wittgenstein; it sets forth a thought that is a possible picture of the world. But it may in fact be false; the man may prove to be my reflection in a mirror hanging in the stairway. While the truth and the sense of sentences were different, then, sentences that were not cast in the form of pictures of the world did not "make sense" for philosophy. Thus the possibilities of the language were just the possibilities of the world. Nothing either impossible or illogical could be said, either in the language or about the world.

The truth or falsity of a sensible proposition was to be shown by treating the proposition like a model, by simply laying it against the world. But, Wittgenstein said, the proposition only "shows" its meaning; there is no explanation of the relation between the verbal model and reality other than the observed correspondence, just as there is no explanation for the logic of the sentence. They are the givens beyond which philosophy cannot pass:

> Propositions cannot represent logical form: it is mirrored in them.
> What finds its reflection in language, language cannot represent.
> What expresses *itself* in language, *we* cannot express by means of language.
> Propositions *show* the logical form of reality. They display it. . . .
> What *can* be shown, *cannot* be said.[4]

Wittgenstein thought that the narrow limits set for philosophy by the *Tractatus* were so much the worse for philosophy; it was necessary, he said, to pass beyond these limits to matters that could not be "spoken about" in philosophical language.[5] What he saw as limitations, however, the philosophers of logical empiricism (or logical positivism, as it is often called) seized upon as virtues. If language really did mirror the physical world, then its limits would indeed be the limits of the possible states of affairs in the world. That view of natural language, they thought, would give them command over meanings, a way of determining whether a sentence expressed a thought about the world or was instead one of the cheats of words. To be meaningful, a sentence would have to say something about sense experience or serve to elucidate other meaningful sentences; in the latter case, the sentence was said to be "analytic," to say something that was true as a matter of logic.

For the empirically verifiable (or "synthetic") class of sentences, the *Tractatus* contained the seed of a problem: how to define the correspondence that was to constitute "verification." For the simplest kind of correspondence, we might be satisfied to make the match instinctively, so to speak, by comparing the proposition with the landscape. But for the logical empiricists that was not the point; there is no analysis, nothing for philosophy at all, if we directly "understand" the sentence.[6] What is wanted is a criterion of verification that can be generalized and used upon reading or hearing the sentence, rather than upon looking at the world and at the sentence. It is language and not individual perception that is at issue.

To formulate such a criterion, even if only for scientific sentences, was a daunting task. It is of the essence of the practice of science that most of its methods of verification are indirect, sometimes elaborately so; that is what makes science interesting. Some propositions, moreover, while verifiable in principle, may remain unverified for lack of sufficient evidence. Still others, like theoretical laws in science, are in principle not fully verifiable, because unvarying causal relations cannot be conclusively established. To encompass everything the empiricists wanted, then, a criterion of verification had to include propositions indirectly verifiable, verifiable in principle, and generally but inconclusively verifiable. As A. J. Ayer summarized their program in 1935:

> I require of an empirical hypothesis, not indeed that it should be conclusively verifiable but that some possible sense experience should be relevant to the determination of its truth or falsehood. If a putative proposition fails to satisfy this principle, and is not a tautology, then I hold

that it is metaphysical and that being metaphysical, it is neither true nor false but literally senseless.[7]

A moment's reflection will show that the definition has been made so general as to define every proposition as meaningful; there is no tenet of religion so farfetched, no magical incantation so weird, that "some possible sense experience" is not relevant to its truth or falsity.[8]

The reason for the failure of this particular program of verification is easy to see: It was tailored to the practice of the physical sciences. So far from searching for a value-free, entirely perceptual standard, as they thought, the logical empiricists were in fact searching for a standard laden with all the judgments implied in science. But the viability of the definition of meaning for the empiricists could not be rescued even if it were separated from the research program of science, even if it were limited to sentences that could be directly compared with the world. Its defects were more radical, as W. V. Quine showed when he delivered its *coup de grace* in "Two Dogmas of Empiricism."

The two dogmas under attack were precisely the cornerstones of understanding for the empiricist: that some meaningful statements are "analytic," while others are verifiable or reducible to a "logical construct upon terms that refer to immediate experience."[9] In language, Quine pointed out, there is never a synonymy perfect enough to give rise to meanings that are "analytic," except in the artificial case when we say, for example, "to be an unmarried man is to be an unmarried man." Every other equivalency depends upon the context in which the sentence and the words in it are formed. We think the sentence "no bachelor is married" is analytic because we know it is being uttered for purposes of a philosophical demonstration, and that "bachelor" is to be taken in the sense that will lend itself to the exercise, rather than in the sense of a person with a university degree or a person temporarily keeping house alone. There is no use of "analytic" in discourse that does not draw upon the notion itself, in a circular way, to create the effect of synonymy.

The destruction of the first dogma concerning the analytic Quine used to undermine the other, of verificationism. He recognized that some synonymy could be preserved if two phrases could be reduced to references to the same physical things. We can say that "the evening star is the morning star" and make the two halves of the sentence synonymous if we know the two things are identical. But we do so only because we know we are in a context in which such a set of physical reductions is to be used to give sense to the sentence. There is an inevitable linguistic element in our treating the sentence as one in which a reduction is called for, and in our shared assumption that the physical equivalency exists. In the end, neither analyticity nor verification can be viewed as the elemental notions of meaning, because their effect is linked to other, unstated usages in the language.

From this basic insight, Quine drew further conclusions.[10] As a matter of communication, of the public nature of language, the references of words and sentences are "inscrutable." I may know as a matter of private knowledge that my picture sentence is accurate, but my listener does not know it. There is no way for me to explain its accuracy, except through other conventional, linguistic means. In the absence of consensus between us, some sort of "translation" is required, as if between languages, and using further linguistic conventions. Our knowledge of things insofar as it is communicable to others is an interlocked whole; sentences are understood and accepted as true or false, not through verification one by one, but in relation to the rest of the language. It appears then that Ayer's definition of a meaningful sentence is not "wrong." It is, instead, correct in a way different from that intended by Ayer: Any well-formed sentence can be given a sense if a warrant can be found for it in the usages of the language.

Some of these conclusions could have been inferred by a perspicacious reader of Wittgenstein's *Tractatus*; in retrospect, it should have come as no surprise to learn that the connection between a proposition and a supposed fact is "inscrutable." Although the empiricists had pushed such implications aside, Wittgenstein himself had not failed to see them. In his later writings he did not so much repudiate as simply abandon the point of view taken in the *Tractatus*. The copy theory of the meaning of sentences, it seemed, had not taken sufficient account of the public nature of language; the correspondences between the world and language, even if they were perceivable, were not communicable.

Language philosophy confronted the basic puzzle that the understanding of language, although social and public, nevertheless shifts with its context. Wittgenstein now said:

> But how many kinds of sentences are there? Say assertion, question, and command?—There are countless kinds: countless different kinds of use of what we call "symbols," "words," "sentences." And this multiplicity is not something fixed, given once for all; but new types of language, new language-games, as we may say, come into existence, and others become obsolete and get forgotten. (We can get a rough picture of this from the changes in mathematics.)
>
> Here the term "language-game" is meant to bring into prominence the fact that the speaking of language is part of an activity, or of a form of life.
>
> Review the multiplicity of language-games in the following examples, and in others:
> Giving orders, and obeying them—
> Describing the appearance of an object, or giving its measurements—
> Constructing an object from a description (a drawing)—
> Reporting an event—
> Speculating about an event—
> Forming and testing a hypothesis—
> Presenting the results of an experiment in tables and diagrams—
> Making up a story; and reading it—
> Play-acting—
> Singing catches—
> Guessing riddles—
> Making a joke; telling it—
> Solving a problem in practical arithmetic—
> Translating from one langauge to another—
> Asking, thanking, cursing, greeting, praying.
> It is interesting to compare the multiplicity of the tools in language and of the ways they are used, the mul-

tiplicity of kinds of word and sentence, with what logicians have said about the structure of language. (Including the author of the *Tractatus Logico-Philosophicus*)[11]

For Wittgenstein, language usages were implicit, learned as it were from the inside and in action by the participants. Many words, for example, have no definition, but rather a series of usages, linked from one to another in a chain rather than joined in a category. Of these, he said: "I can think of no better expression to characterize these similarities than 'family resemblances'; for the various resemblances between members of a family: build, features, color of eyes, gait, temperament, etc. etc. overlap and criss-cross in the same way.—And I shall say: 'games' form a family."[12] There is an enormous number of such family resemblance words. Not only "game," but the word "meaning" itself—in fact, substantially all the abstract terms in a book such as this—tend to shift with usage in such a way as to elude a fixed definition.

Because he saw that other social "forms of life" were, like language, rooted in usage, Wittgenstein was able to suggest the concrete consequences of the destruction of the dogmas of empiricism. The verification thesis is incoherent, reference is inscrutable, understanding is holistic not only for sentences but for the whole city of language, for all forms of symbolic expression, including customs. The problem of interpretation, or "translation" as Quine would call it, is general for all social practice. Whenever we are confronted with the unfamiliar in human action, in the customs of a strange people, or even in the physical world, we are faced with problems of interpretation and understanding essentially similar to the problem of understanding language.

The vision of the world as a web of interpretation obliges us to see that our perceptions as well as our actions and expressions are affected by language. The assumption I have been making up to this point, that we might be sure of our private knowledge, as though the only problem were one of intersubjective communication, useful though it is to underline the public nature of language, is ultimately untenable. The way the world is divided up, what it is that we are expected to see, is established by usage. If we have a large number of words for different sorts of snow, as the Eskimos are said to do, then we will systematically see snow in all those ways; otherwise we will organize it perhaps just as "snow" and "slush." A scientist might be able to find physical justifications for some of the Eskimo classifications for snow, but she will never look for them unless her attention is called to them. Similarly, if we think that the term "primitive custom" implies a people's immemorial pattern of behavior, then when we study the customs of a pre-modern people, we will tend to suppose that they have no development, that their customs are unchanging. We will not look for history unless we suppose it is there. Language tells us what is salient, and what is not salient is not noticed. The cheat of words that older philosophers mistrusted is with us still, but we now accept it as inescapable, a condition of life. When there is no private language, there is no private knowledge either.

Interpretation

Bertrand Russell, still hopeful for a positive philosophy, wrote gloomily about the later Wittgenstein and his circle, "The desire to understand the world is, they think, an outdated folly."[13] His dismay raises a profound question. When once we say that all meanings depend on one another, and that meanings invade perceptions, we are confronted with a radical question of method: How do we interpret anything at all?

Anglo-American philosophers have attacked the problem of method for interpretation in several ways. Some have retreated to the intention of the speaker as the primary source of meaning, a strategy that perhaps makes the problem even more mysterious. Understanding an intention, even at the simplest level, where both parties share implicit acceptance of the language, is extraordinarily complex. As H. P. Grice explained it, the speaker means something by an utterance if she intends (1) to evoke a certain response in the listener, if she intends (2) that the listener should recognize the intention to evoke a response, and if she intends (3) that the recognition by the listener should be a reason for the response. But even these interlocking intentions are not enough to account for the public nature of language; they do not explain why the utterance can be expected to communicate anything to the listener. Additional imputations of intention to the speaker (such as an intention that the listener should also recognize the second and third intentions) do not suffice to break out of the circle.[14]

Philosophers who think that reading the subjective intentions of the speaker is too fraught with danger have concluded, with Quine, that we have to understand utterances as an interdependent whole. In an attempt to explain how we grasp any individual utterance within this holistic scheme, Donald Davidson has argued that "we ought to hold belief constant as far as possible while solving for meaning."[15] In short, we tend to assume that the speaker means what we would expect such a person to mean in his place, an assumption that holds only if there is substantial agreement about our beliefs. When we are on common ground, using a conventional language or engaged in familiar customs, the need for interpretation seems to disappear, to become implicit "understanding." For every problem case of interpretation of a foreign culture or of a choice about facts or values within a culture, however, such understanding offers little guidance. It is in the nature of problem cases that for them we cannot "hold belief constant."

For one philosophical group, then, understanding is a sort of hall of mirrors determination of the speaker's intention by the listener, using a framework of conventional principles. For the other, it is an opaque process of cutting into a web of meanings already largely understood. Although there is a real conflict between them, we have no need to resolve it here because the point is, for us, that they do not supply us with a method. In the attempt to reconstruct such a method lies the genesis of a need for free expression and free inquiry.

Critical Hermeneutics

One approach to a question so drastically without guideposts is simply to treat it as a phenomenological problem: What is it that we do when we interpret something? When the

speaker is talking to us face to face and the implicit understandings are absent or break down, we start asking questions,
getting answers, and asking more questions, to try to guess at
the various intentional levels that Grice described. When the
speaker is physically absent, as in the case of texts and observed
actions, we start asking ourselves questions. In connection
with those questions, we construct a model interpretation that
accommodates our original observation, we search for more
evidence, we compare the model with the new evidence and
begin to repeat the cycle.

   This is the process of hermeneutics—not really a method, but rather the description of what we do when the certainty of method is gone, when we admit that knowledge is bound
up with inquiry. Until recent years, when it has begun to
become clear that the certainty of method is fading, Anglo-
American philosophers have not seemed to take hermeneutics
seriously; it has been the preserve instead of a continental tradition. [16]

   The common ground between hermeneutics and the
mainstream of Anglo-American language philosophy is the assumption that our world is formed by language. In a passage
that might well have come, say, from Quine, Hans-Georg
Gadamer has written:

> In all our knowledge of ourselves and in all knowledge of
> the world, we are always already encompassed by the
> language that is our own. We grow up, and we become
> acquainted with men and in the last analysis with our-
> selves when we learn to speak. Learning to speak does
> not mean learning to use a preexistent tool for designat-
> ing a world already somehow familiar to us; it means
> acquiring a familiarity and acquaintance with the world
> itself and how it confronts us. [17]

Under these circumstances, understanding is a dialogical tack-
ing back and forth by which we cut into the web of meanings
wherever we can, constantly returning to our own interpeta-
tion to tailor it as we go along. There is no possibility of an
entirely neutral standpoint for inquiry. We must always begin
with our prejudgments as a first approximation of understand-

ing and try to modify them in the light of the problem that confronts us. What hermeneutics offers instead of objectivity is a kind of critical honesty, the interpreter's willingness to admit that he starts with prejudgments, and to try to step outside them:

> The hermeneutical experience also has its logical consequence: that of uninterrupted listening. A thing does not present itself to the hermeneutical experience without its own special effort, namely that of "being negative towards itself." A person who is trying to understand a text has also to keep something at a distance, namely everything that suggests itself, on the basis of his own prejudices, as the meaning expected, as soon as it is rejected by the sense of the text itself. Even the experience of the reversal of meaning, the constantly recurring experience in speech, which is the real experience of the dialectic, has its equivalent here. The unfolding of the totality of meaning towards which understanding is directed, forces us to make conjectures and to take them back again. The self-cancellation of the interpretation makes it possible for the thing itself—the meaning of the text—to assert itself.[18]

Some hermeneutic philosophers, taking texts or actions as the models for inquiry, have slighted face-to-face dialogue as essentially unproblematic. Paul Ricoeur, for example, tells us that in a spoken dialogue, the problems of textual interpretation are largely missing, because meanings, references, and intentions can be jointly established by the speakers.[19] That view seems to me in conflict with the critical stance that is the essence of hermeneutics. The most important interpretive act is to be able to treat the familiar as if it were strange, to bracket the ordinary, to step outside prejudgments even when there seems to be no need. It is when meanings are jointly accepted by the speakers in a dialogue that we ought to be most careful to question them, precisely because our joint understandings are cast in the form of language. The "truth" that two speakers implicitly accept may be true at one time, and in one context, but not in another. If we take seriously the view that the meanings of sentences in ordinary languages are all interlocked, that all meanings point round to other parts of the language (some of them not present to our consciousness), and that our understanding of the world is largely formed by language, then we must expect that our ordinary usages will have implications that we cannot foresee, and mask implications that a different usage might catch.

All hermeneutic inquiry in fact partakes to some extent of the "implicit" understanding of face-to-face discussion. The "prejudgement" with which we begin any interpretation and from which we aim to distance ourselves in the effort to understand is also usually "implicit." We cannot begin to understand unless we accept some such judgment as a ground, but we cannot pretend to interpret unless we are critical of that ground, whether it is the unspoken understanding of speakers or any other starting point.

The truth found by critical hermeneutic methods is relative to the purpose of the project and the context in which it is undertaken. Knowledge is always in part practical, always knowledge in application. In this limited sense Gadamer considers the interpretation of law to be the *locus classicus* of hermeneutics.[20] A judge applies a pre-existing body of law, a set of texts, to a present problem. If she is fortunate enough to use a statute or decision that is so recent that the meaning of the sentences comes from her own world, her interpretive problem is similar to a face-to-face dialogue with a contemporary. If the text is old, surviving from a rather different society, then the judge must fuse the meaning in the world from which the law comes (as she understands it) with the meaning in the contemporary world. In either case, the important question is not what the texts meant to those who wrote them, what the writers' subjective "intentions" were, but rather how the words must be understood in connection with a contemporary problem.

Other political decisions, although not so tightly bound up with earlier texts as legal decisions, are elaborated in a basically similar way. Take the case of a decision whether chemical effluent from an industry ought to be allowed to flow into a river. If there is no body of law governing the decision, the policy-maker must decide how to apply more general pre-

existing values of the society to the problem. She is confronted
with some empirical questions for which there is usually relevant but inconclusive evidence: whether the effluent is inju-
rious to people or animals, whether there is any way to eliminate it without destroying the industry, how much it will cost
to eliminate it. Then she must consider how society values a
clean river, and how it values the industry; in the light of all
those things, she will decide whether to permit the effluent at
all, or how much of it to permit. As in the case of the legal
decision, the policy decision is made by applying the interpreter's idea of the existing values of society to a contemporary
problem, to a problem that confronts her and other citizens.

What is true for law and policy is true for all interpretation; it is understanding *for us* that we arrive at, and not understanding for those who originally wrote the text. It is in the
nature of the project of legal interpretation, which is dedicated
to deciding "the case at bar," to make this explicit; it may be
less clear for disciplines like history. The historian is likely to
be in search of a past world as it was understood by those who
lived in it, but in the nature of knowledge, he can only find
that world as it is for him. He must make a history that is
usable for him, a fusion of an unpredictable kind between the
present and the past.

Hermeneutics shares the practical aspect of knowledge
with the creative act. When we want to express something
new, we take a critical stance toward the tradition from which
we come; we either want to make something that is consistent
with that tradition, or in contrast with it. We are constantly in
a question and answer relation with the tradition and our developing work. Any creative work, furthermore, if it is in
symbolic form, becomes a public as well as a private expression. The act is not only for the creator, but for others who
share some knowledge of its tradition and form of expression,
and who will interpret it in a way that draws upon the same
sources as the creator, but is fused with their own points of
view. The relation is reciprocal; interpretation is creative, and
the creative act is a form of interpretation.

Here is the place where critical hermeneutics has gone
beyond merely elaborating and describing a process of interpretation that Anglo-American philosophy of the last genera-

tion has largely taken for granted. It rejects models of ordinary conversation in which we are expected to divine the intent of the speaker, or to "hold belief constant" while solving for another's meaning. The relatively passive notion of interpretation at the root of those formulations is misleading, just because the "implicit understandings" of conversation may as easily in fact be misunderstandings. The conditions of language perceived by Quine and Wittgenstein, where interpretations are not grounded so much in a world outside language as in other meanings, do not imply any such unproblematic model, but tell us instead that the truest interpretation is the one most fully justified by its interconnections in the language. In the world of language, the terms "understanding," "explanation," "interpretation," and "justification" are all interrelated. There is no understanding without explanation, and explanation can only go forward by the dialectical process; in short, interpretations must be justified by dialogue, either open and face to face or silent and by communication with a text (or both, as in the case when speakers discuss a text). The determination of those interpretations is a creative, practical action—a decision—using a language that is shared but never fully interpreted.

The Effects of Critical Hermeneutics

Social Science

Correspondence and copy theories of meaning have always been at their weakest in explaining human actions. There is no "behavior" so simple that it has an invariant significance, or even a complex group of significances, every time it is performed. It has a significance for the people who do it, as well as for those who observe it, and the significance for the performers is something that the observers must try to learn. The significance for the performers is not reducible to some set of physical stimuli, but rather refers around to other acts and significances, as the meanings in a language refer around to other parts of the language.[21]

The effect of the collapse of correspondence theories upon interpretation in the social sciences was suggested in the later writings of Wittgenstein when he described natural language as only one example of the vast number of rule-bound forms of social action. He seems to have thought that we could understand such social phenomena only implicitly,[22] by learning and participating in the forms of life just as we participate in the use of language. It is apparent, however, that social science aspires also to a critical understanding because the limits of implicit understanding—when it is appropriate and when it fails—cannot be supplied by implicit understanding itself. A social scientist examining human behavior tries to find at least two things: what the actors think they are doing, in their own context, and what he thinks the function of those actions is in some different context supplied (consciously or not) by the investigator. Each of these reciprocally affects the other, and is affected by the point of view of the investigator.

Suppose that a political scientist undertakes to study the effects of campaign advertising expenditures on voting behavior.[23] The investigator may find statistical evidence that, at least in the instance of a campaign challenge to an incumbent, the increased expenditure on campaign advertising is directly correlated with an increase in the number of favorable votes. He may make a tentative prejudgment that those results show that "money distorts the electoral process." Without knowing something about how the voters think, however, how they believe themselves to have responded to the campaign, he cannot sustain that judgment decisively. It is not clear, without talking to the voters, that they did not make a reasoned decision, based upon the fact that there was more complete information about the candidates than there would otherwise have been. It is not clear whether there is a reciprocal effect such that the candidate received larger sums of money because he was popular, or the reverse. Evidence can be collected to try to substantiate or refute any of these possibilities; voters and campaign contributors can be interviewed, and the times and amounts of contributions can be tabulated. It is not likely, however, that the evidence will settle the questions definitively. The voters and contributors may explain to their own satisfaction why and how they acted, and yet the investigator may not be persuaded that they understand or are truthful about their motives. A study of the times and sizes of the contributions will probably not resolve the question, because the existence of large contributions either early or late in the campaign is ambiguous evidence at best with respect to the popularity of the candidate. The investigator may decide that, in the nature of such a social question, the subjective motives of the voters and contributors cannot be found with any certainty. He may still conclude that "money distorts the electoral process," on the ground that it is clear at least that the amount of contributions has an effect that does not exist in their absence and is independent of the subjective intentions of the participants. But that is an interpretive judgment that assumes his own definition of what is or is not a distortion of the electoral process; the participants, or an investigator with a different point of view (or the challenging candidate, if he wins), might believe that the increased contributions lessened the distortion of the process.

The example presents a classic set of hermeneutic puzzles. The investigator interprets a pattern of action that has a set of significances for the actors. He thinks he "understands" those significances, yet believes those actions are significant in some way unknown or unadmitted by the participants. His interpretation must be supported by evidence derived from the actions of the same people, but placed in a framework that will explain the evidence in a way consistent both with the participants' and the investigator's understanding. Critical hermeneutics implies that if the investigator offers an interpretation designed to exclude the understanding of the participants, his judgments, so far from being neutral and "value-free," will tend to confirm his own value judgments. His interpretation can never be "objective" but must be an interpretation for him. It is at best a fusion of the points of view of the investigator and the participants, at worst a reflection of the point of view of the investigator.

Natural Science

The interpretation of the natural world is anchored in a knowledge that looks to us rather different from knowledge of the social world. The physical data of the natural sciences are not, in the empirical-pragmatic view usually assumed in our world, part of a symbolic and communicative world, affected by the beliefs of the "participants." As a result there are no doubt some sentences descriptive of the physical world that, unlike sentences about the social world, would evoke nearly universal assent when translated into any language; "deep waters are dark"[24] might be an example. But such sentences do not take us far in science, which requires much more complex and interconnected descriptive sentences. Our understanding of the physical world—the corpus of science at even a very simple level—is linguistic and symbolic as the data are not.

It is just in the natural sciences that the effect of the incoherence of the correspondence theory of meaning is most clear-cut, because it is there that the hope for the theory was originally strongest. If there is no entirely neutral and self-explanatory relation between the sentences of science—its theory—and its subject, then theory will mean somewhat different things to different observers. They can interpret one another's ideas only through a dialogue, by asking and answering questions. Since theory directs observation—by suggesting, for example, what experiment or inquiry ought to be undertaken next—it infuses all our understanding of physical reality. The natural scientist reaches new conclusions about the world through "rationally comprehending the 'go' of things," as Norwood Hanson put it;[25] that sense of the "go" of physics is never purely observational, but theoretical as well. In one of his thought-experiments, for example, Einstein pictured himself riding alongside a light-wave, an image which, in view of his theoretical knowledge, seemed to evoke paradoxical physical results ultimately resolved by the theory of relativity.[26] A theoretical-practical puzzle thus led Einstein to place himself in a question-and-answer relation both to theory and to the physical world. (A "question" of course, could not be put to the physical world directly but only through a theoretical framework.)

Scientific inquiry, whether in communication between scientists or in investigation by individual scientists, is always conducted through a dialogical relation with theory and the data (as filtered through some theory). In his historical sketches of scientific research, for example, Imre Lakatos saw that scientific facts are so embedded in a shared language that it is only through convention that we demarcate "background" from "theory." In one context, the background framework is treated as unproblematic while the scientist tests the theory in light of the "truth" of the framework; in a subsequent context, the unproblematic fact can become part of theory subject to confirmation. As a result, a theory is not effectively falsified by experiment unless a new theory is available to explain the old background facts and the new experiment as well. "There is no falsification," he said, "before the emergence of a better theory."[27] It is the clash of rival theories ("research programmes" in Lakatos' phrase), rather than the clash of theory and "fact," that is the engine of scientific change.

Marxism

The relation of Marxism to the collapse of correspondence or copy theories of meaning and to the hermeneutic tradition is ambiguous. There is no "answer" to the question how Marxism would respond to the picture of language I have drawn here because there are too many versions of Marxism, perhaps as many as there are of language philosophy itself.

A few assumptions, nevertheless, that have consequences for language are common to the Marxist tradition as a whole. Marxists share with Wittgenstein the conception that language, like other cultural artifacts, can never be entirely private.[28] They share with the hermeneutic tradition the view that access to knowledge about cultural artifacts such as language is achieved through dialectical means. In Russia in the twenties, for example, Mikhail Bakhtin and V. N. Volosinov sketched a philosophy of language rooted in the perceptions that "individual consciousness is a social-ideological fact" and that "the immediate social situation and the broader social milieu wholly determine—and determine from within, so to speak—the structure of an utterance." They concluded that *any true understanding is dialogic in nature. Understanding is to utterance as one line of dialogue is to the next. Understanding strives to match the speaker's word with a counter word.*"[29]

The Marxist tradition is in constant conflict over the question whether the linguistic understanding found by dialectical means is objectively real or not. The tension perhaps has its source in the thinking of Marx himself, in his double view that people both shape their world and are formed by it, epitomized in the introduction to *The Eighteenth Brumaire of Louis Bonaparte*:

> Men make their own history but they do not make it just as they please; they do not make it under circumstances chosen by themselves, but under circumstances directly encountered given and transmitted from the past. The tradition of all the dead generations weighs like a nightmare on the brain of the living.[30]

Official government Marxism generally takes the view that the dialectic leads to knowledge of reality; that is part of the reason such governments are inhospitable to free inquiry. For them, some sort of correspondence theory is obligatory. A sophisticated example is *Language and Cognition*, by the Polish philosopher Adam Schaff, in which he concedes that perception is affected by language and that the observer actively participates in cognition through the dialogical process. Only by assuming a complex evolutionary sociology of knowledge, which cuts away layers of false consciousness by dialectical means, is he able to enforce a claim that we get ultimate access to reality.[31] For reasons that should be clear from the discussion of other versions of the correspondence theory, this conclusion seems to me insupportable. If in fact perception is affected by language, it seems impossible to be sure for any interpretation, except by means of faith, that it is "objectively" a true one.

Critical Marxists have differed with official Marxism precisely over the issue of the importance to be given to the symbolic world of meanings. They have taken a position opposed to a copy theory and substantially in agreement with critical hermeneutics, that the world cannot be understood except through linguistic means that are dialectical in nature, and that the relation between language and the reality it supposedly describes is always a reciprocal one.[32] That conclusion seems to me unavoidable for any seriously dialectical approach to language. Many critical Marxists, nevertheless, especially the theorists of the Frankfurt School, have hesitated to draw the same conclusions as I do concerning free expression, for reasons that I shall briefly explore in the next section.

Freedom of Inquiry

The nature of language leaves us in this position: All understanding is context-based and influenced by usage. It is not passively received, but actively created; interpretation is completed through connection with other meanings both openly available and hidden. Sentence meanings, understanding of the social and physical worlds, and creative decisions are all unified as actions taken to solve problems—solutions for us, found for a context, by dialogical means. The question-and-answer pattern becomes inevitable as a result of the realization that sentences are understood only by other sentences.

We begin our interpretation with some basic "take" that grows out of past understandings; the "take" is both necessary and dangerous to the process of interpretation. Any system of authority that dictates a particular understanding, that legislates meanings, cuts off some other avenue of understanding. If the connections between meanings and what they signify is never quite defined, and if language determines, in some measure, what we perceive, then there cannot be a predictable end to inquiry. We cannot be sure that knowledge is "complete."[33]

Although all this may be the "intuitive" consequence of critical hermeneutics, it conflicts at another level with our experience of discourse and interpretation. We constantly conduct inquiries within limitations we think we recognize, that we even call "well-defined." The open-ended world projected in the last paragraph seems, from this point of view, both fantastic and wearisome.

We have such anchors on our discourse, created by personal need or authority, or both, precisely because the process of interpretation otherwise has no limits. Familiar examples are the broad focus of the political campaign in which argument, persuasion, and discussion are almost limitless, up to a fixed date when a vote is taken, or the relatively narrow focus of the legal dispute, in which only the "parties" to the dispute are supposed to be heard, according to complex procedural strictures. But we don't believe that those devices are exhaustive, that all possible arguments will be made or heard through such means; they are ways of making sure that a decision is in fact made and that it can be reviewed and understood because the "accepted" procedures have been followed.

The structures of knowledge we call "disciplines," as well as "styles" or "procedures" within disciplines, are indispensable tools of understanding. It is "natural" for us to create those disciplines, as I shall show in more detail in the next chapter in connection with the psychology of problem-solving, just because there is no discipline that is invariant or necessary for interpretation.

The need for a right to free inquiry is implied in the problems presented by the hermeneutic process of understanding. It is decision-making mixed with the sense that the decisions are open to question. Every prejudgment that begins interpretation, every step along the way, and every conclusion that something is "true" is a decision. If inquiry is to be possible at all, those decisions have to be made, while they must also conflict with our consciousness that the limits we place on understanding are our own limits. Hermeneutics is not true to understanding if it does not keep open some channel of critique parallel to any interpretation, or to any discipline by which interpretations are made.

Critical Theorists, drawing upon the Marxist tradition, point to the limitations created by "disciplines" and similar intellectual structures as a reason for doubting that free discussion ought to be allowed under all conditions. It is precisely because the constraints of authority are so often implicit, are experienced as "forms of life," that we are unconscious of them. We make judgments that we think are "accurate" for a given context without being able to see that our judgments are colored by ideology or unconscious fears. It follows, Critical Theory implies, that the only discourse that the law ought unequivocally to allow is the one that is totally open, without hidden restraints, the "emancipatory" discourse.[34]

This position seems to me in conflict with the essential nature of knowledge resulting from hermeneutic inquiry. I am persuaded that our discourse has constraints, both conscious and hidden from us; what I doubt is that we can tell when our discourse is "emancipatory." We have no standards other than those that are themselves open to criticism for calling discourse "emancipatory" or anything else. Critical theory thus undermines its own grounds for distinguishing the dialogues that ought to be encouraged from those that ought to be limited.*

The realization that we have no reliable yardstick for recognizing emancipatory discourse points toward a rather different question. Do we want all the interpretation that critical hermeneutics affords us? In light of the fact that there is no "true" and final interpretation to which we can attain, why don't we just rely on our traditional limits of discourse, of which we feel we have implicit understanding, and let the rest go? The short answer is that the belief that any discipline has "limits" that can be definitively established is an illusion. There are always questions that can be adequately answered only by breaking down its boundaries, because meanings within the the discipline cannot be self-contained but must finally be referred outside it.

Even an act of interpretation so apparently restricted as a translation from one language to another cannot be limited to a context that is self-defining. Take the case of translation of a prose text, say De Tocqueville's *Democracy in America*, from French into English. We will not be able to carry out such an interpretive project adequately if we treat the text as a fungible "piece of French prose." We have to decide whether to see it as reportage, as more general sociological theory, as political theory, or as some combination of these, and evaluate it in any of those categories. We would translate the book in a certain way if we were to believe simply that it is a work of sociology, and our methods would vary depending on how we evaluate it as such a work. We cannot translate it without thinking about what sort of "book" it is and how it fits into the disciplines of which it is a part, even if, as in De Tocqueville's case, the disciplines have largely developed after the book was written.

There is nothing in the nature of any discipline that prevents us from stepping out of the framework of discourse even more drastically by questioning the validity of the discipline itself. We may decide that one language is radically untranslatable into another, or, to change the example, that the system

*I expand on these issues in Appendix III.

of legal discourse has no independent rules of its own but is in fact the instrument of other forces in society. Questioning the assumptions of a realm of discourse once again affords us knowledge but in a different universe of discourse, a fact that we memorialize by giving such inquiries a new professional label. Arguments that languages are untranslatable we brand as theories of "linguistic anthropology," and arguments that legal discourse is socially determined we brand as "sociology." The knowledge that such radical questioning affords us, moreover, affects our knowlege within the original mode of discourse; we do our law and our translation differently, if we do them at all, after we become aware of such radical critiques.

Are there no universals left for us?* There is at least this one: We are going to go on interpreting language and solving problems. As functioning decision-makers and interpreters, we act as if our understanding were not relative to its context. We take some pattern of discourse as adequate, as if it were objectively correct, for reasons that have a warrant at the time. But one characteristic we know about such patterns is that the warrant may run out in an unforeseeable way. The source for freedom of expression and inquiry lies in the fact that we are certain to make decisions, at the very least the decision to understand a sentence in one way rather than another, while we are not certain about the understanding we bring to those decisions. The need for the freedom lies in the unclosable gap between decision and understanding; the freedom we want is the freedom to search for a new understanding.

In this chapter I have not sought to show more than the need for that freedom. The obligation to satisfy that need cannot be demonstrated by the nature of language alone. I have reserved for Part II of the book the argument about the source of the government's obligation to satisfy the need, which results in the right to open dialogue.

It is still conceivable, although the nature of language as a philosophical matter indicates otherwise, that there are empirical limits on the way people can answer questions that escape the net of philosophy woven in this chapter. It would not be astounding if psychology should find a particular cast to

*The question of relativism is explored in Appendix I.

understanding, a skewed view or a predilection for a limited set of meanings. Psychologists search for such primordial patterns, and there are always possible candidates; Lawrence Kohlberg, for example, argued that there is a natural course of development, an invariant sequence, in the way we think about value judgments. As I shall show in the next chapter, however, the evidence from cognitive psychology on the whole demonstrates that the thinking of children and adults is consistent with critical hermeneutics and that there are no limits to inquiry except the ones we choose to impose.

Chapter II

COGNITION

AND

RATIONALITY

Studying her own children, Melissa Bowerman found that one of her daughters, less than two years old, used the word "moon" in these ways:

> looking at the moon; looking at peel-side of half-grapefruit obliquely from below; playing with half-moon shaped lemon slice; touching circular chrome dial on dishwasher; playing with shiny round green leaf she had just picked; touching ball of spinach mother offers her; holding crescent-shaped bit of paper she'd torn off yellow pad; looking up at inside of shade of lit floor lamp; looking up at picture of yellow and green vegetable (squash, peas) on wall in grocery store; looking up at wall hanging with pink and purple circles; pointing at orange crescent-shaped blinker light on a car; looking up at curved steer-horns on wall; putting green magnetic capital letter D on refrigerator; picking up half a cheerio, then eating it; looking at black, irregular kidney-shaped piece of paper on a wall; "my moon is off" after pulling off a hangnail (a routine usage).[1]

The regularities Bowerman detected in these usages were shape, color, shiny surface, viewing position, flatness, and "broad expanse as background." The source of such regularities for the child are analogies, both of form and function, and sometimes the loose chain connections that Wittgenstein called "family resemblances" (the leaf and spinach are connected, Bowerman thinks, in part because both are green). In a similar way, meanings may be connected because of contiguity, that is, simply because things are found together (the leaf and spinach were seen on the same day).

Through constant communication with others and the dialectic process in her own mind, a child like the Bowerman girl acquires other words for the things in her collection, she imposes other regularities on them, also derived by analogy, by contiguity, and by family resemblance, and she decides the limits and interrelations of those regularities. Every speaker's lexicon contains a vast record of such regularities, in family resemblance words and metaphorical uses (like "national growth" and "expanding market"), that become literal by custom.[2] Although the regularities according to which children use words gradually conform in the main with the usages of others raised in a similar environment, they are always formed as part of the user's individual history. In short, there is no known method for interpreting the meaning of sentences, except the familiar social means of joint communication rooted in the shared web of experience.[3]

Even before she can speak, the infant develops habits of joint communicative action. As she gestures to her mother, often imitating or repeating some pattern the two have developed in the past, so her mother replies, and a vocabulary of expressions and gestures is elaborated.[4] The child's earliest speech takes the form of one-word sentences; the meaning is defined by the purposive action of which the word is a part. If she utters the single work "milk" while trying to open the refrigerator, the child tells us that milk is what she wants. Such a one-word sentence presents the same difficulties of interpretation as an adult sentence, but writ large because of its surface simplicity. In an adult's use of a sentence in discourse, for example, there is usually a relation of "topic and comment" (the sentence "it was your brother who stole it" conveys by its structure that a theft is under discussion); in the infant's one-word sentence the topic or theme is not in the word so much as in the purposive action shared with the other person.[5] The child thus comes to depend on her dialogic communication for sympathetic understanding through a process reminiscent of Quine's philosophical parable of "radical translation," in which we can understand the child only because of the interconnected web of past and present joint action.

The child uses her dialogical habit of mind not only to learn about communication by gesture and language but also about the physical world, the world of objects and operations. Knowledge consists, Jean Piaget said, "neither of a simple copy of external objects nor of a mere unfolding of structure preformed inside the subject, but rather involves a set of structures progressively constructed by continuous interaction between the subject and the world."[6] For Piaget, once the child begins to acquire language, she learns language and the world together, the development of one illuminating the knowledge of the other in a reciprocal relation.

In recent years, investigators of Piaget's school have emphasized the connection between joint communication and the growth of understanding of the physical world. As a child makes the transition from stage to stage of cognitive development, experimenters have found that the child can often be pulled forward to the next stage (for example, to understanding of the conservation of fluids poured from one container to another) when he is paired in the experiment with another child. The less advanced child develops best when his partner is only slightly more advanced, because then he can better understand the explanations; the effect is less pronounced when one partner is well beyond the other because the leader tends to dominate the discussion and to give explanations that cannot be grasped by the other. Similarly, in studying the development of moral judgment (of which more in a moment) among older adolescents, investigators found that a person is likely to develop in judgment through discussion with another only slightly more advanced, especially when the discussion is "transactive"—that is to say, when it in some way engages the arguments of the parties. These experiments seem to me to converge on one point: Communicative interaction is a natural way for children to develop, which works best when the discussion presents a new alternative in terms the child can understand and explain, based on his earlier experiences.[7] The need for a frame of reference in order to entertain a new point of view is a mind-set that the child carries forward into adult life.

As she approaches puberty, then, many of the child's habitual methods for understanding are roughly those of a language philosopher of the last chapter. Language and the apprehension of the world are intertwined. Language itself is a web of meanings, public and at the same idiosyncratic, usually understood holistically and as part of an intentional action. Problems in interpreting the world and language are solved by dialogical means. The difficulty for the child, usually solved by discussion with others, is to find a way to step out of the existing web of meaning so as to take a fresh point of view.

Formal Operations: Search for a Method

Piaget argued that the child's interaction with objects and other people results in definable stages of development, the sequence of which is universal in human society, although not all individuals or societies are expected to reach every stage or to pass from stage to stage in quite the same way. Each of the successive levels may loosely be characterized as of increasing abstraction or detachment. At the level of "formal operations," as Piaget conceived it, a teen-ager finally attains "the capacity to reason in terms of verbally stated hypotheses and no longer merely in terms of concrete objects and their manipulation."[8] While Piaget did not claim a universal method for the interpretation of language, then, he did posit a universal method, formal operations, for approaching scientific problems.

Despite the apparent simplicity of the scheme, however, a reliable description of what it is that adults do when they use formal operations eluded Piaget. The "hypoethetico-deductive" model, which seems to be a first approximation of Piaget's notion, clearly would not serve, as he himself quickly recognized, because it describes so little of what people do when they try to solve problems. If we accept the premise that deduction from hypotheses is part of thinking, and that adults can do it while young children cannot, that still does not tell us much about adult thinking. It does not tell us how hypotheses are generated, and how we decide that one is worth thinking about while another seems to be nonsense. In making the determination discussed in the last chapter concerning chemical effluent, for example, the policy-makers have to decide what is to count as a "harm" to the environment—whether solely effects on humans, or on other forms of life or on non-living things as well. They have to try to evaluate the evidence, scientific or otherwise, that such a harm will occur or has occurred, and what the cost of avoiding it would be (and what is to count as a "cost"). What is considered a good argument, what is recognized as a "reasonable" inference, for the natural sciences as well as for practical social problems, is governed by the interlocking networks of language and belief. The question-and-answer pattern that contributes to the structure of those networks necessarily becomes part of reasoning (in deciding, for example, what is included under a concept or is implied by it). Piaget was finally pushed to speaking of a "psycho-logic," summarized by John Broughton as a "cyclical structural mix of formal argument and empirical fit."[9] With this step, it becomes more difficult to apply the word "formal" to adult thinking, for what may seem formal to one person may seem formless and intuitive to another, and vice versa.

The way our notion of the "formal" depends upon our knowledge and beliefs, as mediated through language, is illuminated by the history of the application of Piaget's theory to the development of moral cognition. Lawrence Kohlberg divided moral development broadly into three levels, similar to those of Piaget: the pre-conventional (obedience to power and satisfaction of personal needs), the conventional (acceptance of authority and search for approval), and the post-conventional, for which moral decisions are generated from rights, values, or principles that could be agreeable to all individuals.[10] As Kohlberg recognized, the implications of his claim were enormous; he was asserting that there is an orderly development established by human nature in the approach to moral questions. He found that relatively few subjects, when judged by his criteria, attained the highest stages of moral develop-

ment. Some of the evidence, moreover, showed a gender difference; more women than men seemed to be at an earlier level of
moral development.[11]

Carol Gilligan, a woman student of Kohlberg's, used
that claimed gender difference to make an argument that some
subjects, especially women, develop in a way that conflicts
with Kohlberg's reading of the higher levels. She found that
many adults make moral judgments that, while "post-conventional," are not abstract and context-free but are instead infused with the circumstances within which the decision must
be made. Their judgments are not "universalizable" in the
sense that Kohlberg then used the term, because those judgments are often organized around personal and "caring"
relations.[12]

Gilligan did not much disturb the general scheme of
levels proposed by Kohlberg; she claimed instead that the
"post-conventional contextual" ought to be recognized as a
legitimate version of the third level. For me, nevertheless, her
research implies a radical critique of Kohlberg's more specific
conclusion that there is one most "adequate" approach to moral
questions. Other experiments have suggested, for example,
that a practical decision for action, arrived at through discussion with others, is more likely than a hypothetical question to
depend upon consideration of the individuals involved and
upon fine-grained distinctions of one situation from another.
Whatever else they may show, this and Gilligan's research imply that there is no final stage of development with a corre-
sponding formalized method for moral decisions. In his own
recent work, Kohlberg has apparently himself concluded that
the last and most "universal" stage in his original sequence is
not a culture-free category.[13]

The critique of "formal operations" in its various guises,
as conducted by Piaget himself and those inspired by him,
reveals that they have not been able to give a coherent account
of a universal method for solving problems, in the realm either
of values or of science. The meaning of the term "formal," like
similar linguistic formulas, cannot be given an entirely invariant definition. That conclusion nevertheless leaves a nagging
doubt, a residual intuition that there is some content to the
notion of a "rational" approach to problems. While we cannot

perhaps formulate exactly what we mean by "rational" in the sense of a specific method, we do label approaches in particular cases as more or less rational. The question remains: Can we give content to that intuition?

Adult Thinking

The rock rolled down the mountain
The rock crushed the hut
The hut was tiny
The hut was at the edge of the woods

In one of a series of experiments designed to test how adults comprehend prose, John Bransford and Jeffrey Franks read these short sentences to subjects, not consecutively but interlarded with others. When they were tested later about what they thought they had heard, the subjects erroneously recalled hearing a complex sentence combining the concepts of the short ones: "The rock which rolled down the mountain crushed the tiny hut at the edge of the woods."[14] This and similar experiments imply a number of things about the comprehension of discourse. The strategy is a continuation of that used by the child. It is holistic: The listeners impose a structure, a framework of meaning that pulls the sentences together. It is intentional: The framework imposed is purposive, with a narrative "drift." It is conventional and contextual: The listeners expect that some scenario familiar from their past lives will be the appropriate frame for interpretation.

The concept of such stereotypical strategies, variously called "scripts," "schemas," or "frames," has proved to be one of the keys to the attempt to construct a model of understanding. When Roger Schank and R. P. Abelson constructed the program they called Script Applier Mechanism (SAM) to enable a computer to read a short, routine story, they found that the understanding they put into the program had to be holistic, intentional, and conventional.[15] There was no hope of understanding without a context; the program had to be prepared to find a overall purposive action integrated into the narrative in order to be able to read it at all. The intention implied even in a very simple story, such as one about entering a restaurant, ordering food, and then paying the check, requires a large scaffolding of presuppositions. Expectations about causal relations (that "ordering" will bring some result, for example) are interlocked with "scripts" for social situations (the "restaurant script" encapsulates the expectations for restaurants). The scripts and plans required for understanding, which are supplied instantly by adults who have spent their lives learning them from a multitude of personal interactions, are of course missing from SAM, which must get them from the model-makers. And however banal the scripts may be, they are often too unconventional for the machine. SAM can read only the most predictable and boring story; people find stories interesting only as they deviate in some way from their expectations. In addition to scripts and plans, humans know many ways to depart from them or adhere to them, more or less legitimately, based apparently on the ability to question and modify existing schemas. Schank and Abelson's model implies, precisely by the ways that it is not like the mind, the dialectical nature of the mind's interpretive abilities. Terry Winograd, one of the most insightful of those who have tried for a generation to program the understanding of language, has concluded: "Although little has been said within AI [artificial intelligence] and cognitive science about how new schemas are generated, it is clear that it must be the result of a history of previous interactions, each of which is mediated through other schemas in a hermeneutic circle."[16]

The strategies used in problem-solving generally are very similar to those used in interpreting connected discourse; interpretation, in fact, is a form of problem-solving. For the listeners in the Bransford and Franks experiment, for example, the short sentences presented a problem until they were integrated in a framework of intention; to understand the sentences was to draw an inference about them. The notions of "understanding" and "explaining" are as closely linked for psychology as they are for hermeneutic philosophy.[17]

It is not surprising that recent research on how people interpret social situations and solve simple social problems has found that adults tend to seize upon heuristic devices drawn from the unreflective understanding of language. One device commonly used is an expectation of "representativeness," that is, the inference of a causal relationship from a resemblance. The resemblance itself may be part of a script or frame; if subjects are given a description of a shy "librarian-type," they will tend to think that a person who fits that description is a librarian, even when they know that the percentage of librarians in the population is extremely small. An "availability" heuristic, through which people seize upon the most immediately accessible solution for a problem as the correct one, supplements the representativeness heuristic. For example, events that have been made salient through a vivid story or an episode are likely to be available in making a judgment; a person who has experienced a crime or heard a bloody account of one is more likely to think that crime is a serious social problem than a person who has heard dry statistics, however persuasive. People also "anchor" their judgments; they tend to stick to their initial estimate of the facts, altering it only a little in the light of subsequent evidence.[18]

These heuristics are, I believe, not materially different from those that are used to learn linguistic meanings. The representativeness device resembles the analogical process by which children assign meanings to words, filled out with an adult complement of scripts and schemas to generate the analogies. The availability heuristic, of course, is the same as the selection of meanings through contiguity. The problem situations "mean" something in an action context drawn from memory in the form of a script or an episode and organized in the same way that language is organized, whether for a child or an adult. A problem situation can be solved only insofar as it can be understood, and the solution projected for a problem is its meaning for the subject. The resulting interpretation is "anchored" because it is part of a complex of schemas with a narrative drift, which is difficult to change unless a new narrative can be found.[19]

It is fashionable to talk as though these findings somehow demonstrate that people do not take a "rational" approach to solving problems. The representativeness and availability heuristics, critics point out, are poor ways of estimating the statistical likelihood of events; a much better way of deciding whether a person is likely to be librarian or whether crime is a serious problem is to examine the numbers of librarians or crimes in the population. The sort of rationality that the experimenters have in mind, however, is rarely available for real problems, especially in the social world. The problems with which people are actually presented are usually not sufficiently circumscribed to have a statistical base to which the problem-solver can refer; when data exist, on the other hand, their relevance is often unclear. Some less rigid notion of rationality must apply as a criterion for solutions to such problems.

Take an example used by Daniel Kahnemann and Amos Tversky to test judgments of probability. The experiment concerns an imaginary lawsuit over an auto accident in a town where, we are told, 85 percent of the taxis are blue and 15 percent are green. A "witness" testifies that a taxi involved in the accident was green, and the "jury" learn that the witness can be expected to be able to distinguish blue from green in 80 percent of the cases. Many subjects will say that there is an 80 percent chance the witness is correct, a conclusion the experimenters think is in error because it ignores the background likelihood posed by the population of taxis in the town. It is not at all clear, however, that the experimenters' underlying assumption—that the jurors ought to judge the accuracy of the witness' testimony by the overall probability that the taxi is green—is correct. If the jury think that the witness is 80 percent likely to be able to make an accurate judgment in an individual instance, it is arguable that the statistical likelihood of blue taxis in the town makes no difference at all. The relevance of the assumed statistical facts to the determination, then, is not at all clear, and is something that the people making the judgment must decide.[20]

A more basic criticism of an experiment such as this, as a test of the ability to solve ordinary problems, is that it resembles only faintly any question that a jury is likely to have to decide. Juries almost never know what percentage of vehicles in a town fit a certain description, and they certainly never know what the statistical likelihood is that a witness is making a correct identification. They make a rough judgment, using the natural heuristics to decide whether they think the witness is honest and whether he was able to perceive the event accurately, and they will generally bring what they know of the background likelihoods into account in making that judgment, just as Kahnemann and Tversky claim that they should. They do not decide the precise bearing of a background likelihood, because they take it into account in judging the credibility of the witness. The natural heuristics are designed for what has been called the "open world," where knowledge is incomplete and the weight that ought to be assigned to knowledge (even assuming it were accurate) is unclear.

The main difficulty for us in the open world is simply how to organize it. The natural heuristics are, if nothing else, marvelous organizers; they supply us with hypotheses from which we can begin to think about problems that are otherwise, unlike the ones posed by the experimenters, quite unstructured. As Allan Collins said in one of the early studies of such heuristics, they are "strategies people have learned in order to give reasonable answers in the face of their incomplete knowledge." While these strategies may be risky from the point of view of statistical accuracy, the alternative, in many cases, is not to be able to think at all. Herbert Simon found in his pioneering studies that there is generally no alternative to the use of heuristics; if the human problem-solver does not restrict himself to a space of "bounded rationality," he may find that he is unable to approach the problem at all.[21]

Open-world problems include most of those that matter to us: important day-to-day judgments, such as whether we like or trust a person, and political judgments, such as the one concerning whether industrial effluent may be allowed into the environment. That is a case where the statistical bases for judgment, and the bearing of such statistical evidence as there is, are likely to be unclear. The decision-makers may know, for example, how much effluent is being released, but they usually will not know how much harm it will do (or perhaps even what "harms" are possible), nor how much the public will or should tolerate. Those are judgments the decision-makers draw from impressions and experience.

Judgments about artistic expression are classic open world problems. In prose narrative, of course, the writer draws upon a host of scripts and schemas in deciding how to express himself; he relies on the narrative drift of such things to make his own meaning clear. The painter relies on her memory of a host of images, her judgment of the effect of the way they were shaped or colored, and their relationship to other images in her own work and thát of others.

Scientific questions, if they are original, are also open-world problems; when they are not—if they have a determinate answer before they are asked—then they are mere exercises of the sort that were posed to the subjects in the psychological studies of natural heuristics. For new problems, the scientist must have some structure, some schema, as a hypothesis into which to fit the problem, and that schema must capture "the go of things" for the scientist. When Einstein conducted the thought-experiment that placed him alongside a light-wave, he had to construct images of himself in motion and (in some way) of the wave itself, using visual images, experience, and the linguistic capacity to make analogies and draw inferences. Most of our day-to-day problem-solving, although much less original and imaginative, is not different in its essentials. We draw upon a similar fund of imagery, episodes, and linguistic frames in attacking a problem.

The trouble with the natural heuristics is that they are too attractive as ways to attack problems. The problem-solver tends to take the hypothesis as the conclusion, with results that are sometimes disastrously inappropriate when they are viewed in a somewhat different context from the original choice. A shy woman may be hired as a librarian because she "seems the type" when she is not in fact well suited to the job, or even when she is better suited to some other job. We have been learning for generations about such misallocations of talent arising from sexual and racial stereotypes, but of course the problem is not limited to social and political choices. The painter may wake up, look at what she painted the day before, when it seemed original and beautiful, and find it utterly banal. The scientist may find that his hypothesis, however imaginative, is disconfirmed by experiment. While individuals do sometimes, like Einstein, have brilliant heuristic insights, for most of us most of the time our proposed solutions to problems turn out to be based on humdrum or inappropriate models.

Even when a proposed solution to a problem can be shown to be inadequate by some standard, the framework in which the original idea is cast is usually difficult to abandon.

Craig Anderson and his associates were able to make a dramatic demonstration of this in an experiment in which subjects were asked to resolve a question concerning a simple social issue: whether people who were prone, or averse, to taking high risks would make better firefighters. Each subject was told a vivid individual case history that pointed to one result or the other, and then was asked for an opinion on the general question. The opinions naturally correlated with the case study, since the subjects had no background information to conflict with the story. The interesting result was that people tended to cling to their opinion even after they had been told that the original story was fiction.

Here is the anchoring heuristic at its most puzzling. Our experience is that people can change their minds, most readily in cases such as this, cases where they have no strong prejudices; there must have been some way, it would seem, that these people could have seen the problem differently. The key turned out to lie in the need for an alternative scenario or framework for a changed opinion. Among those who clung most tenaciously to their original opinion, in the face of the fact that the case history was a fiction, were those who had made a written explanation for their opinion. Conversely, if the subjects were asked to write counter-explanations, to argue both sides of the issue, they were better able to adjust their views to the notion that the story was false. The cold fact that it was false was not enough; they had to be able to imagine the scenario, the theoretical explanation, in which it was false.[22]

The problem with problem-solving is that the thinker does not have within himself enough resources of representative and available models, or does not have immediate access to those that are within him. For us, the world has an argument in the sense of an interconnection of causes, and we can understand it differently only if we can understand a "different argument." Through a lifetime of habit, carried forward from the joint communicative action of childhood, we ordinarily reach such a new understanding through discourse with other minds, either face to face or through the study of their work. Only I myself or another person can present such a discursive argument, and a fresh approach is more likely to come from another person because, having experienced a different history, he may organize knowledge in a slightly different way. By the same token, I will not be able to accept the new approach unless, through similar discursive means, I can assimilate it to something already in my knowlege.

I am not suggesting here that group decision-making is in some way generally superior to that of the individual, just because it involves the interaction of several minds. The position of this book is, rather, that individual and social decision-making cannot be entirely distinguished; they have a great deal in common because the stereotypes absorbed into the natural heuristics are mostly social artifacts. Some of the difficulties that are notorious in group decision-making—the tendency, for example, to reinforce a scenario that all participants share—are in fact structurally similar to the difficulties that an individual thinker faces.[23] In either case, the principal difficulty is to find new approaches, and to find ways to assimilate a new approach to existing knowledge through some discursive means.

Rationality

When there is no formal method of the sort postulated by Piaget for finding solutions to problems and when the effectiveness of a proposed solution is not foreseeable, either because the background information for evaluating the solution is not available or because the relevance of background information as a standard for evaluating the solution is unclear, what weight does the concept of rationality still carry? If an approach is called "rational" in connection with the solution of open-world problems, it must be because the approach is more likely to be fruitful, in the sense that it yields solutions that are found appropriate to a context. The chief characteristic that fits that description, under the psychological circumstances described in this chapter, is the ability to take a new point of view. If one thing we know about theories is that they are likely to turn out inappropriate in some context and according to some standard we cannot foresee, then a rational approach to problems is a readiness to explore new contexts and new theories.

The term "rationality" is often used in the narrow sense of logical consistency; an action or decision is rational if it follows in some deductive way from a premise. Jürgen Habermas has defined a somewhat broader sense of the word, "basing the rationality of an expression on its being susceptible of criticism and grounding."[24] I accept these as proper uses of the word; a decision may be called rational if it follows from a premise, and a verbal expression may be said to be outside the realm of the rational if it is not open to argument. Rationality in these narrower senses, however, seems to center around a method of analyzing proposals already made, while in other usages the meaning of the term extends farther, as in the phrase, "a rational approach to a problem," to include the notion of an ability to canvass alternatives. It may be that rationality in its narrower senses cannot be put to use unless the broader notion, which encompasses a willingness to scrutinize a plan and reject it, is already in place. To be critical is to imagine the possibility of an alternative.

Rationality in the sense that I am using it is linked to a notion of the modern. As Stanley Cavell felicitously puts it, the modern begins "at the moment in which history and its conventions can no longer be taken for granted."[25] To the distinguishing characteristic of the modern temper—that it is self-reflective and self-critical—no doubt a host of influences have contributed. One is the simple empirical realization, shaped by reports of exploration, by modern means of transportation and communication, and by anthropology, the discipline that is their offspring, that there are a host of possible moral and metaphysical views of the world. The growth of literacy itself contributes to the self-reflective temper, by making it possible to record, to pull apart and reform, a set of thoughts. Printing has reinforced the effect by multiplying the number of records of alternative views and making them easily accessible.[26] The chief contributor, itself partly created by these other factors, is the shrinking of the world of the mythical, where nature and culture are seen as one. The mythical view offers a nearly seamless pattern of explanation; as Edward Evans-Pritchard said, concerning Azande witchcraft beliefs:

> In this web of belief every strand depends upon every other strand, a Zande cannot get out of its meshes be-

cause it is the only world he knows. The web is not an external structure in which he is enclosed. It is the texture of his thought and he cannot think that his thought is wrong.[27]

The mythical approach is not irrational, in a society that takes it seriously, because it does form a consistent basis for explanation. It loses its explanatory force, however, under the conditions described in this and the first chapter, when the correspondence between language and the world, between theory and the world, has been attacked so many times that it is neither certain nor natural—when, literally and figuratively, nothing is sacred. In such a world, with a multiplicity of explanatory frames, the fit is never perfect and the rational mind must be ready to try another.[28]

A tradition in philosophy and psychology identifies the rational position as the one that takes a "disengaged" point of view.[29] If this is understood only as the ability to treat every problem as abstract, to reason from any set of hypotheses, it tends to degenerate into a form of instrumental reason, in which values are radically separated from means. If "disengagement" is understood in a different sense, as willingness to abandon a point of view in the face of evidence, and to search for another, then it corresponds to the rationality of the modern temper. This, it seems to me, is the working notion of rationality that survives from Piaget's concept of formal operations as thinking from a decentered point of view and Kohlberg's notion of the moral point of view as "universalizable."

The modern rational approach is plainly not one of the natural heuristics, which are more closely linked to mythical thinking; we suppose that our culturally bound stereotypes describe things as they naturally are, and the anchoring heuristic makes us slow to entertain contrary evidence. If contact with other minds, either through face-to-face discussion or in more passive ways is a main avenue to seeing new hypotheses in addition to those that spring naturally to mind as available or representative, then it is also a road to the rational point of view. The causal relations, of course, are reciprocal; one does not change one's mind just by confronting a contrasting argument or hearing new evidence, nor does one acquire the habit of disengagement and rational search for alternatives merely by being momentarily in the presence of an alternative. Contact with other points of view, when they have been able to persuade us by discursive means we can understand, also trains us to listen to other points of view, to take a rational approach. For example, in a recent study of adult thinking jurors were asked to read two conflicting accounts of an (apparently) historical event and, in another task, to evaluate the evidence in a film of a trial. The investigators found that those who were best able to take a disengaged perspective toward interpretation of the history (as in the phrase, "from the point of view of one country") were likewise best able to participate in the analysis of the trial evidence, because they were able to see the evidence from alternative points of view, and then to respond to questions and change their conclusions about what the evidence implied.[30]

Freedom of inquiry, the access to other minds, is thus linked to a modern rational approach to problem-solving. We may not be able to abandon inappropriate solutions proposed to problems, just because we encounter alternatives, but it is clear that we are less likely to be able to abandon them if we don't encounter alternatives. Cognitive psychology points to this link, not because the mind is "rational" in the sense that it has some set of formal methods for solving problems, but precisely because it does not. It is the peculiarity of the natural heuristics of representativeness, availability, and anchoring, together with the idiosyncracies of different minds and the human characteristic that new points of view can generally be understood only through discursive means, that gives rise to the need for free access to alternative solutions to problems.

There is, finally, no other, more restricted method of inquiry to replace the modern rational approach. The narrowly "scientific" methods—statistical sampling, logic, and the laws of probability—relied on as yardsticks of rationality by critics of the natural heuristics are primarily ways for scientists to check the workability of their hypotheses. Deductive logic, whether or not we view it as an approximation of one of the elements of Piaget's "formal operations," is a way of seeing whether the consequences implied by a hypothesis make sense in the light of other evidence, very much as Einstein did when he tried to state the logical consequence of his thought-experiment. The scientific investigator who does not use those methods has acted "irrationally" in the limited sense that he has failed to try to get around the anchoring heuristic, has failed to try hard enough to find whether there is a context in which his hypothesis will not fit. Generally, however, he cannot find his way to an entirely new approach to the problem except through the natural heuristics tempered by an open dialogical critique.

Repressive Rationality

A principal objection to my conclusion grows out of the view that people are not open minded enough to entertain alternative points of view in a "disengaged" perspective and that correspondingly other minds are not in fact idiosyncratic enough to offer us real alternatives. That view is associated especially with social philosophers of the Frankfurt School, who have argued that decisions, at least conscious decisions outside a therapeutic dialogue, will tend always to be shaped by institutions of domination. The inevitable process of socialization of the child by the repression of instinctual drives is skewed by such institutions, including the patriarchal family and the system of production, so that some alternatives for decision are not so much foreclosed as inconceivable, never on the agenda. Free inquiry and the modern rational approach to problems, as I have described them in this chapter, are in this view simply not going to be strong enough to break through the repression and find those lost alternatives.

In a curious way, this argument from "repressive rationality," as I shall call it, does not seem to make much difference in the need for free inquiry based on modes and habits of cognition.* The argument implies one of two attitudes toward decision-making: vigilant criticism of every proposed decision, with little hope entirely of escaping the skewed dialectic of consciousness, or control of the decision process by some enlightened person or group in the effort to advance the emancipatory and discourage the repressive impulse.[31]

---

*The problems of irrationality are explored further in Appendix III.

The first of these positions would be tenable only if we never had to make practical choices to solve problems. But we do make choices, accompanied by arguments that one choice is better or worse than another. The very notion of a "critique" of those choices implies that there are some resources, however temporary or limited, upon which it is possible to base a judgment. When practical decisions are inevitable, this position comes down to a grudging, even despairing, support for free inquiry.

The second position is incoherent. It posits a "place to stand" for the enlightened, without infection by the subtle poisons of domination. But it is part of the repressive rationality argument that no one can stand entirely outside the system of cognitive domination. Sooner or later, the enlightened must take some actions that are, consciously or unconsciously, repressive in the old pattern. Everyone has seen examples; we should not need Herbert Marcuse to remind us that "in every revolution, there seems to have been a historical moment when the struggle against domination might have been victorious—but the moment passed."[32] The time arrives when the enlightened must come under criticism; but now there is no instrument for it. The struggle for free inquiry begins again.

The repressive rationality argument cannot close off the need for free inquiry because at bottom it shares the basic tenet that we cannot foresee what is the "best" decision for all the contexts in which it may appear. Those who have made the argument know that we approach problems using stereotypes derived from our past knowledge and that we become critical of them only through interaction. Whether or not our minds play tricks on us, we cannot escape from this way of solving problems.

Coda: Language Philosophy and Psychology

Because much of the capacity of the mind for thinking is organized around language or on an analogy to language, the connection between cognitive psychology and philosophy of language is all-pervasive. Of the multitude of parallels, three are salient. One is that language is public, or social, and at the same time idiosyncratic. A second is that, although our knowledge of the world is organized linguistically, there is no warranted method for telling how sentences we utter relate to the world. Third, we are bound to find some method for such interpretations, even though we cannot be sure it is adequate. Thus the heuristics people use for first grasping problems draw upon linguistic concepts that, like language, fit together in systems of belief; but they do not necessarily fit the world, either because they are chosen out of an inappropriate scenario or because the world has changed since the concept was formed. Under these circumstances, critical questioning of the concepts is essential to an interpretation of their interconnection and their possible connection to the world. We find new sources of understanding in other minds because for them concepts may mean somewhat different things and because they may cause us to apply our own concepts in new ways.

Language philosophy, like psychology, participates in the modern passion for self-reflection; rationality is the same for each of them. A rational attitude or approach takes a point of view that is "disengaged" in the sense that it is open to a new point of view, that it always takes a "listening" stance, as Gadamer would put it. Hermeneutics is the modern rational approach to understanding in philosophical dress.

PART II

Free
Expression
and the
Obligation
of the
Government

Interlude

Sketch of a Dialogical Freedom of Expression

Freedom of expression, in the traditional view, has a philosophical basis and legitimacy chiefly for those committed to individualism or to direct democratic government. In a parallel way, for individuals, groups and governments interested in the full interpretation of meanings and the rational solution to problems, freedom of expression has a philosophical basis and legitimacy rooted in the need, in both philosophy and psychology, for dialogue. People may, of course, subscribe to any or all of these philosophical bases; they certainly can say that freedom of expression is essential to individualism, to popular government, and to interpretation. Adherents of any of the theories, moreover, will encounter a similar political problem: Why should the government recognize any such civil rights as against the state?

To have shown that there is a need, whether from traditional or from dialogical sources, for freedom of expression and inquiry does not entail an obligation of the government to respect those liberties. It is a philosophical truism that there is always a gap between the need, whatever its basis, and the provision of rights; yet thinkers never tire of trying to close the gap. It has, for example, been argued that certain liberties, including freedom of expression, are indispensable if individuals are to act, and that it is illogical for a person who recognizes his own need to act to deny such liberties to others.[1] It has of course been argued that autonomous individuals will not find a government acceptable if it denies them the right to decide what they will read and think.[2] Although these are excellent arguments as far as they go, they do not entirely close the gap between is and ought. They show instead that it is illogical or otherwise extraordinarily difficult for a legitimate government to deny certain liberties. Ultimately, it seems that all any political argument can do is to show that the loss due to the denial of a right is great. The larger the loss, the narrower the gap becomes between ought and is. So here, in the two chapters that follow, I shall show that the price paid in irrationality of decision-making and in loss of legitimacy is extremely high.

There is still a possible objection to the conception of a "right" rooted in the need for dialogue: that the nature of language itself makes the notion of any particular "right" so incoherent as to be useless as a guide to thought. If meanings are always open to interpretation, if bodies of knowledge always have a horizon for further criticism, can we say that we know what a "right of freedom of expression" is with enough precision to be able to apply it? Some members of the Critical Legal Studies movement, sometimes drawing on French deconstructionists, have come close to saying "no," a response that at least has the attraction of simplicity.[3]

The argument, for very good reasons, is hardly ever found in so simple a form. The critics are engaged in an attack on traditional modes of legal reasoning, claiming that those modes imply an assumption that the invocation of a "right" can point in a predictable way to a result, without constant reference to the context of the problem and the values that underlie the right. They argue that contradictory value judgments usually underlie existing legal doctrines, a paradox that makes any pretense that rights are "self-executing" especially pernicious.[4] They use modern language philosophy in a way similar to the way I have used it in earlier chapters, to show that a normative sentence cannot be torn out of the context in which it is uttered. They hope thus to reveal the social forms and value judgments that underlie existing claims of right and to advance a different, emancipatory project in their place.

But they do not, because they cannot, utterly reject the effort to use language to express norms; such a rejection, as I have argued earlier, would not be consistent with the way we use language. Like anyone else, the critics cannot begin to think about a problem of policy except from some point of view that limits the possible approaches to the problem. They are bound to try to solve problems, as do other lawyers, by shaping a standard in words.[5] The difference, I take it, is that they are frank to say that the standard is constantly reshaped in the light of the values of society; they reject the notion that rights can be self-contained or self-executing.

That rejection, which I share, is not tantamount to the rejection of the notion of rights as such. Like any other judgment of value, the establishment of a right of free expression is a guide to thought. It does not automatically dictate what decision ought to be made in a case, but constrains the decision-making process in the direction of free expression. And even though it is not self-executing, it can be made more effective by techniques of interpretation that I shall discuss in Chapter IV.

Freedom as it is understood in this book ought to be embraced, rather than rejected, by those who are critical of legal scholarship on the ground that it is not sensitive to the social character of language, because that social character itself gives rise to freedom. So far from being dissolved by the characteristics of modern interpretation, the right of free expression can be seen as a consequence of two of those characteristics, its dual properties that we must, on the one hand, make interpretive decisions and that they are, on the other hand, always open to criticism. It is one right that can be made with the same tools that are used to criticize the formalistic defense of traditional legal rights.

Chapter IV will set forth the political framework for the dialogical freedom of expression, showing why it is concerned particularly with linguistic or symbolic expression, and why government limitations on the topics or participants in public discussion lead to contradictions that tend to destroy the legitimacy of a modern state. Although the establishment of institutions for decision-making that have limits on their scope of inquiry is inevitable, I argue that government failure to permit open debate through some forum on questions of policy leads to errors of understanding and of judgment. Those errors in decision-making, when combined with the deliberate adherence to an irrational approach, undermine the authority of the government, because the populace of a modern state is aware of the logical and causal relations between dialogue and rational decision-making, not specifically but as an implicit part of the experience of living in a modern society.

The force of my argument, even though it is generalized and theoretical, seems to me to depend upon an empirical sense of the practical results of the psychological and philosophical conditions described in the first two chapters. Accordingly, I have introduced it by a short chapter in which I present case studies of irrational government decision-making. I make no pretense that the case studies in Chapter III can prove the arguments of Chapter IV. They only illustrate how failures to perceive or make use of alternatives that may fit the context of a problem can lead to gross errors of judgment, errors that seem obvious in retrospect. They are the sort of failures that would persuade a government to see the point of the arguments of Chapter IV.

The dialogical right of freedom of expression for which arguments are made in these chapters may be viewed as an aspect of freedom of association more than as an aspect of the freedom of the autonomous individual to speak his mind. Because discourse is conducted through systems that are social creations, it depends upon the circumstances of society, such as pictures to look at, texts to read, and other persons to whom to talk and listen. The benefits of discourse are shared by those, whether they are groups or individuals, who participate in the dialogue, either by expressing their opinions or by taking account of other ideas, and all participants have a strong interest in gaining access to the dialogue. Under the dialogical view, then, groups have the same right to expression as individuals, and all have a need for access. Participants in the dialogue may think they need access to information that another party (typically the government) does not want to reveal. They may think they need to hear a point of view elaborated that the media do not care to print. They may even argue that the right of one participant to spend money to express his point of view ought to be limited, typically in an election campaign, on the ground that the sheer volume of speech on one side tends to skew the decision-making process. Although such problems of the "right to know" and the "right of access" arise constantly under traditional views of free expression, the tendency of Anglo-American law runs against the right of access, or in favor of individual and government discretion to limit access, because at the heart of the traditional view is the need for individual autonomy. At the heart of dialogical freedom of expression, on the other hand, is participation, the notion of dialogue in aid of appropriate decisions; the need for a right of access is much closer to the central justifications for the freedom. While problems of reconciling the full scope of individual discretion with the need for access arise for all theories, then, they become more difficult to resolve under the dialogical view. In Chapter V I shall elaborate the ways the balance might be struck, discussing the interaction between private expression and such government-sponsored instruments of expression as independent boards of directors for public media. In the course of the chapter I shall try to understand what the minimum is for a viable system of free expression.

The dialogical approach to free expression implies, finally, that a purported conflict between "collective needs" and "individual rights" is incoherent. Collective bodies, even though their decision processes are somewhat different from those of individuals,[6] need rational decision-making processes quite as much as individuals do. The right of free expression is in the interest of the society as a whole, or any of its units, fully as much as it is in the interest of the individual participants. To set apart some "collective value," such as a system of economic planning or a free-market system, and make it immune to criticism, on the claim that there is no foreseeable circumstance under which society would abandon the system, leads to a contradiction with the nature of interpretation and problem-solving. The value cannot be rationally applied in a new context unless it can be understood, and it cannot be understood unless it can be questioned. To "understand" the application of a value in a particular context is to imagine alternatives, to advance reasons why they are or are not appropriate in the context; to fail to understand the application is to risk an irrational decision. Meanings are disclosed discursively, and if they cannot be disclosed that way, they become mere slogans, not understood but merely heard.

It is a relatively modest, practical right, such as might actually be embodied in law, that is at issue here. My ambitions for it are, I hope, not too grandiose. In particular, I do not make the utopian claim that the right of free expression is "emancipatory" in the sense that it will enable participants to shed the strictures of societal conventions and fears; still less would I try to restrict the right of expression to speech that is designated "emancipatory." On the contrary, the right as conceived here is enmeshed in the social world, and grows out of the difficulties created by social conventions of language and interpretation. We may hope that the exercise of the right will lead to a transcendence of existing social limitations, but I do not see any way we can be certain it will. I am not claiming that free inquiry will always lead to rational results, but only that censored inquiry is likely to lead to irrational results.

Chapter III

THREE IRRATIONAL GOVERNMENT DECISIONS

The great benefit of discussion and inquiry, for the government as well as for private groups and individuals, lies in rational decision-making or, to put it in philosophical terms, in interpretation and understanding. By the same token, the long-term effects of state-enforced curtailment of discussion will tend to be persistently irrational decisions with an attendant weakening of government authority. It is this other side of the coin with which the case studies in this chapter are concerned. I mean for us to comprehend concretely and practically the destructive effects of ignoring alternatives before we pass on in Chapter IV to a more general statement of the source of the government's obligation to respect free expression.

Here I shall outline three cases of decisions both erroneous and irrational, examining in each the influence of limitations upon the decision-making process—limitations upon the persons who were permitted to participate as well as upon what could be discussed. The first two cases, the planning that provoked the Solidarity crisis in Poland in 1980 and the planning for a huge sugar harvest in Cuba in 1970, are drawn from socialist societies. The last, the decision to invade Cuba in 1961, is of course an act of the United States government. My analysis of these cases reaches back, on the one hand, to exemplify the principles in Chapters I and II, and forward, on the other, to illustrate the arguments in later chapters.

From a philosophical point of view, the process of decision in these cases can often be seen as a failure to explain the problem confronting the decision-makers. In the planning for the invasion at the Bay of Pigs, for example, it is apparent that the President and his advisers made a tacit agreement not to examine the proposal in such a way as to be able to see its implications. From a psychological perspective, all three are cases in which the decision-makers had fixed on a scenario for the problem and were prepared to screen out alternatives.

The cases also point toward the reasons why government ought to have an interest in more open dialogue. It is of course true that disastrous errors, to which the limitations on discussion in these case contributed, themselves damaged the credibility of the government. But it is more interesting to observe that the citizenry was aware, at some level, of the nexus between the error and the limitations. It is explicit in the Polish crisis that the supporters of Solidarity were as exasperated by the fact that policies were established in secret as they were by the substance of the policies. An error of judgment may be excusable, they seemed to be saying, but not when it is deliberately courted by an irrational process. The same conclusion is implicit in the reactions of the governments of Cuba and the United States to their errors; in both countries, the process of decision-making gradually became more open in succeeding years. In short, as I shall argue further in Chapter IV, because denizens of a modern state understand and expect to see a rational approach to problems, the authority of the state is damaged when the expectation is disappointed.

It is always difficult, of course, to brand any set of historical decisions as definitively "wrong." What seems at first glance an unqualified disaster, when looked at from another perspective may appear to have hidden benefits. If nothing else, the consciousness of error may cause the participants to change their way of making decisions in the future. In somewhat the same way, it is difficult to identify an "irrational" decision; one that seems erroneous on the basis of its results may be rationally arrived at, and one that is irrationally arrived at may in some cases have excellent results. In an effort to avoid protracted discussion about the definition, I have chosen cases where the participants themselves concede that an error was made. There is an error of judgment for my purposes if the participants (or some significant part of them) as well as outside obervers recognize that the acts did not attain the end sought and were poorly designed to do so. That standard has tended to limit the field to decisions to which the participants took a narrowly "instrumental" approach, but I do not find the cases any less interesting on that account. That characteristic reveals that the problems could not reliably be solved using such restricted methods; often the error of judgment even from a practical point of view lay precisely in the failure to step outside the instrumental context and look at broader value questions. Ultimately, a different decision might have required an inquiry into the most basic values of the society, a possibility to which I shall return at the close of this chapter.

Solidarity and the Polish Economy

The recurrent symbol of crisis in Poland is government action to raise the prices of consumer goods, provoking a wave of strikes and other conflicts with the authorities. When the government of Wladyslaw Gomulka raised consumer prices just before Christmas of 1970, the protest was so widespread that Gomulka had to be replaced as head of the Polish Communist Party. When Edward Gierek's government in its turn raised food prices an average of 60 percent in June of 1976, the workers in industrial centers rose once again; the prices were rolled back. When the prices were nevertheless raised again in camouflaged form four years later, the result was the potentially revolutionary crisis symbolized by the organization of Solidarity.

These repeated government actions and confrontations are only symptomatic of a continuing set of economic problems, never squarely faced nor resolved. Critics outside Poland have agreed upon the main outlines of the problems; more important, independent commentators inside the country agree as well. The Experience and Future Discussion Group, which included disaffected party members and government officials, a sort of "loyal opposition," drafted reports a year before the Solidarity uprising, predicting the crisis and analyzing its sources.[1]

The system of economic planning, solidly established by the time of Gomulka, emphasized investment and growth in heavy industry, without a clear view to the development of markets. Agriculture, which was still largely in private hands, never received consistent encouragement, even though it was able to supply consumer goods and foreign exchange. In a country rich in land and resources, the Poles remained poor.

After the fall of Gomulka, who had gradually insulated himself from news and advice that did not reflect his preconceptions,[2] the decision-making process was momentarily improved. Edward Gierek, at first a popular party leader, did decentralize the planning in heavy industry and tried to pull around him a diversified group of advisers. The classic scenario for socialist industrialization remained at the heart of the plan, nevertheless, and the core economic problem—lack of markets for industrial goods and failure to foster agriculture—continued unresolved. For over five years, Gierek found the money to bridge the gap between consumer goods and industrial investment through foreign loans, but because the problem of what was to be sold to the export market was never confronted, the result was a huge debt. Like the leaders before him, he tried to solve his problem, suddenly and without warning, by a consumer price increase. Rescinding the increase in the face of public protest only put off the day of reckoning for the debt until the actions of 1980 provoked the Solidarity crisis.

The government was apparently never able to gauge the public response to its price increases because from inside the planning-process the increases must have seemed so necessary. It was true that the demand for consumer goods exceeded the supply, and that one way to cut both demand and the continuing increase in foreign debt was to cut consumption. It was true in 1976 and in 1980 that the government needed some economic room to maneuver, that some short-term sacrifices needed to be made if the economy was to be reformed and shifts in the use of resources were to be made in the long run.

It was doubtful, however, that the government was willing to make those shifts—to encourage agriculture and consumer goods—or that the planners were even able to grasp the need for such changes. They had cut themselves off from any thoroughgoing criticism of their basic plan, as well as from many of the incremental suggestions that might have come from a "loyal opposition." In 1965, during the Gomulka years, "the views of the world-famous economist Kalecki, who criticised the plan for its neglect of the standard of living and suggested ways of relaxing the investment drive for the sake of consumption, met with ridicule and abuse at a Warsaw Party conference."[3] Fourteen years later, the Experience and Future Discussion Group was prevented from meeting again after its first bitterly critical reports on the "State of the Republic."[4] It was unclear that any sacrifices made by the public would really be used for reform, in part because the planners were unwilling to imagine the necessary changes.

A related set of difficulties arose out of the system of censorship. The people could neither voice their opinions and desires to the government through representatives and the media nor get reliable information about the economic situation. Public opinion became a rumor mill in which the people believed the situation was different and worse than it was and that it was caused by "conspiracies" in the government.[5] They were unwilling to sacrifice anything of their "jam today" when they had no idea what they might be trading it for.

The Experience and Future reports hammered home the point that the crisis in Poland was more political than it was economic; the problems of economic allocation were not technocratic planning problems, but value questions about how much ought to be spent for what. They were the sort of questions that called for discussion and compromise, for "understanding"; they did not get that discussion because the planners were unable to accept it and the people were prevented from engaging in it. The Group put it succinctly in the conclusion to its report: "Among the deficiencies our society must endure, the most important is not the lack of meat or other goods but the lack of clarity and candor, the lack of trust in the words of our leaders, in official declarations, in information carried in the press or on television."[6]

It is impossible to exaggerate the importance in the formation of Solidarity of the demand for information and dialogue. That was the basis for the sixth of their original twenty-one demands in August of 1980:

> (6) Initiation of real steps to extricate the country from the crisis situation by:
> a. providing full public information on the socio-economic situation
> b. giving all social groups and strata the possibility of participating in discussions on a reform programme.[7]

Some leaders were even willing to make the economic sacrifices the government wanted, if they could only believe they were necessary. One of them told the British reporter Timothy Garton Ash, "We would work a six-day week if we were fully informed about the country's economic situation."[8]

By the middle of 1981, Poland was moving toward a legitimate government, under which the people might understand and criticize its decisions. That possibility has been swallowed up by martial law and its aftermath, chiefly because of the threat of Soviet intervention; the Polish state now governs tenuously, and almost without legitimacy.

The history of the errors of judgment that issued in Solidarity, then, are only superficially errors of "economic planning." To a much greater extent they are the result of a systematically irrational approach to the political decisions that guided the economy, resulting in a stalemate. The government planners and the people were unable to come to grips with reforms for reasons that, although different for each of the two groups—the inability of the planners, on the one hand, to imagine an alternative plan and the unwillingness of the people, on the other hand, to trust any government plan—were both rooted in the fact that they would not or could not communicate and argue out the issues.

Cuba and the Sugar Harvest of 1970

Cuba's Fidel Castro has been called a charismatic leader. Governing by his personal character and magnetism, he is believed, in Max Weber's words, to have "a certain quality of an individual personality by virtue of which he is set apart from ordinary men and treated as endowed with . . . exceptional powers and qualities."[9] The performance of political acts that are out of the ordinary is of the essence of authority for such leaders. Their rule is in constant tension with the routine that is at the heart of most economic exchange and of the instrumentally rational bureaucracy characteristic of modern government; that tension is particularly great in a nation like Cuba that has aspired to modern economic development.

As early as 1964, Castro set the goal of a stupendous sugar harvest for the 1970 season, ten million tons, more than twice what the country was currently producing. The goal was to be a rallying point, a fruitful way to mobilize the people; it was a natural charismatic aim. The country's need was enormous for the liquid capital that an abundance of sugar could supply; as one official put it, "The ten-million-ton *zafra* [harvest] will guarantee our country's second liberation."[10] Finally, and more practically, the Russian government had promised a shipment of harvesting machines, which were expected to be more efficient than the traditional hand work by machete.

When the machines arrived, it turned out that neither the terrain nor the cane itself was suited to them. They would not work, and their failure was no secret; everyone in the country knew that they had not worked. Long before 1970, it was apparent that the costs of producing the great harvest were going to be economically devastating, if it could be done at all. Foreign critics friendly to the government were warning that the feat was impossible, or very nearly so, and that in any case it did not make sense from an economic point of view. Successful or not, the effort was bound to disrupt all the other work in the country for months.[11]

Despite the fact that the prop of mechanization had been knocked out from under the plan, Castro stuck to the goal. He and most of his advisers were revolutionaries, accustomed to winning against unlikely odds. For the charismatic leader, especially one produced out of revolution, the very difficulty of the task, its power to organize the people for a daunting task, was part of its appeal. The government shut its ears to its foreign critics and apparently did not encourage or receive much argument from the mass of people within the country.[12]

The outcome was a foregone conclusion. The harvest fell short by at least a million and a half tons, and the effort distorted the economy out of shape. In fact, worn out by the mobilization effort and apparently unable otherwise to protest, workers had gone on a "slow strike" of absenteeism during the year.[13] In his speech for the anniversary of the revolutionary victory in 1970, Castro himself faced and admitted the error:

> The heroic effort to increase production, to raise our purchasing power, resulted in imbalances in the economy, in diminished production in other sectors and, in short, in an increase in our difficulties. . . .
> Our enemies say we have problems, and in reality our enemies are right. They say there is discontent, and in reality our enemies are right. They say there is irritation, and in reality our enemies are right.
> As you see, we aren't afraid to admit it when our enemies are right. (APPLAUSE)[14]

The Cuban failure had been a classic case in which, when the scenario no longer fit the problem, the leader had nevertheless shielded himself from seeing its implications and considering alternatives. But the long-term political consequences of the failure of the effort were still more significant. At the close of the same speech, Castro began to talk of reform: "Today it is impossible to direct and coordinate this entire apparatus. We must create a political structure to coordinate the different sectors of social production." In later speeches Castro admitted, in effect, that the error was partly due to a failure to listen to local advice. At a national meeting of the block associations (Committees for the Defense of the Revolution) he said:

> As a result of the development of our productive forces, it is necessary for many of the services in the country to be rendered at the city block level. . . . Everybody wants to know what's going on and is interested in everything.
> We are trying to find a way how, starting with our mass organisations, to create other organisations in which the workers, as workers; the Committees for the

Defense of the Revolution; the women, the young people—in fact, everybody—will be represented, so that
they can carry out close supervision of all those activities
on a territorial level. This, in addition to supervision,
control, and participation in those production centers
that already have some development, that have a workers' nucleus. Therefore, nothing will escape supervision
and control by the masses.[15]

Although such political structures had been under discussion
in the sixties, the program was now expedited, and they were
put into effect after the failure of the 1970 harvest. Representatives of local municipal groups, of workers from industries,
and of special-interest groups such as students and women are
organized as local assemblies, which pyramid into a national
assembly. These institutions, called Poder Popular, criticize
economic goals set for local industries and agriculture, criticize
proposals for legislation, and try to untangle bureaucratic errors and misallocations.

The government has made no bones about the fact that
these are not assemblies for root-and-branch criticism of the
government or its plans. Fidel Castro said as much in one of
his 1970 speeches:

Now there are no contradictions in our society; there are
no political parties to represent the landlords, bourgeoisie, and bankers; there is only one party, with one
ideology, and one society, to the extent that we are able
to eliminate all the hangovers from the past. Why, then,
not establish the greatest possible participation of that
society in the struggle for its life, if—as I firmly believe
to be the case—this is the most beautiful thing about a
socialist society?[16]

The institutions of Poder Popular do not have the power to
reject an economic plan as a whole, nor to insist upon changes
in the laws. They can and do complain about proposed plans
and laws, as well as about much more minor things, and the
government takes the complaints seriously. The institutions
are frankly designed to make the centrally governed system

work smoothly by opening its decisions to dialogue and encouraging the suggestion of alternatives, at least at an incremental level. They have changed the nature of Cuban government, as Jorge Dominguez has said, from the "mobilization" style of intense charismatic leadership, to a more pragmatic "incremental" style; they help to coordinate routine with charisma.[17]

Poder Popular is, as it was meant to be, a very limited dialogue. The Cuban government no doubt still makes mistakes as a result of institutional limits on criticism, as well as for a lot of other reasons. Misallocations are still made, for example, as a result of impulsive decisions by Castro.[18] The point for us, however, is that the government saw the necessity for dialogue as a check against disasters such as the 1970 mobilization. Even a government openly and unalterably opposed to "bourgeois liberties," if it is also interested in avoiding unneccessarily irrational decision-making, is impelled in the direction of permitting debate.

The Invasion at the Bay of Pigs

In the United States, unlike Cuba and Poland, the right of the public to criticize government policy, although not unlimited in practice, is broad and well established. For security reasons, however, executive decisions, especially in foreign policy, have often been shielded from discussion and criticism before they are undertaken. Here I shall examine first the effects of secrecy and restricted decision-making on the famous Bay of Pigs fiasco of twenty-five years ago, and then the changes in the structure of decision-making that have intervened.

The decision taken early in the Kennedy administration to invade Cuba with exile forces landing from the sea has been called a "perfect failure"—perfect not only because the Cuban government forces easily overwhelmed and repelled the exiles, but because of the methods of decision-making.[19] It is a pattern by now familiar, not dissimilar to the process in Cuba itself that led to the disastrous sugar harvest nearly ten years later: the selection of a plan of action and a vision of success that is shielded from consideration of its implications and alternatives.

The Central Intelligence Agency had adapted the plan for the invasion from its operation in Guatemala, where its secret agents, working with local people, had overthrown a newly elected government in 1954. The tactics of the coup in Guatemala were quite different, involving as they did a base camp in a country next to Guatemala, no landing by sea, and the potential support of an opposition, both military and civilian, within the country.[20] But the CIA officials were self-confident, accustomed to succeeding; they claimed the analogy was close enough. The Kennedy people did not yet feel sufficiently sure of their own judgment to reject the plan, which was inherited, very nearly complete, from the previous administration. In his biography of Kennedy, Theodore Sorensen has written a description of the decision that is an anatomy of an irrational approach to a problem:

> Supposed pressures of time and secrecy permitted too little consideration of the plan and its merits by anyone other than its authors and advocates. Only the CIA and the Joint Chiefs had an opportunity to study and ponder the details of the plan. Only a small number of officials and advisers even knew of its existence; and in meetings with the President and this limited number, memoranda of operation were distributed at the beginning of each session and collected at the end, making virtually impossible any systematic criticism or alternatives. The whole project seemed to move mysteriously and inexorably toward execution without the President being able either to obtain a firm grip on it or reverse it. Under both Eisenhower and Kennedy it grew, changed and forced decisions without any clear statement of policy or procedure. No strong voice of opposition was raised in any of the key meetings, and no realistic alternatives were presented. . . . No realistic appraisal was made of the chances for success or the consequences of failure. The problems of turning back a preconceived project ready to

go, supposedly without overt American involvement,
seemed much more difficult than permitting it to go
ahead.[21]

Kennedy and his advisers for the most part viewed the
problems of the invasion from what they thought was a practical point of view, focussed on its chances of success as a tactical
military matter rather than on any broader moral or legal concerns; in fact many of them were quite impatient with any
attempt to argue the morality of the invasion. Yet that narrow
approach effectively disabled them, I think, from seeing some
of the practical contradictions implicit in the plan. Two assumptions made by the President and those around him were
that the invasion would not be attributed to the United States
and that the Cuban population would rise up to support the
invasion. A moment's reflection will show that the two are
schematically linked. If the invasion could be successful without the clear appearance of the U.S. military, then the rallying
of the disaffected on the island to the invaders would make it
all the more a "Cuban" matter. There could be very little complaint about the destruction of a government so obviously unpopular.

The Director of the CIA later claimed that his people had
not represented that there would be a "spontaneous uprising of
the unarmed population," and it is indeed hard to imagine
how there could have been substantial support on the island for
the invasion without the complicity of the Cuban army or a
substantial fifth column (neither of which was present).[22] The
fact that the planners nevertheless believed that an uprising
was in the cards suggests that they were unwilling to face the
implications of the possibility that it would not occur. In that
case they would have had to picture the Cuban government as
at least minimally legitimate and the people as willing to defend it, and they, in turn, would have had to picture themselves as having attacked such a government; conversely, if
they had been able to picture those situations, they would have
seen how improbable the uprising was. Thus, I think, the
desire to avoid thinking about the "morality" of attacking
Cuba led to an avoidance of the realistic possibilities of failure.

It seems that the CIA and the President's advisers were

working with different and conflicting scenarios: The CIA expected quite a lot of U.S. military support, while Kennedy did not want to give any support that would openly link the attack to the United States. The two scenarios were fused for purposes of planning by the vague hope of support inside Cuba. Once again, if that ill-defined assumption had been examined to see what it implied, and if the alternative that in fact occurred had been contemplated, the conflict between the expectations might have been clarified. Because of his own scenario excluding all U.S. military involvement, moreover, Kennedy made a decision that was a tactical error from the point of view of the invaders. He refused to order a second air strike to cover the landing at the Bay, and thus made it much easier for the Cuban government to repel the invaders. If he had thought the scenario through beforehand, he would have seen that the air strike was necessary, and he might have seen that the invasion "with no open U.S. involvement" was an incoherent scheme.

The administration scotched the possibility that forces outside the circle of advisers would force the President to see the consequences of the plan. Those reporters who got wind of the invasion and asked the government for confirmation were told to keep quiet about it in the interests of security. The *New York Times*, although it did publish three stories mentioning the possibility of the invasion, gave the matter less prominence because of the government's caution. Yet after the fiasco at the beach in Cuba, Kennedy said to Turner Catledge of the *Times*, "Maybe if you had printed more about the operation you would have saved us from a colossal mistake."[23]

What could he have meant? Certainly Kennedy had heard people, including Arthur Schlesinger, Jr. among his own advisers, opposing the invasion. Did his words merely express a wish that press exposure had made the political situation different, so that the element of secrecy and the fiction of "no U.S. involvement" would have been destroyed? They expressed that wish, no doubt, but perhaps also a little more than that. Kennedy seems to have thought that he needed more persuasive and vivid arguments to call his attention to the political consequences of the invasion, to the incoherence of the plan, and to its slim chances of success. Reporters like Tad Szulc of the *Times* knew that it was unrealistic to expect an uprising in Cuba, and that the hand of the United States could not be concealed. More important, a number of journalists, including James Reston and Edward R. Murrow, saw some of the moral and political consequences of unprovoked aggression against a small nation. The press, perhaps, had the power to bring those issues forward in a way that could not have been ignored; the media, for example, might have spelled out the implications, both instrumental and moral, of the projected invasion, and might even have given a clear idea of what the Cuban response was likely to be.

The process of making foreign policy decisions of this sort in the United States has changed in the intervening years, not only because of the Bay of Pigs itself, but because of apparently similar patterns of decision-making during the war in Vietnam. There is no doubt that the decisions to escalate that war, taken from 1963 until about 1970, were not irrational in the same way and to the same degree as the 1961 decision about Cuba. Kennedy himself, and Johnson after him, arranged to have more varied and flexible intelligence information. Yet the controversy over the executive decision-making process during that period continues to center precisely on the question whether or not that process was "rational," either in the sense I have used the word in this book or in some other sense. Leslie Gelb, who had been in charge of the assembly of the Pentagon Papers for Robert McNamara at the Defense Department, argues that the system was rational in the narrow sense that "the core consensual goal of postwar foreign policy (containment of communism) was pursued consistently." He goes further, however, to say that "virtually all views were considered and virtually all important decisions were made without illusions about the odds for success."[24] It is difficult to see how that claim can be entirely true, at least in the way I have tried to think about the consideration of alternatives in this book. If it were true, then the "consensual goal" should have been brought into question. Gelb himself notes that skeptics in the intelligence services lacked influence with their superiors (not to speak of the President) precisely because "the shared images were too strong."[25] What Gelb is saying, in effect, is that for the most part the officials did their job; they called the shots as they saw them and did not lie to themselves or their superiors.

It is clear, all the same, that thoroughgoing criticism of the assumptions of U.S. policy did not get much exposure.

This view is confirmed by one of the most notable skeptics among the intelligence advisers, Thomas Hughes, at that time Director of Intelligence for the State Department. In 1965, for example, he argued (apparently correctly) that escalation of the bombing in North Vietnam would strengthen rather than weaken the resolve of the North Vietnamese. [26] Yet the President and his immediate advisers went on believing that they could force the Vietnamese, through the bombing, to be "reasonable" and negotiate; they never really saw the matter from the point of view of North Vietnam. One reason, Hughes wrote in 1972, was that opinions such as his were often filtered out at the inner circle of decision: "These . . . estimates were read and rejected by the contingency-paper writers, whose own quite different assumptions went into their policy papers—which in turn went forward from the State and Defense Departments to the White House." He went on to say that the underlying intelligence estimates could have been given their proper emphasis, could have been forced upon the consciousness of the executive, if they had been circulated to a joint committee of Congress:

> The proposal goes very much to the question of the environment in which estimative intelligence is listened to and hence the environment in which Presidential decisions are ultimately reached. By ending the Executive's current exclusive access to estimates, and converting them genuinely into what their name implies—*national* estimates—the President and Executive officials below him would be less able to turn off the estimative process in moments of dissatisfaction or embarrassment. [27]

Something very much like Hughes' proposal has actually occurred. During the seventies Congress seized the initiative to establish Intelligence Oversight Committees, which are briefed on projected intelligence and counter-intelligence operations. Through such committees, as well as the War Powers Resolution of 1973, Congress has forced its way into all foreign policy decisions, whether secret or not, that involve military aggression. [28]

The shift toward decision-making shared with Congress not only widens the debate, bringing more diverse opinions to bear upon a decision, but also gives those opinions some of the power that President Kennedy wished they had when he spoke to Turner Catledge in 1961. Sometimes power has to be exerted to force people to listen, to take advice into account when, as Gelb puts it, "shared images are strong." This is one of the senses in which it is said that "information is power" in the realm of politics; if information can be kept away from those, in the press or in Congress, who have the power to force officials to take it into account, its effect can be blunted or avoided.

The narrative of the Bay of Pigs and the subsequent changes in foreign policy decision-making make for a cautionary tale. They remind us that simon-pure expression of opinion, without regard to its source or the forum in which it is made, does not necessarily cause anyone to look at new alternatives. It is just for that reason I have included the example; I don't want to be thought of as pretending that the presentation of alternatives invariably is effective (or for that matter that the alternatives are invariably good ones or lead to an appropriate result). I think the story does suggest, nevertheless, that the failure to generate alternatives, whether or not they are accepted, has still worse results. If there were no evidence that could be assembled into a record like the Pentagon Papers, there would be no way to decide why decisions are wrong nor to propose changes. Once generated and disseminated, there is at least some hope that ideas will take on persuasive force; the worst case occurs when the authorities can prevent information both from being generated and from being disseminated. Something very close to that had happened before the decision to invade Cuba, and that was one reason that the invasion was permitted to occur.

Conclusion

The reflections in the last few pages concerning developments in United States military foreign policy during and after the Bay of Pigs suggest that important decisions of the sort discussed in this chapter are linked finally to basic value-policy choices in the society. Indeed, that is undoubtedly a principal reason why prejudices in these cases were so strong that the leaders were unwilling to consider alternatives. As the Bay of Pigs invasion is linked in the American mind to containment of Communism, which has been, in Leslie Gelb's and Richard Betts' words, the "core consensual goal of foreign policy" since the late forties, so the Polish economic crisis is linked to the core decision to emphasize central planning of heavy industry, and the Cuban sugar fiasco to the core decision to accept charismatic leadership toward economic prosperity.

In light of those links, it may seem utopian to suppose that the leaders could have made alternative decisions in the three cases. I am not claiming, however, that a society is obliged to abandon its basic policy in order to entertain new alternatives. Even though a basic policy may be reaffirmed, for one reason or another, after it has been examined, its consequences will be clarified. Thoughtless acceptance of the policy of containment, for example, had accustomed United States officials to the belief that governments like that of Cuba do not enjoy strong indigenous support; questioning the policy might have led to questioning that belief as well as the viability of the invasion. A fresh examination of the policy of centralized industrialization in Poland might have led (and may yet lead) to the view that it could be harmonized with the development of agriculture, and a fresh examination of the unquestioning acceptance of Castro's leadership might have led to the realization that the plan for the 1970 harvest was rooted in an illusion. After such a reevaluation, the basic policy may still be accepted for the society, but if it is not examined at all, then its applicability, its meaning for the decision at hand, will not be clear.

It is true, of course, that governments sometimes have to make quick decisions; there are times when it is nearly as important to take some action as to take precisely the right action (although the cases in this chapter do not seem to be of that type). We have basic structures of policy and value just so that we retain a framework for decision, so that we do not have to approach every case as an original question. Often the existing framework does supply a plausible choice when an emergency decision has to be made; if the inquiry is limited to an instrumental approach to the problem, however, there is always a risk that the decision chosen will not be the appropriate one and that a broader inquiry would yield a better result. Furthermore, if criticism in some forum is not encouraged after the action has been carried out, there is the added risk that the decision-makers will never understand why the core policy did not work and will make a similar error again.

While a government may limit the rationality of its decisions, then, and may sometimes feel obliged to do so, it cannot exclude the consequences, regardless whether it is a "planned" or a "market" society. The three governments in this chapter compromised their inquiry by limiting both the participants and the agenda for discussion. Decisions were made by a closed group, or by a leader with the advice of such a group, according to a preconceived scenario, hardly questioned by any of the participants. The scenario was not subjected to criticism from outside the group, even though its members were the least likely candidates to be able to imagine alternatives to it. In short, having adopted a framework that violated basic principles of hermeneutic understanding and problem-solving, those governments paid a considerable price in rationality and legitimacy for the resulting decisions. As I shall show in the next chapter, governments ought to recognize free expression in order to avoid systematically paying such a price.

Chapter IV

POLITICAL
PROTECTION FOR FREE
EXPRESSION

For many Anglo-American political philosophers, individual rights are part of a social contract theory of the state. In this tradition, if freedom of expression is essential to the autonomy of the individual, then the individual conditions his consent to the government upon the preservation of the freedom. John Rawls expresses the idea generally in connection with his social-contract scheme: "It seems that equal liberty of conscience is the only principle that the persons in the original position can acknowledge." Scanlon puts it still more sharply: "The harm of coming to have false beliefs is not one that an autonomous man could allow the state to protect him against through restrictions on expression."[1] In the world of individualism, a state that does not recognize such rights is simply not legitimate.

If we view freedom of expression as derived from the need of individuals and groups for dialogue in aid of understanding and problem-solving, then the issue of the state's obligation to recognize the need is presented anew; the arguments from individual autonomy and social contract do not apply in the same way. The arguments that can be made to show the state's obligation under the dialogical view are nevertheless compelling enough, I think, on other grounds. These arguments do share with the social contract theory an emphasis on the legitimate authority of the state; as I shall show in the course of this chapter, a modern state that limits participation in discourse to certain speakers or certain subjects tends to damage its own legitimacy. The arguments can be brought into focus if we consider first just what sort of speech is to be protected.

What Is Speech?

How shall we define this "expression" about which the question of the state's obligation is raised? Thomas Emerson, in his well-known distinction between "speech" and "action,"[2] chose a definition that seems confusing; speech, after all, usually *is* action, of a particular sort. But Emerson is pointing in the right direction. The action that speech embodies may persuade others to act, but it is still, as Scanlon puts it, "expression which moves others to act by pointing out what they take to be good reasons for action."[3] It is expressive action that speaks to the mind through an "argument," using the word in the sense of a symbolic action that conveys an intention, even when the argument is presented in something as simple as a schema or an image. The essence of the notion of "speech" for purposes of political protection is that it puts forth an argument that must be understood, that is susceptible to explanation or response through other arguments before any other sort of action is taken. The words of Justice Brandeis in *Whitney v. California*[4]—from which both the epigraph and the title of this book are drawn—are the touchstone of a working distinction: if speech can be answered by more speech, then it ought to be eligible for protection.

This definition does not include absolutely every use of the spoken word, or every symbolic action. Some are not arguments to be understoood or answered, but are mere signals; the example familiar to lawyers is crying "fire" in a crowded theater. Some are uttered under circumstances where a reply is, as a practical matter, all but impossible; a false statement of ingredients on a retail package of food is perhaps an example. The effect of answerable expression, taken together with its interpretations and answers, is unpredictable. The meaning of such expression is not self-evident; it depends upon the context chosen for interpretation or other answer by the one who listens or looks and those in the dialogue with her (which may include herself at another time). If she hears a political talk, she has to consider how to take it: for its apparent truth-value, as a reflection of the personality of the speaker, as an oblique reflection of social or economic problems, or as something else. If she finds the talk somewhat persuasive on its face, reflection by herself or discussion with others may lead her to think that it is only clever propaganda or the expression of an unbalanced mind. If she looks at a painting, she has to find a context for it, find a way to look at it: as representative of a style, for its place in some view of the history of art, or according to some standard for a "good" picture of this sort. Any of those contexts may influence the others; if she finds the picture beautiful at first, comparison with other paintings may convince her that it is a banal example of a style with which she was unfamiliar, or persuade her that it is more original than she had thought.

Nothing except expression through symbolic means is unpredictable in its effects in quite the same way. Other harms that the state frequently punishes sometimes serve symbolic means; a punch in the face may persuade one to be more polite in future. But a punch in the face has other, physical effects as well. Answerable expression, until it is answered or acted upon in some non-linguistic way (if action is called for), provokes only interpretation and answer.

Protection of Freedom of Expression

The obligation of the government can be put in a nutshell: A modern state, even though it establishes institutions that impose limits upon their own discussion for the purpose of reaching determinate decisions, if it is nevertheless committed to rational decision-making in the sense that I have used the term, must permit those institutions to shape their discussions as they see fit and encourage expression in forums outside those institutions upon the ground that the fullest dialogue contributes most to such decision-making. In the light of the arguments made until now concerning the nature of language and its interpretation, the heuristics for solving problems, and the definition of expression for our purposes, I think the obligation set forth in this bald proposition can be shown to be very strong. Its implications can be revealed best by studying the consequences of two sorts of limitations on expression— first of limitations on the subject matter and then of limitations on the participants.

Limiting the Subjects of Discourse

A proposal for action, such as a policy decision, is understood through dialogue much like any other bit of language. The context of the proposed action is bound up with its expected consequences; based on our expectations we guess whether it seems to fit the situation. We understand the "meaning" of the action through its supposed consequences, elaborated in a dialogue; there we imagine the consequences verbally or in images or both, we criticize that imagining, and then we imagine the consequences again. Alternative proposals or amendments to the original proposal for action are always in the wings, to be brought forward and compared in the light of the supposed consequences, just as alternative interpretations of texts or other expressions are available when, as a result of discussion, our previous understanding does not seem to fit the context. Limiting the imagining of possible consequences and alternatives, whether through sheer stubborn attachment to a single proposal or through censorship, formal or informal, disables the participants, whoever they are, from fully interpreting and understanding the proposal. Such effects were apparent in all the cases discussed in the last chapter. In Poland, the relative effectiveness of the economic plan could only have been interpreted by considering alternatives; in Cuba, the probable effect of the harvest could have been perceived only by trying to imagine its consequences and its alternatives. In the case of the United States attack on Cuba, the President's advisers had made an unspoken agreement to treat the proposal in an instrumental way, as though "how to do it" were the only question. But the failure to think about the legitimacy and

strength of the Cuban government, which was part of the refusal to consider broader moral questions, was linked to the
instrumental problem. The context in which the proposed invasion could be understood, and in which criticism might be
crucial, was not predictable.

The conflict between limitations on the subject matter
for discussion, on the one hand, and the nature of linguistic
interpretation and the rational approach to problems, on the
other, is illustrated most strikingly, in modern societies, when
an effort is made to make some set of concepts "true" for all
purposes, to place them beyond criticism. This is commonly
done informally, through custom or prejudice; thus in the Old
South before the Civil War, it was anathema to question the
propriety of the institution of slavery. A system of state censorship formalizes and bureaucratizes such controls; the results are
similar, although more hidden, when the government simply
takes over the media instead of censoring the private press. All
such programs, formal or informal, can be viewed as attempts
to turn answerable, interpretable expression into a triggering
mechanism, like a signal to action. But because the expression
in fact remains interpretable, the results are peculiar.

It turns out that the boundaries of the forbidden cannot
reliably be drawn. In the Old South, for example, freedom of
thought withered, not only in relation to slavery but generally
as to all topics, because no one could predict when a discussion
might suggest a new idea about slavery or race. Religious or-
thodoxy was encouraged, and scientific ideas about geology
and the descent of man were discouraged for fear that they
might call into question the domination and separation of
races.[5] Censorship, formal or informal, in every society where
it is found, tends to spread over uncensored knowledge like a
stain. I myself observed the effect at work in Nicaragua in
1984 through the censorship of the newspaper *La Prensa*. Although the standard of censorship was said to interdict only
reports of military matters or product shortages that might
cause panic, it was used to suppress, for example, an article
about a collision between a military vehicle and a civilian bus,
and another reporting the public announcement of a government plan to put the economy on a war footing, which mentioned problems of scarcity.[6] The interpretive activity of apply-

ing a verbal taboo, however it is defined, destroys its limits because its applications cannot be predicted.

The "Black Book of Polish Censorship," a file of directives to the press bureaucracy prepared by their Central Office and spirited out of the country during the crisis of the middle seventies, exemplifies the ways that censors try vainly to control interpretation. Like other developed systems of censorship,[7] the Polish rules contained general directives for policy decisions:

> 89 In connection with the reform made in the structure of local officials and the territorial division of the country, I should like to emphasize that consistent with the text of Comrade E. Gierek's address made at the 17th . . . Central Committee Plenum, it is the task of the press, radio and television to explain and propagate the reforms throughout the society.
>
> Hence, the mass media should not take up those problems which could evoke undesirable repercussions from the public.

The Central Office tried to help in the application of such general orders through an enormous number of other rules specifying how they were to be used. They range from the most painfully detailed:

> 103 No information on George R. Feiwel's book *The Intellectual Capital of Michael Kalecki; a Study in Economic Theory and Policy*, published in the United States, should be permitted.

to some that seem of middling generality:

> 88 No materials should be permitted which give information about the current level of pollution or which point up the phenomenon of the progressing pollution of Polish sections of rivers flowing from Czechoslovakia as the result of industrial operations in our country.
>
> On the other hand, information on the pollution of

these rivers caused by industrial activity in Czechoslo-
vakia may be permitted.[8]

But the proliferation of directives can only solve problems of
application that have already come up; they cannot tell the
censor what to do for the unforeseeable next problem. Through
the hermeneutic process, he tends to suppress anything that
colorably fits his general definitions. The Polish writer Stanislaw Baranczak tells, for example, why his editor wanted to
change the phrase "liver sausage" as it appeared in one of his
poems: " 'Liver-sausage'—she explained to me gently and pa-
tiently—'is the cheapest pork-butcher's product. The poem
gives the impression that the average Pole often eats liver-sausage, and this in turn may be understood as an assertion that
there is a meat shortage in Poland.'"[9] Every society with a
system of censorship is rife with similar stories; dissenting
writers and artists like Baranczak always have a treasured favor-
ite. Although the stories are sometimes offered as evidence of
the "stupidity" or "irrationality" of the censors, they seem to
me rather to suggest the opposite—the constant intrusion of
rationality through the appearance of alternative meanings for
the policies underlying the taboo. The elaboration of meanings
by the censor is the mirror image of the rational approach to
solving problems; it is, if you will, the rational approach to
avoiding solutions to problems.

Agents of the state ordinarily seek to suppress expression
because they suppose it fits in some explosive way with concepts that are already abroad: that obscenity will feed destructive sexual fantasies, or that criticism of the government will
hook onto pervasive dissatisfaction with society. But the "blank"
in information and communication created by censorship is
not effective to eliminate those ideas because it does nothing to
change the scenarios and schemas that are supposed already to
be dangerous; they go on and change in new ways unless they
are answered. If answerable expression is important enough to
be suppressed, it is important enough to be answered, and
suppression does not take the place of an answer.

The effect on the public mind is exaggerated if the populace knows, as they usually do, that there is some censorship,

even if they do not know the nature of what is suppressed. Then the "dangerous" underlying ideas become rumors, as in Poland in the years before Solidarity; public opinion manufactures crises and conspiracies, for lack of reliable information. Poles who were concerned about industrial pollution, for example, may well have thought that pollution was worse than it actually was, because of censorship under the rules in the Black Book. And the lack of information, or the publication of soothing information, fails of its effect because everyone suspects that any conflicting information has been suppressed. The "official" story does not trigger reassurance, because the story is insulated from answer and interpretation; rumor takes the place of any other answer.

Viewed as a general matter, then, censorship illustrates the philosophical and psychological nature of answerable expression; it shows that its interpretive and problem-solving character have no limits and cannot coherently be subject to a prescribed set of interpretations. But the effects of censorship are exacerbated in practice because it never does occur "as a general matter," but rather as a political matter. As such it tends to make decision-making irrational not by excluding some random group of alternative choices, but by excluding alternatives in an especially skewed way. The hope of the censors, at best, is to create a climate favorable to the government and within that framework to facilitate its pet projects, whether they be industrialization, the encouragement of agriculture, or some military endeavor. They will try to suppress expression that fails to accord, however vaguely, with those scenarios. If there are problems, unstated or ignored, with the existing system or the pet project, then the really dangerous opinions are going to be those that raise those problems; they are the ones that the censors will be most vigilant to suppress. It is the plausible opposition and the information genuinely damaging to the program, rather than the obviously crazy proposal, that the censor will find most unsettling. The nature of interpretation naturally makes it impossible for the censor to restrict himself to any such self-destructive program, but he is sure to catch, in addition to everything else he gets in his net, the most important alternatives to and the most dismaying consequences of the government's ideology and program. Censorship thus condemns the government to working with those proposals that obviously fit existing scenarios, without being able to see the most likely sources of error.

The clever censor, if he gives any justification for his work at all, is likely to reply that, without the salutary threat of the black pencil, the scissors, and the occasional arrest, society would never be able to shape a discussion so as to decide upon and carry out a government project. But that claim is too sweeping. The need for a determinate decision-making process does not justify any censorship outside the process; and even within the decision-making institution, there is no reason why its participants should not be able to decide what they want to discuss. Policymakers, and even their critics, may decide that a course of action is workable in view of its expected consequences and of the alternatives with their consequences. But it can only be understood as correct in the light of criticism; the concept "correct" is scarcely even usable except in a context where alternatives have been canvassed. We may take the proposal and our method of evaluating it as a model for a similar problem in the future, but only as a quick way into the problem, and not as a cast-iron plan immune to criticism.

Naturally we do not approach every problem afresh, as though it had no antecedents. We organize boundaries for discussion as continuing disciplines, designating them as "law" or "political science" or something else. Those boundaries are useful, however, not because we fail to criticize the way they are set, nor because cannot step outside them, but rather because we do criticize them. When a social or political question is cast as a legal problem, we commonly start the discussion by complaining that the context is too narrow, that we must take a broader approach; at least one editorialist will surely say that "it is not the job of the courts" (or the legislature, as the case may be) to resolve the matter. We pursue the legal analysis only when we are convinced it is adequate. In short, disciplines survive constant criticism of their terms and boundaries because that criticism shows that they are useful heuristics, ways to start thinking about problems. We agree to use the discipline when we think it is useful and not because we are forced to do so.

Censorship is difficult to shape into anything like a "discipline," to be used as an heuristic approach to the problem of what it is appropriate to say, because its alternatives, no censorship and censorship based on some other set of policies, are not subjects for discussion. The tendency of a system of censorship to swallow up the uncensored is accelerated by the fact that the rationale for the censorship is itself not subject to criticism. The censor reaches for the farfetched interpretation of a phrase because there is no "discipline" for the censorship that tells her to do otherwise.

Our analysis of censorship, as a matter of language as well as of politics, puts us in a position to see the fallacy of a relatively subtle version of censorship, often discussed by American scholars.[10] A distinction is sometimes made between "political" speech, that is, speech obviously about problems of statecraft and powers of the government, and "artistic" or "commercial" forms of expression, for example, which are far from the center of political debate, as a predicate to an argument that political speech ought to receive more protection from control by the state than non-political speech. I claim that such a distinction will not work. First and most obviously, it is impossible to state any linguistic distinction that will hold as between the "political" and the "non-political." Take the case of "liver sausage" as a political concept. If I had to take my stand upon a phrase chosen at random in order to defend the critical-hermeneutic position that meanings are never self-evident, that absolutely anything can be political in a proper context, I would be hard put to it if "liver sausage" were the words picked out of the hat. But the Polish editor had no trouble at all seeing the politics in "liver sausage," and the phrase serves as well as any other to show the malleability of meanings.

Nevertheless, it is fair to say that such an argument describes no more than the nature of language; we might still be able to decide through the hermeneutic process roughly what is "political" for us and what is not. The distinction between the "political" and "non-political" fails, finally, not so much because of the nature of interpretation as because of the nature of censorship. There is no reason for the state to take an interest in any expression except for political reasons, and expression is political by virtue of the fact that the state does take an interest in it. Those who advocate the distinction may say that some varieties of state control of expression, of obscenity, for example, are not directed to any problem central to the political process, but only, let us say, to the "quality of life." If the state, nevertheless, chooses to control expression affecting the quality of life, then it makes that into a political matter. The breakdown of the distinction appears very clearly in recent controversies over the definition and control of pornography. Some feminists have sought to define pornography as expression (particularly in pictures) that connects sex and violence toward women, drawing on evidence that such expression tends to degrade women in the mind of the viewer; they have sought in turn to censor such pornography as a way of reducing the incidence of violence toward women.[11] It is plain that there is no issue that is of greater political importance to those who have advocated such laws than reducing violence toward and degradation of women. Pornography, as newly defined, is marked as a "political" matter by the institution of censorship in this case just as clearly as the price of meat was marked as a political matter by the censors in Poland. Censorship, in the end, cannot slip into the system under the guise of controlling something "unimportant"; if answerable expression is not in some way important, the state does not bother with it.

Governmental authorities often use a related technique, by which they control or punish action that is connected to answerable expression as a way of controlling the expression itself. Local lawmakers in the United States have from time to time adopted measures against "disturbance of the peace" or "littering," for example, that are drafted so as to appear to be ordinary police controls; the statutes have then been used to control speeches and demonstrations or political leaflets.

American constititutional law has viewed the two sorts of legislation as rather different. "Disturbance of the peace" is described as a concept too vague to be applied in a case that implicates answerable expression; because the statute does not punish anything specific, it can be manipulated by the censor to control expression.[12] "Littering" is not called vague when it is applied to a political leaflet, presumably because it is thought that, in ordinary usage, the concept of "litter" is more concrete than "disturbance," and that a leaflet fits within the concept.

The courts instead say that the governmental interest in controlling trash in the streets must be embodied in a statute "narrowly drawn" so as to reach the trash problem with as little interference as possible with expression.[13]

In both cases, however, the courts are engaged in an interpretive process that is the mirror image of the censor's. Just as it is natural for the censor to expand the construction of any statute in order to control answerable expression, so it should be the job of legal interpretation to narrow the construction. While the censor's interpretation may be branded "vague" or "overinclusive" depending on the nature of the law, the court's underlying purpose remains the same: to use the interpretive process to narrow the scope of statutes to allow more scope for expression.

Censorship is a laboratory, then, to demonstrate a number of interesting things. On the one hand, the peculiarities of the way it is elaborated and of its effect on the public exemplify the irrationality of subject-matter limitations and at the same time show that a rational approach cannot be entirely suppressed. On the other hand, through its exclusion for political reasons of a body of approaches to problems, it increases the irrationality of decision-making. Censorship thus writes large the more general problem of the risks involved when alternatives for understanding or action are excluded from consideration.

Limiting the Participants in Discourse

Limits on the participants in a discussion are so common as usually to provoke no notice at all. At one extreme are the least controversial, which have little more than administrative convenience as a rationale: the need to ensure that a decision is made within a reasonable time, or to limit the scope of its effect. The limitations on the size of the jury in the Anglo-American trial, or on the participants in a litigation through rules of "standing," may be understood in this light. A significant characteristic of such decision-making bodies of limited jurisdiction is that, in practice, no one supposes that such a group will exhaust all the possible or even all the useful arguments in the matter before them. Although the decision of the group may be "final" in the legal sense for the purpose of ensuring that a definite decision is made, we nevertheless do not consider it final in any other sense. We seem to recognize that such a group runs a risk of failing to canvass major consequences or alternatives to the chosen decision, that its rationality is limited together with its jurisdiction. In societies that do not enforce censorship of subject matter, citizens and the media criticize the decisions of judges, juries, and every other sort of administrative body after decisions are made and sometimes while they are still under consideration.[14]

At the other extreme are limitations that are openly partisan, for the purpose of shaping decisions in a special way. A small group or a "vanguard" that runs the state in the interests of a class, for example, often allows no participation in decisions from outsiders. And in between the two extremes are decision-making bodies that, although chosen with particular "interests" in mind, have limited jurisdiction. The foreign policy decisions of the executive of the government, for example, are often taken in secret for security reasons and after discussion with advisers who, by some standard, are thought to have "sound" opinions. The decisions of these groups, of course, are open to criticism by people outside their jurisdiction just like those of any other administrative body (if the critics are not censored), on the ground of the inherent limits to their rationality.

A limited ruling group that purports to act in the interests of a class (passing for the sake of argument the problem of defining a class) cannot predict what decisions will turn out to be in the interests of that class. There is evidence, for example, that the development of the trade union movement in the United States has been in the long-term interest of the capitalist class, and that the development of free-market incentives in Communist China has been in the interest of the peasant class, outcomes that most representatives of business in the United States and of the peasants in China would not have foreseen fifty years ago. If the ruling group excludes consideration of some approach as contrary to the interest of the class it represents, then it necessarily runs the risk of error in selecting the decision that is, in the light of all the alternatives and conse-

quences, most in the interest of the class. The Polish bureaucrats under Gierek may have thought their policy of industrialization was in the interest of the working class, and Fidel
Castro no doubt believed the same about the great sugar harvest of 1970; nevertheless in retrospect it appears that the refusal to entertain alternatives led to a result that was not in the
class interest.

The dynamics of the situation are not substantially different, even when the oligarchy try to act in their own selfish
interests. Although they may suppose that no one could know
their interest better than they, it is notoriously the case that
interested parties have a difficult time seeing the consequences
of and alternatives to their schemes. The Polish bureaucrats
may have thought before 1980 that their economic plan would
at least be in their own interest, by preserving their privileges
and prerogatives, but it proved not to be any more in their
interest than it was in the class interest.

As a way of approaching problems, a group with limited
participation is potentially much superior to an outright limitation on the subject matter for discussion. The group can
increase the rationality of its decisions by insisting upon the
elaboration of alternatives, by being broken up into subgroups
for preliminary decisions, by appointing a member or members as "devil's advocate," and by having a cooling-off period
for the reconsideration of any decision. All of these measures
were used in foreign policy decision-making in the United
States after the Bay of Pigs episode.[15] In the case of a group
chosen for partisan purposes, however, the inherent limits on
their ability to consider alternatives is in fact usually exacerbated by the way the group is constituted.

The selection of members of a group on account of their
adherence to some interest is necessarily skewed. Each of them
is identified by some standard as stereotypically "right-think-
ing"; if it were not so, then some other person would have been
chosen. They all have a similar habit of mind, and will tend to
exclude similar alternatives. The implications are easiest to see
if we imagine such a group trying to adopt a more rational
method of decision-making. Let us suppose they appoint one
member of the group as "devil's advocate" to make counter-
arguments to the proposals typically made in the group. One
issue that the devil's advocate will want to raise is the wisdom

of the limitation on the membership in the governing elite. Why appoint a member of the existing group as advocate in this artificial way when the arguments could be more naturally presented by someone outside the group who in fact adheres to them? When considerations of national security are not at issue, the reason must be that the elite does not seriously want to consider any alternatives the devil's advocate will offer. The elite is selected as it is precisely because of its prejudices, and it expects to make decisions in accordance with those prejudices. The devil's advocate, cast in a difficult position, is likely to cease to be a gadfly. A version of this appeared in the group of advisers deliberating about the Bay of Pigs in the Kennedy administration. Although participation was limited primarily for security reasons, the group in fact appears to have been chosen in a skewed way, heavily weighted in favor of such "tough" plans as the invasion of Cuba. The result was that a potential advocate for an alternative, such as Arthur Schlesinger, felt intimidated from vigorously objecting. If the dissenter does not trim his sails in this way, he is likely to resign or be forced out of the group. He is subjected to a *de facto* subject-matter censorship, the indirect result of the limitation on the membership of the group. That censorship extends to everyone in the group because all are constrained from playing the devil's advocate.

Variations of the pattern appear repeatedly in the actual workings of ruling elites. As some members try to introduce greater rationality into the deliberations, they find themselves ridiculed or excluded. They then become disaffected, like the Experience and Future Discussion Group in Poland in the late seventies. It is a characteristic crisis of a ruling elite, a sign that its power is weakening, when members criticize the government because they cannot make their alternatives heard. They are indignant because they have, in effect, been subjected to censorship.

It is rare that a partisan ruling group does not engage in subject-matter censorship as well; limitations on subject matter and on participants, although they are analytically separate, are in practice usually found together because they spring from the same impulse to limit the prospect of alternatives. The combination gives rise to those "blind spots" so notable in ruling elites: their inability to see the economic or revolutionary crisis even when it is nearly upon them, and people inside and outside the government are warning them about it, as happened repeatedly in the seventies in Poland.[16]

The costs in rationality exacted by state schemes to limit discussion in order to advance a chosen program are enormous. The political motives that bring about subject-matter censorship or the formation of closed decision-making elites, or both, increase the risk of error inherent in any limitations on discussion, because such institutions systematically blind the participants to the most persuasive arguments against their proposals. The psychological and philosophical nature of interpretation makes it impossible for them to do this in a coherent way, but they can do it well enough to exclude consideration of many viable alternatives.

Although the free expression I envision in place of such restrictions no doubt presents the prospect of a disputatious politics, in which similar proposals may be made repeatedly, even under circumstances where they are unlikely to be accepted, that prospect itself suggests a benefit from having many forums open for discussion. We cannot predict at what point a proposal, even though it has been heard before, will hook effectively onto ideas that are already accepted so as to seem to fit the case. It depends on the nature of the decision-making body and on what other arguments have been given; it may even depend on the person who makes the argument. President Kennedy recognized this in his remarks about the press after the Bay of Pigs, as did Thomas Hughes when he advocated congressional discussion of intelligence information during the Vietnam war. No doubt Kennedy did not expect to hear any arguments from the press that he had not heard before, nor Hughes to hear any from Congress that were new. Their hope was that the arguments would "take" as they had not before, because of the way they were presented or the person who presented them.

Authority

Although the consequences for the state due to limitations on free expression are serious, a ruling elite might well think that, as I have described them up to this point, they are not too much to bear. The ruling group may believe that the actions of the government could not withstand rational scrutiny because, for example, economic decisions are determined by bribery and personal influence; they are likely to think that free criticism presents too much of a risk even if it might be in their long-term interest. And regardless whether the government is corrupt or not, the limitations on participants in and subjects for discussion also serve to conceal from the ruling group for a time just how irrational its decisions actually are. The group can keep the consequences of and alternatives to their policies away from themselves as much as from anyone else, as happened in Gomulka's Poland. In fact, because the decision-making group in such a situation is chosen on account of its adherence to a particular pattern of thinking, it is easier for them to persuade one another than to persuade others that their policies are successful. The ruling group thus may underestimate the costs of limiting dialogue, or believe that they have no real choice but to pay them. The price of suppression of free speech for a modern state, however, is more than a loss of understanding; it is a loss of authority as well.

The citizen of such a state expects the government to take a modern rational approach to its problems. Whether or not she is familiar with the arguments made in the first two chapters of this book, or similar arguments, she lives in a world infused by the consequences of them, because they are descriptive of how interpretation and problem solving are done under modern conditions. If the state purports to explain society and solve problems in a way that is inconsistent with the modern citizen's understanding, then limitations on discussion will drain its authority.

The force of this point is made easier to see by comparing life in such a modern state with an idealized traditional way of life, in which both the denizens and the government (if any) are satisfied to understand the world and to solve their problems by reference to myth. In the world of the Azande as described by Evans-Pritchard,[17] for example, the meanings of the actions of people as well as of physical occurrences are explained by a view of the supernatural that integrates all the knowledge of life. Words, like other actions, may have magi-

cal effects within that world of mythical significances. Freedom of expression would seem to have no place in such a society, because the abuse of words may be thought to visit supernatural dangers on the people and because understanding is
circumscribed in every case by the all-encompassing tradition.
Such a mythical system may be "rational" in the sense that it
can explain the world in a way that is adequate to the life of the
people, and the problems of authority attendant upon limitations of discussion may not arise.

This book is concerned not with such traditional societies, but rather with the enormous number of governments,
from the most centralized to the most democratic, that purport to solve their problems in a way that is consistent with the
modern rational search for alternatives. Such governments frequently try to have it both ways, mixing the sacred or the
mythical with the rational. They set apart some beliefs as beyond question, either because they are claimed to be of supernatural origin, as in a hybrid modern theocracy, or because
they are claimed to be "natural" and immutably true, as in the
case of an inflexible Communist or free-market ideology. A
modern state may try also to get some of the benefit of charismatic authority, by shielding from question the acts of its leader. But the nature of questioning essential to understanding
tends to destroy the walls surrounding the artificially "sacred."
In Cuba, for example, the effort to modernize the economy in a
way that would supply a greater abundance of goods and services to the people led to criticism of the leader's decisions and
to the formation of institutions to increase discussion about
consequences of and alternatives to proposed policies. I am
not, of course, trying to force all modern states into a single
mold of "modern development," whether industrial, techno-
logical, or otherwise; on the contrary, I am trying to leave open
the widest range of choices. Once a range of non-traditional
choices is opened, however, it cannot be arbitrarily closed off.
A set of beliefs cannot be shielded from the modern habit of
inquiry once the government has ventured upon that sort of
inquiry.[18]

Governments sometimes take a desperate measure, characteristic of totalitarian fascism, against modern critical understanding. They try to create a "modern myth" in which every-

thing is to be explained as if through a traditional world view. Such measures always seem unstable, partly because the myth after all is not traditional, and many people will refuse to accept it. More important, insofar as such a government tries to solve its problems by modern means, as it often will in the case of economic or scientific problems, the myth must begin to dissolve. The attempt to adhere to the myth leads to grotesquely irrational decisions in such societies.

The prevalence of a particular set of beliefs no doubt makes a difference in the rapidity with which the dialogical habit of mind will affect the society as a whole. For example, ideas that can be plausibly presented as emanating from a "foreign enemy" can often be excluded from discussion; that excuse for censorship has been used in the Soviet Union consistently for sixty years, and sporadically almost everywhere else. Similarly, if the state has a charismatic leader, his actions may be shielded for a time by enthusiam for his rule, although that enthusiasm will tend to break down in the face of irrational decision-making as modern habits of understanding come to be the norm. Finally, the interest in which the government claims to act may affect the temporary plausibility of limits on free expression. If the government purports to act in the interest of the working class, for example, it may seem superficially reasonable to prevent those who do not speak for that class from expressing their opinions, as has been done in Cuba. The most obviously unstable situation, on the other hand, is created when the government does not permit expression by the people it claims to represent. In Poland before 1980, for example, critics were acutely conscious that the government did not allow free expression to the working people in whose interest it acted. After the Solidarity strike began in Gdansk in 1980, the opposition Polish League for Independence stated: "The ruling party has been brought before a tribunal of the class from which it allegedly derives its pedigree and in whose name it pretends to govern."[19] Solidarity gained legitimacy precisely because it was a working-class organization, trying to gain access to understanding for those who were the government's source of authority.

In the long run, the scope of the demand for free expression does not depend on whether the government calls itself a liberal democracy, a socialist democracy, or something else. It depends rather on the attitudes of citizens to interpretation and problem-solving, and whether the government purports to act in accordance with them. Those expectations may lead to a demand on the part of citizens to listen and be heard even in a state in which they do not have the legal power to make the decisions themselves, either directly or through representatives. Their concern is to minimize the risk that a "wrong" interpretation will be accepted or acted upon or, if a factual question is at issue, be recorded as a judgment of history or science. Once they grasp the premise that discussion is essential to understanding, citizens know that discussion must take place in as open a system of discourse as possible if those who have the power to decide are to be sure that they know what they are talking about and that they have not failed to take anything into account. The citizens will not suppose that only workers have something to say in their own interests any more than they suppose only bourgeois have something to say in the interests of the bourgeoisie. If a topic or a source of opinion is excluded from discussion, then the inference is strong that there is something the government does not want to understand, or does not want the populace to understand. The exclusion implies that for some reason, corrupt or otherwise, the government aims to make a decision that is wrong for the context in which it is made. When citizens with such attitudes see themselves or others excluded from discussion, they do not "believe" in the government's position because dialogue is the only basis for belief they know. They cease to accept the government's authority because it is not consistent with the world as they understand it.

It is of course possible for a government to operate at the point of a gun and without authority. But rule entirely by violence does not, under modern conditions, confer legitimacy. Quite the contrary. The claim to authority implies a notion of understanding that leads to the need for free discussion, and such a group can give no justification through its approach to problems why it should remain in power. If the ruling group of the moment is replaced at gunpoint by another, there is not a ripple of complaint because it makes no difference who holds the gun. The moment the group lets its guard down, it is swept away, and the familiar lesson is that violence is not a sign of strength but of weakness.

Conclusions

All the arguments made in this chapter reinforce one another. The risk that important alternatives or consequences for policies will be neglected, always attendant on restrictions on the subject matter or participants in a discussion, is exacerbated by the political circumstances under which censorship is imposed and elites conduct discussions. The fact that such restrictions tend to become malignantly irrational under conditions of modern inquiry is the basic reason that modern governments lose their authority insofar as they repress free expression. A state not governed by traditional myth must foster free expression in the interest of its own authority as well as of rational decision-making.

The practical force of a right of free expression, shaped through the arguments made in this chapter, should appear most vividly in the character of legal problems and doctrines that are expected to arise in a state that recognizes those arguments. I foresee several sorts of legal issues, none of them entirely alien to the existing legal world of free speech, but all cast in a different light by the new approach.

Speech Acts

When expression is answerable in the sense that I used the term at the beginning of this chapter, it should in general be protected from official punishment. Censorship should not be excused upon the ground that a class of answerable expression is not "political" in nature or is not "important" to society, because it is impossible to tell with any accuracy just what sort of expression will prove to be political, and because censorship is not undertaken unless the expression involved is important.

A more difficult question concerns the borderline between "speech acts" and other sorts of action. Decisions must be made whether actions—strikes and street demonstrations, for example—that have both expressive and non-expressive aspects are to be treated as speech to be protected from state control or not. The threshold question is whether the act conveys an argument that is as a practical matter interpretable or answerable. If it does, then the questions remain how important the control of the non-speech aspect is for the state and whether the motive of the government is to act against the expressive or some other element of the act. The impulse of the censor, under such circumstances, would be to catch as many speech acts as possible within the net of a statute that purports to control other acts. The government can show that it encourages free expression by establishing standards, opposed to the censorious urge, that limit the "vague" or "overinclusive" interpretation of statutes.

Administrative Limits

Just because there are no linguistic and psychological limits on discussion, we are obliged to impose them all the time in order to reach determinate answers. We do it through agencies so necessary and commonplace that we do not conceive of them as restrictions on expression—through limits on the size of groups, through time limits on debate, and through institutions of representation. Such structures nevertheless always create a risk that the discussion will be insufficient, that the better answer or interpretation will not be found. It is important that the risk should not be increased through systems of censorship or boundaries on participation in an institution, imposed from outside the institution and designed to advance a certain agenda of alternatives and exclude others.

The criticism of the actions of any administrative body and of the way it is constituted, in the larger society outside of its decision-making process, should not be controlled by censorship or limitations on participation. Free discussion of decisions of such groups is the only way to ensure that they are as rational as they can be and that they are not used as covert systems of censorship. Accordingly, an indicator of an effective system of free expression, in a society honeycombed with specialized decision-making bodies, is the existence of at least one sort of forum, one arena in which no limits are imposed by the government and all the putative errors of the specialized bodies can be aired. The increase in the number of such forums, of course, increases the likelihood that alternative ideas will be found and will be heard.

Toleration

The principle that there can be no predictable limits on discussion in the open forum leads to the glib conclusion that all opinions must be tolerated. The concrete application of the principle, nevertheless, may still give us pause; as a practical matter it is not very difficult to think of opinions that are unacceptable under any circumstances we can imagine. The most obvious candidate, under the arguments I have made here, is advocacy of a comprehensive system of censorship; another, more notorious, is advocacy of genocide against a racial or religious group. The question is: Must we tolerate advocacy of ideas that we would under no circumstances put into practice?

The very fact that we say that a policy of censorship or genocide is inadmissible under any circumstances implies that we imagine what would happen under such a policy; we know what the alternative to the idea we advocate is and the consequence of our own opinion as well as its opposite. The failure to take the alternative and its consequences into account is to fail to understand our own opinion. If the unacceptable opinion is important enough for us to consider suppressing it, furthermore, it is important enough to answer. It will be connected, through fantasy or linguistic meaning or both, to opinions that some people in the society find attractive; it is essential to come to grips with those fantasies and meanings, to try to explain and answer them. Even though we cannot conceive of the opinion as "true" as a matter of policy, it may be a reflection of social or psychological conflicts that cannot be touched except through a response to those fantasies. Understanding the opinion in a context different from the narrow "policy" context makes its toleration essential.

There is a still more basic reason for tolerating opinions that are unacceptable as practical propositions: It is a guarantee of the rationality of the government. It demonstrates that the state takes seriously the need to decide questions only after examining the implications of all alternatives. The government prejudges nothing as "out of the question," neither the most cogent nor the most absurd opinion. Absolute toleration is a categorical statement that all possibilities can be canvassed when decisions are made.

Who May Speak?

Any person or group that may be persuaded by a speech act, or may give an answer to one, should have the freedom to speak. For special political reasons that I shall examine in the next chapter, the government has no such right, although some independent bodies under government sponsorship should have such a right.

Access to the Dialogue

Individual self-expression, and the freedom of the press and of association that accompanies it, is important under any theory of free speech. Under the dialogic theory of free speech and expression, however, centered as it is upon understanding and decision-making, access to the dialogue is just as important; in fact, participation in the social process of understanding meanings and solving problems is a predicate to self-expression. It is this emphasis that presents the most challenging questions of application for the theory of freedom of expression, because it raises a potential conflict between individual expression and participation by others. Nevertheless, unless they seize complete control over the media, governments cannot avoid the conflict; in every non-totalitarian system, no matter how committed to free enterprise, some balance is struck between private and government-sponsored speech. The search for elements of balance that may yield a relatively open dialogue rather than a covert system of censorship is the subject of the next chapter. The solutions discussed there are, as I shall show, particularly important for underdeveloped countries that have minimal resources for private media. In the course of the discussion I shall try to sketch the minimum conditions for a viable system of free expression.

Chapter V

ACCESS TO THE DIALOGUE

Although the U.S. Supreme Court has always recognized a right to listen to or read information that a speaker wants to publish, until recent years it declined to recognize a constitutional right of access to information controlled by government or by anyone else. Twenty years ago, in a case concerning the unsuccessful attempt of a citizen to overturn a ban on travel to Cuba so that he might acquaint himself with conditions there, the Supreme Court held that "the right to speak and publish does not carry with it the unrestrained right to gather information."[1] The Court applied the same limitation to attempts to force access to government operations and information—to a case, for example, brought by news reporters to gain access to and take photographs of a jail where conditions were said to be inhumane. "There are few restrictions on action," the Court's opinion said, "which could not be clothed by ingenious argument in the garb of decreased data flow."[2] The justices were hinting that they would not recognize a "right of access" as an aspect of freedom of expression because the limits of the right were not foreseeable; in particular, it was not foreseeable whether the right could be limited to government information.

In 1980 the Supreme Court finally shifted its position

slightly, ruling that the press and the public could not be excluded from a criminal trial merely because the prosecution and defense had agreed that they should.[3] The justices tried to avoid creating a generalized right of access to government proceedings by basing their opinions for the most part on the tradition that American trials are open to the public. The attempt was not entirely successful because a recognition of some of the elements of a dialogical right to participate lies behind the tradition itself. The opinions emphasize, for example, in the words of Justice Brennan, that "closed trials breed suspicion of prejudice and arbitrariness, which in turn spawns disrespect for law."[4] Those phrases, of course, embody a special case of the general argument made in the last chapter that the public will lose respect for the government if they are barred from understanding and commenting on an official action even when they cannot actually participate in it, for example, as jurors or parties.

The court system, moreover, is a particularly strong candidate for public scrutiny because of its avowed purposes in the common-law system and the resulting authority it confers on the government. A trial is the model for a rational decision-making process conducted by a limited group of people (judges, lawyers, witnesses, and sometimes jurors); it is a circumscribed inquiry that is nevertheless supposed to find a "truth." In order to fulfill such a function, the court's process of decision must be explainable by argument, and it must always be subject to criticism from outside the proceedings; otherwise its rationality is unnecessarily limited. I think the Supreme Court senses these characteristics of trials without analyzing them in quite the same way, and for that reason has ensured a right of access to them.

The fact that the trial process may present the perfect case for a right of outside criticism does not quite explain why the Supreme Court has been loath to expand a constitutional right of access to official actions outside the courts.[5] The Court's continued hesitation suggests that painful conflicts of policy about whether a more general "right of access" or "right to know" exists, or ought to exist, are still unresolved. Those who favor a right of access have tried in general to limit it to government information, while those who oppose it often fear that such a limitation will not hold. Concealed in the notion of a right to enlist the aid of the state to get information that is otherwise insufficiently available, the opponents see an implied judgment that the existing sources of information and opinion, largely private in the United States, are inadequate. In the interest of the right to know, the government is liable to make decisions about what ought to be known or what knowledge ought to be encouraged, and conversely about what ought not to be known or ought to be discouraged. The virtue of the right to expression pure and simple is, as James Goodale of the New York Times put it,[6] that it is "self-executing"; the government makes no pretense of trying to aid in understanding and consequently leaves people entirely free to say and think what they please.

There is certainly much in this argument; it is true that government aid to knowledge does tend to become sponsorship, or an attempt to "balance" disfavored opinions. But underlying the argument, in many cases, is a faith, implicit or explicit, that all the information and opinion, all the access to the dialogue essential for both personal and group decision-making can be supplied through the mechanism of free personal expression and an independent, private press.[7] In the presence of such a faith, a right of access or a right to know must seem a dangerous and unneccessary interference.

I cannot share that faith. Belief that the present-day popular media will present a great range of alternatives for the solution of problems, undertake fundamental criticism of institutions in cases where it may be needed, or present a framework for discussion that is not systematically skewed toward the status quo, seems to me unjustified. To argue the issue at length, describing the accumulation of evidence about constraints on the media, is beyond the scope of this book and should not be necessary at this point in time; reports have been issuing since the end of the Second World War expressing alarm at the restriction of communication in the mass media.[8] When newspapers depend on advertisers for a large part of their revenue, as they have now done for generations, there is a natural drive to unify the papers in each locality in such a way as to maximize the effectiveness of the advertising dollar. For that and such other reasons as rising costs, the number of newspapers drops constantly and those that remain are becoming aggregated in a few hands. Concentration by itself might not lead to blandness and uniformity of opinion; there are still maverick editors and reporters, and magazines that supplement the newspapers, at least on some issues. But for the most part, all those media are so dependent upon the good will of their advertisers that they hesitate to attempt any far-reaching criticisms. Although television broadcasting on a national scale is concentrated in very few hands, within the local markets formed by towns and cities there are often effectively more television channels than newspapers; the development of cable television holds out the promise of a wider range of expression, which has not yet been realized. Television news is nevertheless heavily dependent on that of the leading papers and television presentations generally are turned bland by the aversion among sponsors to the controversial. When print or television reporters do show a reforming zeal, it is likely to be thwarted by the unwillingness of officials, in the absence of a right of access to government information under the law, to reveal the truth about their knowledge and their actions. In liberal societies, alternative media used by a few critics constantly scrutinize the mass media and received opinion, but they do not often bring new alternatives into popular consciousness without the support of the mass media themselves. Frequent electoral campaigns hold out the promise of somewhat more critical discussions about public issues, which might in turn be reported in the popular media. The need to court special interests, however, in order both to pay the increasing costs of political campaigns and to avoid offending those independent political action committees that have an axe to grind, dulls the will of candidates to attack controversial issues.[9]

As a result of all these forces, a range of alternatives is often missing from discussion of public issues in the media. An example I find illuminating grows out of a discussion in Charles Lindblom's *Politics and Markets*. There Lindblom argues that liberal democracies ("polyarchies," in the terminology he uses) do not engage in central economic planning, not because of any demonstrated inconsistency between polyarchy and planning, but because private enterprise controls the system of decision-making in such a way that central planning is effectively not on the agenda. Lindblom goes on to say that conflicts between business and liberal government are not evidence of the lack of control by business, but merely of disagreements within a accepted range of alternatives. In his review of the book Aaron Wildavsky argued that the effects of such business "vetoes" on issues of public policy are in fact much more diverse than Lindblom allows. He commented: "Unless corporations are to lose on every try, they must stop some things that they do not like; since they are very often divided on subjects such as free trade and oil prices, some corporations must veto, and some fail to veto, some of the time."[10] The oil-price example is a curious one because it seems to me that it tends to prove Lindblom's point. During the "oil crisis" in the early 1970's, there were indeed a great many businesses that were seriously harmed by the price increases. Although the mass media constantly editorialized about the crisis, they did not, to my knowledge,[11] advocate a radical intervention by government such as control of the oil market and central planning as a solution to the problem. Corporations may have been divided over issues concerning oil, but not so divided as to favor a proposal that would suggest a breach in the free-market ideology as a whole. As Lindblom might put it, such a proposal was simply not on the agenda.

The skew in discussion created by the agenda-setting power of the media presents a particularly acute problem for the theory of liberty in this book, dependent as it is on philosophical and psychological notions that envision reaching decisions through the dialogical comparison of alternatives. Facing the problem, however, does not get us very far toward solving it. The underlying philosophical and psychological theories also tell us that, as a practical matter, the best of discussions are never more than approximately complete. We may be fairly sure that something will be left out of any discussion of a problem, but since we do not know in advance what the "best" or "right" solution to the problem is, it is difficult to tell whether the discussion ought to be extended or expanded to search for more alternatives. Although we talk of bringing "balance" to a dialogue by the introduction of a range of new alternatives, we use the concept of balance only in its roughest sense, because it is usually not clear that the new alternatives are better than ones we have not thought of, or indeed as good as the ones already on the agenda. We may think we know when a dialogue is out of balance, in short, but we don't correspondingly know when it is in balance. We are going to have to rely on the usual unsystematic heuristics for problem-solving to decide what may be promising alternative views and how much they ought to be encouraged. The most we can do is try to create legal structures that may somewhat compensate for the most obvious systematic biases.

The absence of a faith in the private media as effective instruments of dialogue, moreover, does not reduce the dangers of goverment interference. It is still true that government officials are going to try, when they have a chance, to foster ideas that are consistent with their existing programs, and to discourage the alternatives. For the dialogical approach to free expression, nevertheless, participation in dialogue and the presentation of new alternatives is so important, so much more central than it is to more traditional theories, that we must run the risks attendant upon government sponsorship or aid to knowledge, just as we run the risks attendant upon private sponsorship or aid to knowledge.

In reality, because government participation in and sponsorship of communications is already pervasive, the state leaves us very little choice but to run at least some of the risks. In every modern society, from the most liberal to the most repressive, government constantly talks to the public; the apparent dominance of private expression in liberal societies is a matter of degree, of comparison with societies in which state intervention is still more complete. The political problem is not to prevent or eliminate state communicative action but to shape it so as to increase access to understanding while minimizing the dangers of control. The touchstone for government aid or input to communication should be, in general, that it will add to the amount of information or opinion from all sources that already exists, rather than decrease it. Government action for the purpose of cutting down the amount of expression will be suspect except in cases where there is some private monopoly control of information and there is no other way except limitation to break that control. Finally, at a minimum, one or more media ought to be left totally free of government action as a critical brake upon any efforts at "balance." In poorer countries where private media are weak or non-existent, the government should establish institutions that will diversify its monopoly and act as a control on official opinion.

There are a number of ways for the government to aid or sponsor knowledge. The least controversial from the present perspective is that of access to information created and held by the government, discussed above as part of the constitutional debate in the United States over a "right of access," but more specifically dubbed the problem of "freedom of information." Slightly more difficult is the issue of speech by the government itself. Most complex and delicate, finally, are the problems of government aid to access to knowledge and decision-making.

Freedom of Information

Freedom of information, which we may define loosely as access to facts and opinions in the control of the government that the government does not reveal as part of its own expression, appears in a number of ways. It may be found in a formal Freedom of Information Act, in an ombudsman or other oversight institution; most informally, it is found in "whistle-blowing" officials who secretly leak information to the press or risk their jobs by doing so publicly.

The potential for distortion that arises when the government tries to bring "balance" into discussions in society, either through fostering a point of view or by entering the discussion itself, which will be more fully discussed in the pages that follow, is all but non-existent in the case of freedom of information. The official material sought can be chosen by people outside the government, without official interference concerning how it ought to be used or what inferences ought to be drawn from it. Freedom of information, of course, raises other political risks, such as the possibility that officials will not express themselves freely if they think they may be quoted, that investigations into criminal misconduct may be curtailed, that foreign governments will be embarrassed if negotiations with them are revealed, or that "security" information, particularly of a military nature, will be compromised. Although those dangers may tip the balance in favor of the concealment of information for a time, they never eliminate the countervailing danger that the government will fail through lack of discussion to take relevant factors and arguments into account. The discussions concerning the Bay of Pigs and the escalation of the bombing of North Vietnam were conducted in secret for what were thought to be excellent reasons, but they do not on that account escape the charge that they were irrational. The dangers from exposing the facts, furthermore, especially if they concern breaches of security, however compelling they may seem to be before a decision is made, generally cannot justify concealing information about past actions. The revelation of the factors that have gone into a past decision, on the other hand, may be extremely valuable in criticizing the decision and trying to make a better one the next time, as Robert MacNamara saw when he ordered the assembly of the Pentagon Papers and Daniel Ellsberg saw again when he exposed them to the public.

Access by citizens to information held by government and to knowledge about its processes of decision-making thus seems to be one of the minimum elements—necessary but generally not sufficient—to satisfy the need for participation in society's dialogue of understanding and decision-making. Knowledge about government plans and policies is often necessary if individuals and groups are to decide what actions they are able to or ought to take, and it is impossible for the government itself to take the most rational approach to problems except through a dialogue that takes account of opinions outside the government, opinions that must be skewed and truncated if they are based on misinformation. If the society has a developed system of media, the benefit of access to government information is to some extent self-executing; journalists will find and expose at least some of the important aspects of the information. If the media are weak, then of course the benefit of access to information is reduced; but if the government can withhold information at will, the development of media will be much less important as an instrument of knowledge. Government concealment and distortion has an effect on knowledge and decision-making similar to that of censorship: It tends to conceal the most cogent internal criticisms and the most damaging information, although government will be unable to set coherent limits on what ought to be withheld. The media, no matter how elaborately developed and open in their criticism, are effectively censored with respect to government decision-making.

The emphasis in the traditional views of free speech upon personal expression has encouraged a curious blind spot about the value of freedom of information; until recently it has been protected in most western countries in a patchy and unsystematic way. Although Sweden has a tradition stretching back two hundred years which has resulted in a Freedom of Information Act and the institution of the ombudsman, the larger European nations have not always been so open. England, so far from having a freedom of information act, has an Official Secrets Act which, together with a long-standing tradition of official reticence, tends to discourage the revelation of information that might be embarrassing to government. France has had a custom of bureaucratic secrecy, buttressed by laws penalizing "outrage" and "offense" in criticism of the government. As of 1978, it has a new Freedom of Information Act, the effect of which is not yet clear. In 1981, the ministerial Committee of the Council of Europe finally recommended to all of its members the adoption of such laws. [12]

The United States Supreme Court, in declining to create a constitutional right of access to official or other information, declared that the issue was one of "policy which a legislative body might resolve one way or the other."[13] During the sixties and seventies, a period of unprecedented social pressure and criticism of the government, Congress, as a step toward closing the gap in effective political discussion left by constitutional doctrine, finally passed a freedom of information act. Although the law has been very useful, bureaucrats have put constant pressure on the courts and Congress since its passage to widen the exemptions for large categories of government documents.

Government Speech

Government engages directly in a large amount of speech. Some of it, like the publication of standard economic data, is not controversial, but partisan communications are quite common. Executive officers freely call press conferences to announce policies, or to criticize the legislature or some foreign nation. Legislators allocate money to have their debates printed, and to record the testimony and results of hearings to establish new laws; they report investigations that are intended to reform other branches of government, and sometimes even the legislature itself. So long as these forms of expression do not exclude private research and commentary in the same fields, they are rarely viewed as infringements of the free speech of others. At the same time, although government speech may be a valuable part of the dialogue for understanding, we do not think of the government as having a "right" to speak, because there is no one against whom to enforce the right. Put in more practical terms, if the legislature chooses for one reason or another to curtail government publication, research, or other expression, the agency that is curtailed has no recourse as a matter of right.[14] It often does, of course, have effective political means of redress.

The problem becomes more complex as the government moves beyond direct expression on its own behalf toward aid or sponsorship of the speech of others.

Government Aid to Private Speech

The least obtrusive government aids to communication are facilitative, like tax exemptions or the cheap mail rate that prevails for publications in the United States and some other countries, including many in the third world. Reduced mail rates can be be used as instruments of censorship, by singling out publications for exclusion from the privilege, as has been done in the United States in the past and is still done, for example, in Tanzania, where only government-approved publications enjoy the privilege.[15] Special mail rates act as a real facilitation for free expression only when they are applied in the simplest way, automatically and across the board, to a whole category of media, with no discretion to refuse them.

More sensitive are the cases where, instead of extending some sort of privilege like the mail rate that can be expanded as the media expand, the government supplies facilities for communications. Typical cases are auditoriums and parks used for public speaking, which are of course limited spaces. The issue of access to such forums comes up frequently because governments constantly refuse the use of them to their critics or to purveyors of controversial entertainment. It is clear, nevertheless, that such "public forums," as they are called under United States law, have a censoring effect unless they are made available, whether by rental or gratis, without discrimination based on content.

In countries with a large private sector such as the United States, many public facilities for communication will be marginal; if the government refuses a service, there is often a practical alternative. In underdeveloped countries, on the other hand, it is frequently necessary for the government to supply facilities if they are to exist at all. That sort of market power over communications offers a greater temptation toward government control and at the same time implies a correspondingly greater need for non-discriminatory administration. Newsprint, for example, is a scarce resource in most countries, both because they do not manufacture paper and because they have to spend precious foreign excnange to get it. Paper becomes a bone of contention between the print media and governments in third-world countries because, without some objective standard for allocation sucn as past circulation, the supply can be manipulated as an almost invisible form of censorship. Tanzania, for example, has used restrictions on paper imports as a weapon against the non-government press; in India the issue reached the Supreme Court in 1973, when it was held that the government could not arbitrarily limit the size or circulation of a newspaper by limiting its supply of newsprint.[16]

If the government wants to ensure neutrality in administration, it may establish a governing board independent of direct state control to dispense scarce communications resources.[17] As they move beyond merely administering a monopoly, such bodies take on a life of their own, and may be essential instruments for fostering free expression in poorer nations.

Government Sponsorship of Communication

The device of a governing body insulated from government is commonly used for media of communication, either to open channels alternative to the private media in a developed system or as a way of supplying capital while affording a measure of independence in a new system. Independent governing boards have been used throughout the western world for television and radio broadcasting. In Great Britain the dominant force has been the British Broadcasting Company, established with a board somewhat insulated from politics. West German broadcasting has been divided into regional systems, with insulated governing bodies for each. The French system has changed over time, under constant pressure to reduce tne number of state appointees on the governing body and to break it up into smaller units. In the United States, as an alternative to commercial broadcasting, itself heavily regulated by the Federal Communications Commission, the federal government has established and partly funded public television through independent corporations.[18]

In the nations of black Africa such corporations have been used not only for broadcasting but for the print media as well. When Zimbabwe became independent in 1980, the government took a controlling interest in the newspapers, which were then centered in a South African press group, and assigned it to a "mass media trust." There have been similar bodies in Ghana and Zambia, as well as an apparently still more independent trust managing two papers in Kenya. By the standards of many western journalists, these must seem like poor protections for freedom of the press, especially in the print media, where we are accustomed to a largely private system. Nevertheless, in parts of the third world, the alternatives may be even more restrictive. A few African countries have no newspapers at all, and some have only an official press.[19] The press operated under a trust arrangement separated from the government may be the most viable alternative, at least in the short term. The existence of such an insulating structure is an index of the intention of the government to encourage free expression, rather tnan merely to engage in government speech. It is true, of course, that the "independent board" for such communications may turn out to be censorship or government speech under another name; recognizing that it is more palatable for them to interfere with free expression in the guise of an independent body, the government may set up a mere puppet body, or obtain influence over a private body. And even if the government sets up an independent body in all good faith, it frequently happens that public officials cannot resist the temptation to tamper with it.

The board of a government-sponsored medium that has any independence is usually engaged in an effort, over many years, to minimize official interference. The independence of broadcasting, or on the contrary its notorious politicization, has been an issue for two generations in France, and a major issue in at least two elections. The management of French broadcasting, although still not free of censorship, has become gradually more decentralized, with progressively smaller direct state representation on the boards, as the legitimacy of the government has come partly to be linked to broadcast independence. In a similar struggle, German broadcasting has been increasingly subject to political pressure in informal ways outside the legal structure of the television authorities; such intervention is viewed as a scandal nevertheless, which creates pressure on the government to stop it. In the United States, the structure of decision-making in public broadcasting has changed, partly in an effort to become more independent and diversified; the Public Broadcasting System was formed to coordinate and distribute programs, and the local stations now vote on the funding of programs. In Africa, the independent boards for the media are often quite weak; Elihu Katz and George Wedell, in *Broadcasting in the Third World,* say of the autonomous public broadcasting corporations modelled on the BBC in some countries that their "independence is largely notional and that the original BBC principles of public service, as distinct from government, broadcasting have been adjusted to fit the less politically stable conditions of Africa."[20] Yet such boards, if they are not a total sham, are different from and more creative than direct control by the government; the mass media trust in Zimbabwe does serve to insulate the press somewhat from complaints by government ministers. The establishment of such boards is most important where resources are at a minimum, because the push for editorial independence cannot even begin until such a body exists. The problem is to create legal structures that will tend to strengthen its independence.

The cardinal such legal rule is, quite simply, that the managing board should have a right, as against the government, to freedom of expression. It is this that will distinguish the board's actions from speech by the government itself. As a corollary, the board should usually have editorial discretion to select its style and point of view and to reject material that fails to fit its format. The learned journal in a state-run university is expected to select its articles and the public television corporation to fund its programs according to some standard of merit established by itself and not on a first-come, first-serve basis. Constitutional law in the United States has begun to recognize such rights for public media corporations; the Supreme Court recently ruled that a section in the statute for public broadcasting that forbids "editorializing" by any station funded by the Corporation for Public Broadcasting is so excessively broad as to infringe on free speech.[21] On the other hand, as such a body comes close to controlling a resource or an entire medium, it has an increasing obligation to represent all points of view and to "balance" any position it takes by giving an opportunity for reply. The independent boards in charge of the infant media in some third-world countries, if they take their job seriously, will sometimes find that they have to try to offer a forum for the whole range of public opinion.[22]

The members of the governing board, its funding, and its decisions should all be insulated from governmental pressure as much as possible. The boards of the British Broadcasting Corporation and the U.S. Corporation for Public Broadcasting are perhaps more successful than the broadcast monopolies of France and Germany in escaping direct political control, even though they are still subject to heavy pressure from time to time. Board members are beholden to the people who appoint them, and the corporation as a whole is subject to reorganization and sometimes to financial manipulation by the government. Because they are largely funded by franchise fees levied on television and radio receivers sold to the public, the French, German, and British corporations are more nearly independent in this respect that the U.S. corporation, which is kept on a very short tether by legislative appropriations. Its lowest point was perhaps in 1972, when for political reasons President Nixon vetoed its appropriation. Finally, procedures for the conduct of relations between the government and the corporation should be established and followed with great care. Deviations from them will give rise to an inference that the government is acting for reasons of politics or censorship, or both.[23]

In sum, there are four basic elements for the independence of a media governing body. It should have editorial freedom, except when it is a monopoly, it should have independent funding and management, and its procedural relations to the government should be explicit.

Government Encouragement of Balance

Intervention by the government to create a "balance" in an ongoing dialogue is a venture much more perilous for liberty than merely intervening to add a voice to the discussion through government speech or aid to speech; liberal governments, nevertheless, have frequently tried it. The most sympathetic case for an intervention in the interests of balance, as I suggested in the last section, occurs when there is concentrated control over some forum for dialogue, which may lead to the restriction of discussion and to irrational decision-making unless a conscious effort is made to introduce other opinions.

Great Britain, France, West Germany, and the United States have each independently adopted a policy of balancing the dialogue of ideas in broadcasting. The decision was first made when the media were new, and there was an apparent natural limit on the number of broadcast bands. One source of the policy, nevertheless, has also been the governments' fear that the broadcast media, because of their psychological power, could be used to skew public attitudes; the fear is accompanied by skepticism about the ability of a private, commercial system of programming to reflect sufficiently diverse points of view. France and West Germany created state broadcasting monopolies, administered by independent governing bodies, precisely to prevent any group or party from obtaining dominance over the media; balance or impartiality in programming is one of the overt aims of that control. In the United States, privately owned broadcasting stations licensed by the Federal Communications Commission have a duty under the "fairness doctrine" to open their programming to opposing points of view when they take a position on a subject that turns out to be controversial, while the Corporation for Public Broadcasting is directed to observe "strict adherence to objectivity and balance in all programs or series of programs of a controversial nature." In Britain, both the BBC and the Independent Broadcasting Authority are enjoined to take care that "due impartiality" is observed for controversial subjects; the Programme Complaints Commission was set up to consider charges of unfairness.[24]

The administration of a requirement of "balance" or "impartiality" raises an immediate dilemma, both administrative and theoretical, because no one knows what a "balanced" discussion would sound like. The United States and Great Britain have found perhaps the best solution to the puzzle by leaving it as a matter for private complaint from the public. Under the fairness doctrine in the United States or the Programme Complaints Commission in Britain, the party with the opposing point of view can protest to the official body and, if she is successful, present her answer. Similarly, when the broadcast media are opened to the candidates in a political campaign, they can be made open equally to all. In such cases, the larger framework of discussion in society determines what is controversial and the broadcasting system responds (approximately) by presenting all sides.

The problem becomes acute wnen the government tries directly to impose its notions of "impartiality" by bringing pressure on the broadcaster to publish a reply or change its policy; governments have done such things repeatedly in all four societies. On their face, these are acts of censorship; the results, however, are in practice usually more interesting. In all such disputes, there are at least four parties: the government, the broadcaster, whether private or an independent governing body, the other media and the public. All of them engage in an open wrangle about the underlying controversy, about the possible positions concerning it, about what a balanced view might be, and about the motives of the government in bringing the pressure. In short, where the broadcast media are not operated directly by the government but have some independence, and there are other independent media as well, the dispute about "balance," even though it is ultimately unresolvable, leads to a larger debate about the underlying issues and the government's motives. When the broadcast media are operated by boards insulated from the state, the issue becomes indistinguishable from the issue of their independence. The government cannot bring its pressure without expanding the debate and paying a price in public confidence if it is thought to be acting as a censor.

The broadcast media are no longer in their infancy in the four countries, and with the advent of cable and satellite broadcasts, the broadcast spectra probably are no longer resources that are naturally "scarce"; in any case they are not more scarce than the resources used by the print media. As a result, it is frequently argued that the rather uneasy attempts to balance the dialogue in the broadcast media ought to be abandoned, or, less frequently, that the same policy ought to be applied to obtain access to the print media.[25] It seems to me that both approaches miss a more complex process in which the political system attempts to compensate for the inadequacy of the dialogue in the commercially supported mass media, by enforcing a right of access to one class of media, while leaving others completely free as a control on the speech in those media and upon government censorship. Under this view, the same treatment need not be accorded every medium, providing that some are free of a putative duty to be "fair" or "impartial." As long as the public has the power to initiate complaints of unfairness, and as long as the dispute is public, as it is in the four countries, the danger of censorship is minimized.

Broadcasters have claimed that the process I describe leads to blandness and the avoidance of controversy on television and radio. Although there is some truth to that, the effect is minimized by the presence of other media that will, in however skewed a way, comment upon, and ultimately force television to report on, controversial matters. Recurrent complaints about the fairness of television programs show that it is never really closed to controversy. More important, the broadcasters' claim ignores the fact that the alternative to the existing compromise under present circumstances is likely to be the concentration of all the mass media in the hands of a relative few, with no right of access. While the mixed approach to the mass media in the four countries, with a qualified effort at balance and a right of access in one medium but not in others, is a ramshackle structure, it is probably preferable to that alternative.

The popular image of freedom of speech in the Anglo-American world envisions the individual or the private press embattled against the state. My sketch of government influences on expression, including freedom of information, government speech, government aid, and attempts at balance, is intended to suggest, on the other hand, that those political systems which value free expression are often doing something rather different. They are sometimes concerned with completeness of dialogue, with rational decision-making, as well as with individual expression. While all such devices of government influence, with the possible exception of freedom of information, can be and are used as levers of censorship, they also point toward the possibility of a mix of private and government-sponsored expression that can afford a broader range of alternatives in the mass media than either can do alone. This possibility, and the forms of government action that underlie it, may be still more important for underdeveloped nations than it has been for the western liberal democracies.

Underdeveloped Nations and the Balance of Speech

In the past fifteen years, the search for the elusive "balance" in expression has become a catchword for third-world countries. Using UNESCO as a forum they have sought to combat what they perceive as overwhelming dominance by Europe and the United States over information and the media.

There is plenty of empirical evidence to support the dominance thesis. Some of it concerns outright acts of imperialism, either official or unofficial, to corrupt or control local media. The Central Intelligence Agency, for example, has funded media in foreign countries to influence the public or the government. Most notoriously, in Chile the CIA paid large sums to the newspaper *El Mercurio* and other media to run items against the election of Salvador Allende in 1970; after Allende had been confirmed by the legislature, the agency spent still more money for stories calculated to destabilize the government. In Canada, to choose another example, after American film companies had been enjoined under the United States antitrust laws from conspiring to control the distribution and exhibition of films in their own country, they nevertheless continued the same practices across the border, with the effect of restricting the development of an indigenous film industry.[26]

The most important and massive evidence, however, has no such conspiratorial cast; it is a function rather of the historical priority and economic dominance of western technology. Television, for example, where it is found in the third world, is to a large extent supplied with imported programs, because many countries have only the simplest facilities for television production. Although American commercial television in 1970 used only one percent imported material, as small a percentage as mainland China, third-world countries typically used 30 percent, and often more than half, foreign programs.[27]

The flow of news, chiefly through international news agencies, which affects both the electronic and print media, has provoked the most bitter complaints from third world countries. The major news agencies, which are centered in the western nations, emphasize news drawn from and directed at those countries, even though two-thirds of the world's people live in underdeveloped countries. A count of news stories for one month showed that 80 percent of the news reported by the United Press, and 50 or more percent of the news reported by Reuters and Agence France Presse, was concerned with western Europe and North America. Of the correspondents maintained by major international news agencies in 1980, only 4 percent were in Africa, and 11 percent in all of Latin America. Third-world countries complain that much of the news that is reported is written in a patronizing or prejudiced style. The flow of news, moreover, in Africa at least, has historically tended to be in the direction of the central office and then back to the (present or former) colony, rather than among the African nations themselves, because the lines of communication among African countries were not as well developed as the international news wires and the other connections to the developed world. There were, of course, perfectly bona fide economic reasons for the situation; there was very little market for news in Africa, and the agencies spent more to collect news there than they ever received in fees; the demand in western countries for news about their own cultures, on the other hand, has always been strong. The fact that the situation came about for understandable reasons, however, only ensured its continuation.[28]

Many of the third-world countries in UNESCO began to push for a "New World Information and Communication Order" (NWICO), a phrase that, despite the outcry the United States and the western press have raised against it, describes no specific program at all, but rather a general ambition to stem western dominance of information and the media. On the one hand, it often threatens nothing more menacing than a search for a real dialogue in communication; as a UNESCO resolution put it in 1980, one of its aims is "respect for the right of the public, of ethnic and social groups and of individuals to have access to information sources and to participate actively in the communication process."[29]

Some supporters of NWICO, on the other hand, have argued at UNESCO conferences that the press has a duty to support rather than criticize third-world governments and their development projects, that a standard of "accuracy and objectivity" should be imposed on news reporters, and even that government ought to be the source of news.[30] Although such proposals have not been adopted as UNESCO policy, they are used by officials in their own countries to explain and excuse repressive internal actions; theirs is a version of one of the most powerful ideological tools for justifying a system of censorship, "the exclusion of foreign ideas." They play upon fears—a case like the CIA corruption of Chilean media is the paradigm—of a situation where the speaker has no real interest in participating in a dialogue, no interest in finding serious answers to problems, but only in subverting the government. The prospect is particularly terrifying if the source of communication seems enormously powerful compared with local sources. And in the public mind, it is not very difficult to taint the news with the fear even in cases when what comes over the international newswires is not of this subversive variety.

Some western critics seem as intransigent, in the other direction, as the repressive third-world ministers. Americans in particular, coming from a society in which almost everything in the media is concerned with and produced by their own culture, find it very difficult to imagine what it is like to be surrounded by films, music, and news from a foreign society. They are doubly suspicious of third-world attempts to balance the cultural dialogue because in their ideology of the press there is hardly any place for government at all. An American observer at a UNESCO conference in 1976 reported darkly, "Unseen presences at the conference were the experts whose work underlay the working paper. The conference proceeded on their assumptions, woven throughout the paper, that people have a right to receive communications and participate in communications, and it is within the power of governments to guarantee this two-sided right." At the end of 1984 the United States went so far as to withdraw from UNESCO, accusing it, among other things, of hostility to "free press" and "free markets."[31] The free-market rhetoric seems to me only to encourage, in ways I shall explain more fully in a moment, the cynical response that some third-world countries have had to western-style freedom of expression.

Neither the view that the press ought to be controlled and foreign ideas excluded nor the view that the state has no proper role in shaping the media can contribute much to communication policy. The real question, ignored by both extremes, is what can be done, consistent with the needs of developing countries, to encourage and protect free inquiry. There are institutional ways, I think, to encourage international and indigenous media competitive with the dominant institutions of the developed world.

Take the case of the major international wire services. The charge of cultural bias, whether it is true or not, has had little effect on news reporting. The news agencies might change their ways in reponse to shifts in demand, or to a lesser degree in reponse to isolated pressures, but in the main no official agency has the power to change the way they report the news. A practical response to the wire services would be to establish alternative international news agencies that might report news in a way that suited the third world nations and reporters; those agencies could "balance" news from the major national news agencies in a literal sense, by creating more news and not by limiting it. Such projects were tried, in a small way, during the seventies. The Non-Aligned News Pool was established, but it was never very strong because the pooling countries mistrusted one another's news as well as the pool, because the western press agencies disliked it, and perhaps because UNESCO did not devote large resources to it. In 1980, UNESCO established the International Program for Development of Communication to act as an umbrella organization for communications projects; its effectiveness is not yet clear.[32]

A strong alternative news agency was a natural project for funding by an organization such as the United Nations. Its board would have to be independent of UNESCO control under U.N. practice, and it could be insulated from the national governments as well; they would not participate unless they chose to do so.[33] If the underdeveloped nations lacked the capital to pursue the project, UNESCO could supply some of it. If electronic links for the exchange of news between the third-world nations were missing, funds could be allocated to create those links through already existing international satellite communications. It is such a natural project, in fact, and such an obvious approach to problems of cultural domination, that it is difficult to avoid the conclusion that it was not pursued in a major way because the participants did not care to solve the problems. Western representatives were no doubt reasonably satisfied with news supplied by existing media. Officials from some underdeveloped countries seem to have been more interested in using western domination as an excuse to control discussion within and the news that gets out of their own countries than they were in creating new sources of information.

The situation in third-world broadcasting, like that in the international news agencies, illustrates the futility of complaining about domination by the developed world without proposing some sort of alternative. It is true that television broadcasters in underdeveloped countries use a large proportion of imported material, but until local production facilities are built, the only alternative is to have less television. After the left-wing military government came to power in Peru in 1968, for example, television stations, having formerly used 60 percent imported programs were required to use 60 percent Peruvian programs; the situation changed very little, nevertheless, because Peru was unable to produce that much original material. Radio, on the other hand, presents a much more hopeful prospect for cultural independence. The production and broadcast of programs is relatively cheap, as is the production of receivers; the receivers, moreover, can often be locally manufactured. In nations having little or no newsprint, with poor systems of transportation and a high rate of illiteracy, radio is a more important medium than newspapers and television. In Latin American countries such as Peru itself, indigenous radio has a long tradition; its influence is so pronounced that it has been made the stuff of satire in Mario Vargas Llosa's *Aunt Julia and the Script Writer.*[34]

Political structures that encourage free discussion while they balance the force of communications from richer nations are possible, then, even in quite poor nations. There may be good reasons, under the dialogical theory of free expression, for a government to try to prevent its culture from being inundated with information from abroad, especially when the country is newly formed and has a weak sense of identity. It would have been surprising for the new government of Zimbabwe, for example, to have stood by and let its newspapers be run from South Africa; even in the United States, powerful and independent as it is, there are legal limitations on the ownership of media by aliens.[35] It may seem necessary to a new government to censor or seize the means of communication, particularly when they are controlled from abroad, in the interest of consolidating its legitimacy. As I argued in the last chapter, however, the danger to a rational approach to problems, and, ultimately, to legitimacy, is very high. As soon as possible, the media should be insulated from government control through institutional devices such as those I discussed earlier in this chapter. There are so many effective tools for balancing the dialogue through government speech itself or government sponsorship of indigenous speech that there is no good reason, over the long term, for any government that pretends to modern decision-making to exclude all news or criticism from foreign cultures, not to speak of criticism inside the culture. Within this framework, public and private measures can be combined to create the conditions for modern rational decision-making and a sense of personal liberty through print as well as electronic media.

The government should encourage the print media through exemption from taxation and non-discriminatory distribution of newsprint. If private capital, expertise, and markets are insufficient to support a newspaper, a corporation insulated from politics in the selection of its board, in its finances, and in its procedural relations to government should be used to create one. If there is a privately owned newspaper, the government might establish another through such an autonomous corporation in the interest of expanding the discussion. The supranational wire service discussed above, with special links between underdeveloped nations, could be used in support of the newspapers, but imported publications and other wire services should not be excluded.

If a poor nation is interested in encouraging discussion among the people, while resisting outside domination, it might put its resources for electronic communications into radio, rather than into television. At least one station could be left free of government interference, through private development if possible, or at the very least through an autonomous corporation. Non-discriminatory government supports, such as exemption from taxation, should be available for radio just as they are for print. If there are not enough local resources to support or staff alternative stations, UNESCO funds could be used to subsidize them.

One central aim of any program ought to be to keep some communication free of governmental attempts at "balance." If there are sufficient resources, one source in each medium ought to be unencumbered: one television channel, one newspaper, one radio station. At the very least, one source in one medium should be left open, as a check upon the others and on the state. Finally, in every case, freedom of access to official information must be observed; however weak or strong the media may be, such freedom will make them more effective.

These seem to me to make out minimum conditions for a system of free expression. I have tried to envision those structural elements that, as a practical matter in a society of restricted resources subject to information pressures from other societies, seem essential to keep alive a modern rational approach to problems. Nevertheless, even these exiguous elements are often not found in the countries that protest cultural domination. Part of the reason, I think, is that both the developed world, particularly its Anglo-American representatives, and much of the third world are prisoners of the same rhetoric about freedom of expression. The western liberal ideology imagines a legal structure, not reflected very accurately even in their own systems, that systematically resists state-supported efforts to expand and balance the dialogue. For the most part, poorer nations know that such a structure is simply not available to them; they cannot have media without government aid. It is a situation that encourages third-world representatives to take a comfortably repressive view that "freedom of expression" is a luxury of systems that are alien to them, systems especially that are wealthy and culturally dominant.

Within the shell of the ideological quarrel between the developed and underdeveloped countries there is concealed the pearl of a genuine difference. The western societies really do rest much of their authority on the promise of the development of the individual, as the third world countries rest theirs primarily on the promise of the development of the society. The consequence of the third-world view, however, ought not to be repression, but rather an expanded dialogue. It is the last turn of the screw of cultural domination for third-world officials to be persuaded, or to be able to persuade others, that freedom of speech and inquiry is inextricably bound up with the colonialism from which they have tried to escape.

This is the tragedy of the polarization of UNESCO. Although it was one of few avenues to expanded expression for the poorest countries, some of them nevertheless rejected the liberty UNESCO might have afforded them, thinking that, as the west conceived it, liberty was an alternative to development. They failed to see that, because liberty is essential to decision-making, it is essential in societies dedicated to collective needs.

Conclusion

It is characteristic of problem-solving that the person or group who makes the decision is always limited in some way, if only in access to ideas and time to deliberate. In Chapter IV I emphasized the resulting need for outside criticism of such processes; decision-making, always more or less irrational, can be made more rational if it is enveloped in a broader public dialogue. I have drawn on those general principles in considering the problems of access and balance that arise out of the dialogic theory of free expression. A realistic, concrete comparison of communications practices in very different societies in the light of those principles reveals an interesting landscape of institutions. In systems that have any vitality, expression deriving from the state—freedom of information, government speech, government-assisted speech, or risky attempts at balance—is in constant tension with private institutions of expression. So long as independent media persist, the mix of institutions can produce a useful dialogue, perhaps more complete than either can produce alone. The most important principle for any government to grasp is that the open dialogue is not to be a grudging concession, but ought to be encouraged and preserved, through legal rights, as indispensable both to modern rational government and to legitimacy.

PART III

Procedural Rights and Individual Rights

Interlude

Dialogues and Disputes

In its broadest terms, the question posed in this book has been whether some rights may be derived from the characteristics of human language and problem-solving. In modern philosophy of language and psychology, as I showed in the first two chapters, understanding the meaning of sentences in ordinary language has proved to be a central branch of problem-solving. As a paradigm for cognitive psychology, the understanding of language is the model for the organization of knowledge and many other aspects of thinking. The project of interpreting language, as illuminated by its indeterminate, hermeneutic character, has seemed to point naturally, if not precisely inexorably, to a need for and a derived right of social discourse. That right is secure unless the philosophy and psychology underlying it are rejected; in that case, I believe, we would live in a very different, myth-bound, scientific and social world.

The right to speak and listen in the forum of the society as a whole is not the only characteristic of the political system that is linked to linguistic problem-solving. Official bodies such as courts and administrative agencies solve problems using language in ways that are not in essence different from those used in the larger society, even when they require limita-

151

tions on the participants, the topics, and the manner of presentation, as a means of reaching determinate decisions in a reasonable period of time (sometimes nevertheless very long, as American court proceedings demonstrate).

In societies where knowledge is bounded by myth, such agencies often use magical methods to solve problems. Sometimes it is thought that the causality of events is supernatural; thus, for example, a tribe may believe that death is ordinarily brought about by sorcery. The factual inquiry will be directed to determining what sort of magic was used and by whom. Other matters such as theft may be taken as caused by human agency but knowable by supernatural means. The fact-finders may have a trial by battle or by some other ordeal in their search for the perpetrator, otherwise concealed from ordinary human knowledge.[1]

In societies that take a modern rational approach to problems, the work of such agencies is a classic exercise in making decisions through language. Dispute resolution, in particular, ordinarily consists in part of an attempt to determine the facts of a past event, reconstructed from written and oral accounts. There is no "event" before the court that is entirely independent of the words of participants and witnesses. The dispute is commonly resolved by placing all the verbal constructs in a context of value judgment—law and custom—which is itself memorialized in language through the memory of the judges, the arguments of advocates, the records of other decisions, and generalized statutes. The "interpretation" of those value judgments, their application to the concatenation of accounts, is the resolution of the dispute. It is significant that, as I noted in earlier chapters, the society as a whole recognizes that the methods used by the tribunal are continuous with problem-solving in general; people will usually criticize the facts found or the law made by the court, either in the light of what was adduced there or in the light of entirely new factors.

It is easy to infer from arguments made in earlier chapters that there are more and less "rational approaches" to this sort of dispute resolution with limited jurisdiction. In a transitional stage, societies sometimes adopt modern rational methods of solving problems, for example, yet retain a vestige of magic as a "court of last resort"; if the judges are not satisfied

with the testimony of the witnesses, or if the case is too socially explosive to be trusted to human agency, some supernatural test may be used. For disputants who accept the linguistic resolution of problems, however, the rational approaches
should be more legitimate, should confer more authority upon
the tribunal. What I claim, and what I shall try to show in the
next chapter, is that procedural rights are vested in disputants
in the interest of making the approach to the resolution of the
dispute rational—in the sense that alternative understandings
of the facts and law are canvassed as widely as possible— and
in the interest of making the disputants as well as the larger
public audience aware of the fact that a rational approach is
being used. Accordingly, as in earlier chapters, I shall consider
procedural devices from many legal systems, with the hope of
finding what those systems consider to be essential to rational
fact-finding and application of law or custom.

   I shall be concerned in the next chapter with procedural
rights in the narrow sense, that is, with those rights that are
believed to contribute to a "fair hearing" (passing for the moment the definition of "fair," which will be considered in the
Chapter VI). I shall talk more about "civil" than "criminal"
procedures, because the interest of the courts and the political
system purely in the fairness of procedures is more clear-cut in
civil matters; that interest is not so overlaid as it is in criminal
matters with substantive concerns about protecting the defendant from the executive power of the state. I am, for example,
not concerned with those special protections built into the
criminal trial in America and to some extent in other countries
that are supposed to protect the defendant's right to privacy—
the rights to refuse to testify and to exclude from the case
evidence that has been seized unlawfully.[2] I do not, in fact,
emphasize procedural "due process" under the Constitution as
contrasted with procedural rights that come from statute or
custom; I am interested in due process as part of a continuum
of procedural rights, insofar as it seems to mark the minimum
standard of inquiry that is acceptable in the American system.

   I shall also be concerned only with procedures in the
classic adjudicatory "triad," in which the parties submit their
dispute to some sort of official or body that has a license from a
political authority to make a binding decision.[3] I realize that

similar decision-making processes are used in cases of negotia-
tion, when no third party is present, and in cases of mediation,
when the third party has no power to issue a binding decision;
it is a chief point of this book that similar methods are used
whenever problems are solved in the modern world through
the use of language. I limit the discussion to the judicial triad
because it is there that the issue of state intervention to resolve
disputes first begins to intrude, and it is only in cases of state
intervention that the issue of "rights" arises in any clear-cut
way. Civil rights are defined by and in relation to political
power, rather than in private relations; it is hard to picture a
question of procedural rights as between two parties trying to
negotiate a matter privately, for example. The parties may use
methods of inquiry similar to those of a court, but we do not
say that they have a "right" to such methods. On the other
hand, I do not mean to limit the discussion to "courts," as we
often understand the term, with a judge who has a specialized
function of resolving disputes; I include in the definition administrative agencies, as well as the councils of elders or chiefs
who hear cases in less developed societies. In many of the latter
cases, of course, the political authority is quite diffuse, and the
power of the judges to bind the parties may be largely a matter
of custom. In such cases, the notion of "rights" to specialized
procedures is correspondingly weak. It is, nevertheless, a striking fact that, as I shall show, the procedures of the tribunals
are similar in significant respects to those of our more familiar
"courts."

Chapter VI

PROCEDURES
FOR DISPUTES

A little over ten years ago, the United States Supreme Court took up the question of what rights public high-school students have when they are threatened with suspension for disciplinary reasons. The students in the case had been suspended for periods of up to ten days because they were accused of having participated in some of the school disturbances that were so common in the early seventies. The case thus concerned a low-level administrative proceeding, of the sort that occurs constantly but rarely reaches the Supreme Court; a great many people (including some of the justices who sat on the Supreme Court) took it for granted that high school principals had almost complete discretion to discipline students, at least for periods of time as short as ten days.

A bare majority of the Court nevertheless held that "due process of law" required "that the student be given oral or written notice of the charges against him and, if he denies them, an explanation of the evidence the authorities have and an opportunity to present his side of the story." The Court, the majority explained, was trying to fashion rights for the minimal administrative case, where formality would be out of place:

> There need be no delay between the time "notice" is given and the time of the hearing. In the great majority

of cases the disciplinarian may informally discuss the alleged misconduct with the student minutes after it has occurred. We hold only that, in being given an opportunity to explain his version of the facts at this discussion, the student first be told what he is accused of doing and what the basis of the accusation is.[1]

The majority was able to cite language from precedents—none of them, to be sure, concerned with anything so commonplace as a school suspension—running back more than a hundred years. If they had reached outside their own constitutional law, they might have cited precedents and maxims from every developed legal system running back for centuries. The principle captured in the Latin phrase *audiatur et altera pars* (let the other side also be heard) is called an element of "natural justice" in English administrative law and appears throughout the civil law system, both in continental Europe, including the socialist states, and in Latin America.[2] Although the maxim by its literal terms calls only for the person brought before the tribunal to be heard, it is always thought to imply a requirement of notice of the charge, if only so that the respondent will know what he has to answer.

Despite—or perhaps because of—its antiquity and its nearly universal acceptance, the underlying purpose of the bare-bones procedural protection of notice and an opportunity to answer is still debated. Very roughly, there are two schools of thought, which we may call the "dignitary" or "individualist" school and the "decisionist" school. Those who adhere to the first school have relied upon the interest in the integrity of the person to urge the expansion of the recognition of rights to a hearing, arguing that the hearing itself has value for the participants, apart from its effects on the outcome of the proceedings. John Thibaut and Laurens Walker, for example, who have conducted some of the very few empirical studies of attitudes toward procedural rights, have concluded that the parties to a proceeding personally prefer a system in which they have control over the presentation of evidence and argument in their behalf; they perceive such a system as more "fair."[3]

The other school has emphasized the importance of the hearing, as well as other concomitant procedural rights that we will come to in this chapter, to the outcome of the proceeding; procedural protections are believed to contribute to "accurate" or "correct" results. Almost no one in either school entirely rejects the views of the other; hardly anyone would like to argue that the right to a hearing contributes only to dignity and not to a preferable outcome, or vice versa. In the high-school suspension case the Supreme Court refused to choose, saying cagily that the right to a minimal hearing would serve to prevent "unfair and mistaken" decisions. In deciding what sort of hearing must be given and when, the Court has tried in a later decision concerning social security payments to strike a balance among three factors: the risk of an erroneous decision, the cost to the government of affording a hearing, and the "private interest" involved in the case.[4]

The contrast between the two schools, the reliance on the one hand on "accuracy" and on the other on "fairness" to the individual litigant has been misleading, I believe, because the use of terms such as "accurate" and "correct" has tended to conceal the nature of the inquiry used in disputes. In the typical case, the "facts" at issue are actions—physical acts or speech acts—taken by people in the past. The actors themselves and those who observed them must tell what they saw and heard; thus any understanding of what happened, correct or not, is an interpretation of intentional linguistic actions both in the original actions and the recounting of them. The way to get at an approximate meaning of actions and words is through listening to or reading an account, making a tentative interpretation, and then searching for alternatives through questions or through another interpretation. The "notice" basic to all procedure supplies one interpretation of the facts, and the response given through a hearing supplies a new interpretation of those facts, or other facts that give rise to a new interpretation. It is for similar reasons that in developed legal systems, at least in cases when accuracy is of great importance, we require the third-party decision-maker to be impartial; we fear that a person who has an interest in the case will be committed to a scenario or script that would disable him from a rational approach to the problem.

When the evidence is oral, the third party hearing the matter almost automatically asks questions to try to resolve differences and choose an interpretation. When the evidence is in writing, he may require some argument from the parties about the meaning of documents in order to resolve the dispute. Finally, whether the facts are oral or in writing, whether they are disputed or undisputed, they must be interpreted in the light of the values the decision-maker brings to bear upon them. Dispute resolution, in short, is a version of the familiar hermeneutic circle of the interpretation of linguistic meanings. A "correct" interpretation is uncertain in the way that meanings are always uncertain, and in the way that understanding of past actions is always uncertain; it is at best correct for the parties, the interpreter, and perhaps for the audience in society.

The "decisionist" and "dignitary" rationales for procedural rights now begin to look much more alike. Any *a priori* decision by the tribunal about what facts ought to be considered, how they ought to be viewed, or what value judgment ought to be applied has a necessary tendency to lead to a result that is incorrect in the sense that it does not best fit the case, because the consideration of alternatives is the only rational approach to the resolution of problems of meaning. For a hermeneutic inquiry such as a legal decision, participation is thus a source of accuracy because it is a chief source of possible alternatives. No doubt, as Thibaut and Walker found, participants favor the hearing method of resolution, in which they decide what facts and arguments are to be presented, as distinguished from the procedure by which the interpreter entirely controls the proceeding, because they sense that the hearing method tends to results that are correct *for the case*. If they experience the demand to be heard as a demand of "right" and the denial of participation as an attack upon their personal dignity, they do so in large part because in the absence of participation they sense the loss of something essential to dispute-resolution. Fairness and accuracy are indissolubly bound up in the hermeneutic process; when the interpreter shows that he is open to only one scenario, one schema for the dispute, he denigrates not only one of the parties, but the decision process itself.

Some commentators on procedure have been reaching out toward such a view, rejecting the dichotomy between accuracy and participation, and saying that a hearing should be tailored to the facts and values in the case.[5] The U.S. Supreme Court has suggested that it is a matter of degree, that some issues may really require a tailored hearing, and some may be so cut and dried as to require much less interpretation. In a case concerning the recovery of excess social security payments, the Court said that a written procedure was permissible for the relatively mechanical act of determining the fact and the amount of overpayment, at least initially, but that a more careful oral hearing was properly required for the value-laden decision whether to waive recoupment of the money on grounds of "equity and good conscience."[6]

The hermeneutic source for the right to a hearing is writ large in the history of procedure. The development of modern procedure in the civil law system of Europe is parallel to the modern rational approach to the understanding of language, not in the literal sense of conscious or causal relation (although that is sometimes present) but in the sense that the tools of non-magical procedure have tended to be those of critical hermeneutics.

The resolution of disputes through divine intervention, either in trial by battle or in trial by ordeal, at least had the attribute of formal certainty. It showed who was "right," without the doubt that always lingers in trying to decide who is telling the truth, or what is meant by statements in documents or recited by witnesses. Medieval procedure, even after it had passed beyond trial by supernatural means, still sought to close the gap between meaning and reality, as if frightened of the chance for difference of opinion inherent in verbal evidence. Jurists of the *ancien regime* tried to minimize the inquiry that is natural to language through methods that were as "formal" as possible. The proceedings were largely written and secret— mysterious—partly in hopes of making the results seem as little open to question as possible. Although witnesses were used, their number and type was counted and assigned a certain weight depending on their status, sex, and interest in the case, as if they could be given an "*a priori* arithmetical value."[7] In a criminal case, if a defendant would not confess and bring his own testimony into line with the accusation so as to eliminate all doubt about the verbal account of the facts, he could not be convicted except upon the evidence of two eyewitnesses. In some jurisdictions conviction in a capital case was not permitted at all without the defendant's confession, a dramatic demonstration of the fear of interpretation.[8]

Much of the abhorrence of the elusive nature of verbal truth survives down to the present day; especially in civil-law countries, the fiction has prevailed that the system of the law, even though it is expressed in language, must be complete and gapless, supplying a predictable result for virtually every case. The fiction was a cornerstone, for example, of Max Weber's analysis of modern law and rational bureaucracy; he imagined such a predictable system to be essential to a modern integrated economy. He could not see how the relatively context-based methods of determination—the common-law case method and the jury trial—used in Anglo-American law could endure in modern capitalist systems.[9] The search for a positive point of interpretation has been the obsession of lawyers, of course, as it was of Weber, and as it has been to a considerable extent of social science as a whole.

A revolution in dispute-resolution was at work in the civil-law system even while the lawyers clung to the myth of a totally formal system. The law has been passing from a written, secret procedure to an oral, public one. As Mauro Cappelletti puts it, "The idea of orality . . . for nearly two centuries, has been the symbol for the most important reform movements in the field of procedure, at least in the Civil Law world."[10] An oral proceeding, the reformers have believed, would contribute to the reliability of the trial process, by bringing the parties before the judge to argue out their points and answer questions, would make the process more legitimate by subjecting it to public scrutiny, and would incidentally speed up the disposition of cases. While in France the oral and public aspect of the trial has principally appeared in the argument of the facts and law before the judges, in other systems it extends to the presentation of evidence as well, in a manner more similar to the Anglo-American system. The civil-law movement to orality (*muendlichkeit*) was most complete in the German-speaking world. The Austrian Civil Code of 1895 introduced a "trial by colloquy" among the litigants and the judge, and contemporary West German procedure calls for such a trial, as often as possible in a single hearing. Even in countries where orality has not progressed so far, it is recognized as an ideal.[11] The European Convention on Human Rights provides only that in civil and criminal cases "everyone is entitled to a fair and public hearing within a reasonable time by an independent and impartial tribunal"; but the fact that the Convention does not specify whether proceedings should be oral or written has prompted a legal adviser to the Council of Europe to ask rhetorically "if the rule of publicity in hearings and issuing judgments does not entail the rule of orality."[12] Some such rule seems to be implied by the ancient and basic right to notice and a hearing, when combined with the proviso that the hearing should be public.

The movement toward publicity shows the continental reformers' intuitive grasp of the critical and dialogic nature of inquiry into facts and values. They understood that publicity would lend the proceedings legitimacy because, as I suggested in earlier chapters, it would permit a critique of the hearing—its procedures, the evidence adduced, and the values expressed in the result—by the larger society. It is the state's willingness to subject the decision-making process to such a critique that, to the modern mind, guarantees that the tribunal has taken a rational approach.

In the United States, as we saw in the last chapter, the public now has a First Amendment right to attend a full-fledged judicial trial, and a similar rule apparently applies to administrative hearings.[13] The right of the parties, as distinguished from the press and public, to have an administrative proceeding opened to the public if they choose is a rather different question under American law, a question of the fairness of proceedings rather than of freedom of access and expression. In a case that shows the confluence of the notions of accuracy and legitimacy in the concept of procedural fairness the District of Columbia Court of Appeals held that a civil servant threatened with dismissal had a constitutional right to an open hearing. The Air Force had been seeking to fire Ernest Fitzgerald, as part of an alleged "reduction in force," through a civil service hearing routinely closed to the public. Fitzgerald claimed that the proceeding was really a covert attempt to punish and intimidate him for blowing the whistle on wasteful

Pentagon procurement practices. By the time his case came up, he was already a symbol of public criticism of secret decision-making and a conduit to wider public knowledge and criticism. A closed hearing in his case would have been bound to convey the impression that it was just one more in a series of decisions rendered suspect by their insulation from scrutiny in the society as a whole. The court, moreover, conveyed the strong impression that there was in fact a better chance of an impartial decision in a public than in a private proceeding. An open hearing brought the double benefit of increasing the likelihood of a rational approach to Fitzgerald's case and ensuring that channels of criticism of both the Pentagon and the Civil Service Commission were open.[14] Publicity thus becomes an element of procedural due process in the U.S. system just as it is a fundamental procedural guarantee in the civil law system.

The civil law reformers saw "immediacy" and "spontaneity" as concomitants of orality in litigation. They expected the new procedures not only to be more expeditious than the old written procedures, but more responsive to the nuances of the case.[15] Trial under the Austrian Civil Code, which was the model for others, has been described as "a meaningful three-cornered dialogue" conducted according to the "Socratic method."[16] Although the Anglo-American system, traditionally devoted as it is to *viva voce* methods, has had little need for such a reform movement, the courts in recent years have had to think explicitly about the benefits of dialogical procedures in the course of deciding when the right to a hearing ought to apply. In the landmark case of *Goldberg v. Kelly*, which concerns the right to a hearing before the termination of basic welfare benefits (and requires a more searching proceeding than a school suspension), the Supreme Court wrote:

> Written submissions do not afford the flexibility of oral presentations; they do not permit the [welfare] recipient to mold his argument of the issues the decision maker appears to regard as important. Particularly where credibility and veracity are at issue, as they must be in many termination proceedings, written submissions are a wholly unsatisfactory basis for decision. The second-hand presentation to the decisionmaker by the case worker has its

own deficiencies; since the caseworker usually gathers the facts upon which the charge of ineligibility rests, the presentation of the recipient's side of the controversy cannot safely be left to him. Therefore a recipient must be allowed to state his position orally. Informal procedures will suffice; in this context due process does not require a particular order of proof or mode of offering evidence.[17]

Dialogic methods of procedure are not restricted to developed societies such as those of the United States and Europe, with their right to notice and a hearing and their evolution in the direction of public, oral and immediate proceedings. Hermeneutic methods, whether called by that name or by any name at all, are used whenever and wherever an effort is made to resolve disputes by non-magical means, using inquiry through natural language. In societies without a strong sense of contrast between the litigants and the political authority of the judge, the use of those methods may not give rise to a notion of a "right" to a particular procedure but rather to a custom or practice. Hermeneutic methods are nevertheless constantly at work, I think, both in sifting the facts and in applying values to the facts. In the pages that follow, I shall talk first about the nexus between facts and values, and then about methods and concomitant rights connected to fact-finding, although I recognize that the two sorts of inquiry interpenetrate and are bound up together.

Facts and Values

Legal systems afford great scope for face-to-face dialogue among the parties and the decision-makers concerning the relation between the facts of the case and the values of the society, as embodied in its laws. British and American lawyers make an oral argument, in most cases, both civil and criminal, when they appeal to higher courts. They always sum up in a case tried before a jury; the United States has gone so far as to accord a criminal defendant a constitutional right to have his case argued at the close of the trial, even in a non-jury case. In France, the central part of the trial, the part to which orality

and publicity apply most consistently, is the argument between the parties before the court concerning the relation between the law and the facts.[18] In the more informal courts of
simpler societies, such an argument is often all there is to the
trial.

Trials in tribal communities differ, of course, from those
in industrialized societies. Because the parties in a rural village
dispute ordinarily must continue to live together after their
differences are resolved, a principal aim for a local court is to
enable the parties to get along within the common values of
the community. The judges' approach to disputes tends to be
"multiplex," in Max Gluckman's phrase, to expand to cover all
the problems between the parties, in an effort to ensure that a
modus vivendi is restored. Among the Lenje of Zambia, for example, village dispute resolution pulls in all interrelated griev-
ances, while a trial at the local court formally established by
the central authorities will deal only with one isolated dispute
at time.[19] Tribal village courts tend to differ from more formal
courts in their notion of what we call relevancy, and not in the
way they argue or reason out the case.

The importance of dialogical argument in dispute resolution, whether it is multiplex or not, lies in the interdepen-
dence of fact and value. At every stage of a dispute, norms
guide the decision-maker's interpretation of the evidence; he is
likely to find an account more or less plausible depending on
how it accords with normal behavior. If we expect exchanges to
be made at prevailing market rates, for example, we are immediately puzzled when we hear that an exchange has been made
for much less or more than the going rate. Similarly, in a land
case before a Trobriand Islands local tribunal, one party testified that a branch of bananas had been offered, claiming that it
was in payment for the use-rights in the disputed land. Since
such a gift was too small to give rise to use-rights, the judges
interpreted it as a special payment intended to confirm and
continue pre-existing use-rights.[20]

The norms applied both in interpreting the evidence and
in finally deciding the case are themselves open-textured, subject to interpretation. Central to a party's presentation of his
case as a whole is an argument about what law is applicable
and how it ought to be applied. Describing the trial of dis-

putes among the Tswana of southern Africa, John Comaroff and Simon Roberts write: "Tswana disputants construct and rely upon a 'paradigm of argument': that is, they attempt to convey a coherent picture of relevant events and actions in terms of one or more (implicit or explicit) normative referents."[21] Examples of such arguments appear repeatedly in anthropological reports from widely scattered places, particularly in land cases, for which the bare chronology of actions concerning the disputed property is often well settled, but the understanding of those actions is disputed. In the Trobriand Islands case, for example, it was accepted that the bananas had been tendered; the question was about the significance of the act.

The construction of the paradigm of argument is, of course, entwined with the interpretation of the facts. As the party argues the case before the tribunal, there is a complex interplay among questions of fact and law. The party is asked how the norm can be applicable in the way he claims it is in light of the probable facts, and then he is asked how the facts could be as he claims them to be in light of the norms. Such is the typical course of legal argument before the French, British, or American courts as well as before those of the Tswana or the Trobrianders. The novice lawyer in the English-speaking world is ordinarily advised, in trying his case or arguing it before a jury or a judge, to find a theory, a thread of plausible fact that will tend to accord favorably with the law. The "facts" as verbally reported and the norms are interdependent and must be adjusted to one another continuously until a result is reached that seems best to fit the case, an adjustment that is difficult to make except through a live dialogue.

Analyzing the Facts

For Anglo-American jurists it has been a great pastime to extol their adversarial system of litigation and by the same token to denigrate the civil law system of the Continent. At the source of that invidious comparison lies the belief that only under the common-law system do the parties have control of the evidence to be presented at trial and of the way it is to be presented, whether through direct questioning of friendly or cross-examination of unfriendly witnesses. English-speaking lawyers are fond of quoting Wigmore's opinion that cross-examination "is beyond any doubt the greatest legal engine ever invented for the discovery of truth"; in 1975, Judge Henry Friendly was finally provoked to ask drily why, if that were true, other legal systems had not seen fit to import the engine.[22]

Part of the answer lies in the fact that the common-law system does not differ from others quite so radically as its practitioners like to think it does. When Thibaut and Walker studied peoples' attitudes toward procedural justice in the United States, France, and Germany, they found that subjects preferred, as most fair, a system in which the parties, rather than the judge, could control what evidence was put into a hearing. The authors called the latter the "adversary system" and thought that their results demonstrated a cross-cultural hankering for such a system among those who did not enjoy it. I suspect that what they may show instead is that all these nations prefer their own systems, which in fact differ very little in respect to the parties' control of their own cases.[23]

Under procedures of both the common-law and civil-law courts, parties have long had a right to know what it is that witnesses have said, and to rebut or support their testimony with other evidence. As long ago as the thirteenth century, the defendant in a French criminal case received copies of the testimony against him and had the right to rebut and reply and to bring witnesses in support of his defense. The contemporary European Convention on Human Rights, in words similar to those used in the Sixth Amendment to the U.S. Constitution, provides that a criminal defendant has the right "to examine or have examined witnesses against him and to obtain the attendance and examination of witnesses on his behalf." Although neither the Convention nor the U.S. Constitution has found it necessary to give an equally specific description of the procedural rights of the parties in a non-criminal case, a legal adviser to the Council of Europe has suggested that the refusal of a tribunal to listen to the witnesses for one side or the other can rise to the level of the denial of a hearing. The question is rarely presented as a matter of principle or constitutional law because procedural codes and customs in England and America as well as on the Continent accord rights to civil litigants that are close to those enjoyed (if that is the correct term) by a criminal defendant.

The civil- and common-law systems differ most in the way that evidence is presented at a trial. Under the civil-law system, the judge or his delegates examine the witnesses; the parties or their lawyers do not subject the witnesses to direct or cross-examination, although they may suggest questions to the judge. There is no doubt, however, that witnesses do get cross-questioned and impeached under the civil-law system. As early as 1260, at the moment when the French king abolished trial by battle, he simultaneously replaced it with a system of inquest in which the judge's delegates were required to question the witnesses "subtilement."[24]

A face-to-face dialogue with the witness, to draw out potential contradictions in his testimony, to find the places where it is consistent with other evidence, or to clarify ambiguities or hedges in meaning, has everywhere been used, even in quite "primitive" societies, at least when the method of dispute-resolution does not rely on fighting, or an appeal to the supernatural, or both. Lawyers are not used at all in most systems, and as a consequence such questioning is usually done by the judges, although in some places the parties are allowed to pose questions as well.[25] Some thirty years ago, Max Gluckman in *The Judicial Process Among the Barotse of Northern Rhodesia* was among the first to point out how general is the impeachment of witnesses in tribal courts. The dispute that Gluckman calls "The Case of the Violent Councillor," for example, in which councillor Saywa was accused of assaulting one of his villagers who was quarrelling with Saywa's son, was resolved by the judges almost entirely through the cross-questioning of the councillor. Saywa had claimed in his defense that he was merely intervening in the fight between the villager and his own son. Part of the questioning went as follows:

"When Y [the villager] came into your courtyard, why did you not tell him to sit down, and then summon your children and the men of the village, so that you could enquire into the dispute between them?"—Saywa hedged: "They are binding me with lies."

Solami, head of the court, pressed him: "Why did you
not make them sit down so that you could judge between
them?"—Saywa: "I did not do this."[26]

The court also impeached Saywa over the manner of his fighting with Y, if in fact he was trying to make peace, and over his
failure to appeal an earlier judgment if he was in fact not at
fault.

It can be argued that the dialogical methods of questioning used by tribunals in simple economies throughout the
world have been borrowed from the European legal systems
imposed by imperial adminstrators. That claim is difficult to
test, because legal systems which have received intensive study
have in most cases experienced penetration by Europe as well.
Even though it is true that tribal courts often did adapt European legal methods—in many cases, for example, they abandoned supernatural methods under pressure from colonial ad-
ministrators—it is striking that so many of them found the
dialogical method of cross-questioning congenial, from whatever source it was derived. Its prevalence suggests that it is a
rational development in any non-magical system of trial.

Although they are in widespread use throughout the
world, dialogical methods of testing evidence emerge as issues
of "right" only in a system like the Anglo-American one,
where the questioning is the prerogative of the litigants rather
than the judge. Where the modes of inquiry have become matters of right, moreover, the legal doctrines of evidence have
tacitly come to reflect the critical-hermeneutic character of the
inquiry and the psychological effects of different sorts of questions.[27]

Distinctions made in American law concerning the propriety of questions track parallel distinctions in cognitive psychology. There are witnesses who are impartial as between the
parties, but so far as we know there is no such thing as a
witness who is neutral in the sense that her memory, as she
recounts it through language, records the past like a camera.
The witness' memory is at least in part organized by language,
as we saw in Chapter II, and the framework for that memory is
typically the scripts and schemas that the witness finds familiar
or congenial. As studies by Elizabeth Loftus and others have

shown, the witness' account of her memories can be altered by the terms of questions put to her, a characteristic the courts use to try to manipulate the witness into a relatively neutral position. Before the witness gives testimony, the court either does not know what she will say, or expects her to give testimony favorable to the person who has called her; the framework of schemas and scripts concerning the case in the mind of the witness should, in general, be assumed to fit those expectations. The questioner who calls the witness is required to ask questions that do not suggest an answer; the common law says that he is not permitted to "lead" the witness. By the same token, the courts permit leading a witness who has said that she cannot recall the facts unaided, in order to supply the witness with a framework to trigger her memory.

Once the witness has testified, we can infer what framework he brings to the facts; in general we will find that at least some of her account is helpful to the person who called her. And here, on cross-examination, is the place that the common-law tradition permits "leading." The term itself is indicative of the psychological function of the questioning, to suggest to the witness a script for her memories that is different from the one she has already expressed. Cross-examination is often used, of course, against a consciously untruthful witness simply to indicate to the trier of fact the inconsistencies in her story, but its psychological roots are deeper than that. It is most effective when it is used to suggest to a susceptible witness another view of the facts.

Still more interesting is the sort of question that contains a significant assumption, the "when did you stop beating your wife" question, forbidden in the common-law tradition for any witness, either on direct or cross examination. A reason commonly given for barring such questions is that they are tricky to answer; a witness has to affirm or deny the premise in the question in order to answer it. A more profound reason is that the assumption in the question is likely to be incorporated into her memory by the witness and to be recalled as a "fact" by those who are listening. In studies by Elizabeth Loftus, subjects were shown a film of an accident and then were asked, "How fast was the white sports car going when it passed the barn while travelling along the country road?" A large percentage of the subjects later remembered seeing a barn, even though there was none in the film.[28] In short, the scenario in the question became part of the subjects' scenarios.

The nature of the trial as a hermeneutic inquiry, dependent on dialogue for knowledge, is crystallized in the rule of the common-law courts against the use of hearsay testimony. In practice the rule is, as every law student in the English-speaking world has been taught, a bar against the use of testimony from persons who are not in court to be cross-questioned. As a first approximation of the reason behind the rule, the courts say that they want to be sure that questioners can clarify ambiguity and vagueness in the apparent meaning of the witness' words. More broadly, the rationale is that the best interpretation of the witness' testimony in the context of the case can only be known through questioning. The court must be able to hear the witness' reaction to proposed alternatives, to compare them with other evidence, to evaluate them in the light of the norms, and then to hear still other alternatives offered to the witness. The ways the witness' testimony might best be understood are often not foreseeable and cannot be revealed without a dialogue. In the United States, the right to try to find that interpretation and convey it to the trier of fact is considered so important that the Constitution guarantees a criminal defendant the right to "confront"—that is, to cross-question—the witnesses against him.

Conclusions

Upon reflection, it should not be surprising to find direct, oral procedures in such relatively simple societies as the Barotse or the Trobriand Islanders. It is in fact more puzzling that doctrines favoring the orality, immediacy, and publicity of proceedings, including the face-to-face questioning of witnesses, should prevail in developed societies like those of the United States and Europe, and not only prevail but have become stronger in the last hundred years. Max Weber pictured the law of the modern state as one of increasing "formal rationality," supposing that substantive rules and procedures could be devised such that courts would be able to obtain predictable results in almost every case. Yet the fact-finding and law-applying aspects of procedure in modern states have in many respects become more informal, in the sense that Weber might have understood the term. They are more nuanced, more suited to the individual case.[29] The notion of procedural "formality" shared by Weber with an earlier generation of legal scholars has gradually been undermined by the modern view of language and of the way problems are solved when they are cast in a linguistic framework. It is no longer plausible to suppose that the interpretation either of evidence or of legal precepts according to the formal model would be either just or accurate. Dialogical inquiry, most effectively conducted face to face and subject to criticism by other institutions and people, is not only the simplest but also the most "accurate" and "correct" way of resolving problems of evidence or of law, or of the combination of the two.

If justice outside the criminal courts is perceived as distant and bureaucratic in industrial societies, the reasons are not to be found so much in the formality of contemporary procedure in the intense professionalism of judges and lawyers, in the expense and delay of lawsuits, and perhaps also in their narrowness. Although the dialogic methods of procedure are well tailored to the sort of holistic, multiplex dispute resolution that Gluckman found among the Barotse, the systems of western Europe and the United States have not used those methods, in general, to broaden the scope of dispute resolution. There is a strong sense that if procedure were more multiplex, more inclusive of the lives of the disputants, it would become less generalized, less able to treat litigants as equal before the law. Where such a view prevails, mere hearing procedures, however oral, immediate, or public they may be, will not be able to dispel the feeling that legal proceedings are detached from other actions in society. It is the price we have paid for a tradition of abstract rights.

Conclusion

THE PLACE OF RIGHTS

Many institutions of the modern polity have been shaped by the effort to solve problems clothed in language; such problems involve questions of interpretation and choices of action that can be adequately decided only through discussion. Procedures for courts and administrative hearings fit this description so closely that they may be conceived as special applications of the general method of linguistic inquiry. Such procedures are used in any modern rational system of dispute resolution, but they are assured to the parties as matters of civil "right" primarily when the parties, rather than the tribunal, conduct some part of the inquiry. The right of free expression may be seen as a still broader "right of method," a right to inquire into the propriety of administrative actions of the state, or freely to seek methods to solve any other sort of problem; like procedural rights of inquiry, it is a need cast in the form of a civil right in order to restrain the interference of the state.

It is possible, then, to talk about the dialogic functions of political institutions quite apart from issues of rights; to some extent we did exactly that when we examined the work of courts outside the common-law system in cross-questioning witnesses. On a much larger scale, the system of checks and balances that appears constantly in modern constitutions, using the courts to monitor the legislature, often dividing the legislature itself, and using both the courts and the legislature to monitor the executive, serves the purpose of having policy questions discussed by one body and then criticized and re-discussed by another. The power that each body often holds over one or more of the others forces each of them to take criticism into account.[1] The shift in foreign policy-making power between the President and Congress during the past twenty-five years, brought about by the war in Vietnam as well as such incidents as the Bay of Pigs, as traced in Chapter III, shows that a source of the change was a sense that the executive branch had made decisions without sufficiently taking alternatives into account. The shift was designed, clearly though inadequately, to force the kind of flexibility in decision-making that the executive did not seem to have (while introducing other sources of rigidity due to conducting foreign policy in the open and in front of the press and the electorate).

I touch here upon the relations of political institutions outside the relatively narrow world of civil rights as a reminder that the effects of the peculiarities of language are not limited to the issues of rights to expression and participation and the like, and that the presence of such rights does not by itself ensure an optimum solution or even a rational approach to problems. The right to speak in the forum of society as a whole is necessary but not sufficient; it does not, of course, guarantee that expression will be taken into account, or understood, or even heard. Institutions for policy-making, as discussion in earlier chapters has shown, always present some risk of an ill-informed decision, and one function of the political process is to shape institutions so that the risk is as small as possible; they must add to the right to speak some power to force officials to listen.

A full discussion of the critical-hermeneutic function of the relations of political institutions is beyond the scope of this book. It is more useful, I think, to close the book by exploring the place of civil rights in the social world of dialogue as I have sketched it in earlier chapters. I return to a question that was central in the Introduction: What is the place of the individual in this scheme of rights? In conventional liberal theories, that place is secure; the individual is the basic unit of political action, the bearer of rights, although groups may often assume rights similar to those of individuals. When the rationale for rights is rooted in such social actions as the interpretation of language, on the other hand, the distinction between the individual and society cannot be drawn in the same way. When all understanding is thought to be interdependent with that of other minds, the notion of an entirely "individual" or "private" thought is transformed. The question of who or what is the bearer of rights becomes again problematic. In past chapters I have talked about rights both of expression and of participation, for groups as well as for individuals, passing perhaps too smoothly over the question why or how we should continue to center rights in individuals or indeed in anything at all.

We can decide who or what is the holder of civil rights under the dialogical theory only by going back to the origins of the argument. The purpose of a right to free expression or of a procedural right is to enable the individual and society to understand meanings and solve problems. The only appropriate holder of such rights is one who can contribute an interpretation to discourse; she must be able to participate by using language and similar symbolic structures. It has been one of the underlying themes of this book that only persons, acting individually or as a group upon their common decision, are capable of this sort of participation. The point is so basic, so short and direct, that it is difficult to grasp its importance. Its force can perhaps be seen best if we try to conceive of the alternative.

Consider the problems raised by the notion of any system for interpreting language or solving problems that is made by humans but is not itself human, such as an elaborately programmed computer. Even though computers do solve some problems more rapidly than humans, play complex games, and even use words in limited ways, there are good reasons to think that a manufactured contrivance cannot be got to do what humans do when they exercise dialogic rights.

Language, as it has been described in this book, is a juncture of common and idiosyncratic elements. Understanding it is at once a participation in the public, social history of the language and a reflection of personal history. That uneasy dilemma is the source of the perennial dialogue carried on to determine meanings. The scripts, plans, and goals that Schank and Abelson found they had to specify to the computer as a predicate to its understanding of the simplest group of connected sentences were an attempt to represent the public history of the language, its social assumptions. Yet those frameworks never afforded any but the most mechanical powers of reading. We might assemble an enormous staff of socially and linguistically sophisticated programmers to write still more of that public history—except that they would not be able to do it. They would have to find which meanings are in the public domain and which in the private, a problem in interpretation not only enormous but in the end insoluble. It is inherent in the interpretation of language that users do not agree about which parts are common and which idiosyncratic; one interpreter's commonplace is another's oddity. Even if there were a portion of the language for which all the lexicographers could agree that it is held in common, that portion would still be organized differently for each of them, interconnected with the rest of his language in idiosyncratic ways. There is, of course, no source of authority to settle the disagreements among the linguists. Their language has been created by the community of speakers and writers, acting without an arbitrator, and none can be found to replace the community. Even if the linguists assigned an authoritative meaning to every conceivable word and sentence, through an exhaustive dictionary and grammar, sentences would be uttered that were not accounted for in those texts, because the language is still constituted through the idiosyncracies of the members of the community as well as by the public history of the language (supposing the latter to be knowable).

The attempt to imagine a model of "thinking" suggests dilemmas similar to those presented by the model of a language-interpreter, but raised to a still more problematic level. When a psychologist tries to simulate some aspect of "thinking," be it language interpretation or memory, he expresses in abstract terms his own concept of that aspect; he does not, in short, escape from his own thinking. Expressing the concept in some form such as a computer program, physically outside the thinking of the experimenter, does not avoid this limitation.

To be sure, the computer does seem to give an "objective" answer for the problem posed to it. The beauty of the machine experiment as a hermeneutic tool is that it enables us to formalize our thoughts and reveal exactly how the proposed model works. If the investigator can see some respect in which the model fails to "think" and is clever enough to be able to model that new aspect, it may seem that he is gradually bringing the program closer to thinking. All the machine can give, nevertheless, is a formal statement of the investigator's internal dialogue concerning the attempt to define an aspect of thinking. "Thinking," either as a general concept or broken down into its supposed components, is not a limit to which one approaches, but a linguistic construct which itself presents all the problems, both individual and social, of interpretation. Years ago, when an experimenter in artificial intelligence was asked to assemble a list of factors as candidates for the formal description of "behavior," he concluded: "We have considered the problem of turning this set of concepts into a full-scale mathematics of behavioral systems, finding that this may be impossible owing to the lack of any generally applicable criteria for delimiting what a 'behavior' is."[2] The programmer cannot tell, even as matter of private conviction, whether he has got his machine "thinking" (or "behaving"), because once he translates the term out of ordinary language into computation language he has no way, independent of language, of telling whether he has the same thing or not. Furthermore, if the researcher were convinced that he could specify mathematically all the characteristics essential to thinking, he would encounter basic disagreement from others, either because the concept is organized differently for them or because his explanation of the concept is understood differently by them. The psychologist brings to the concept, and to his attempt to interpret it in computable form, the idiosyncratic as well as the public history of the concept; the relation between them is unspecifiable except through linguistic means, which are themselves subject to interpretation.

The attempt to simulate thinking presents us with a

Chinese puzzle of problems within problems, of which the linguistic problem of interpretation is only one. We are imprisoned within our thinking, unable to say what there is about it that is idiosyncratic and what is similar to the thinking of others, except through the tools of language, within which we are also imprisoned. Yet the concepts we use to interpret "thinking" seem even more ill defined than those we bring to bear on other interpretive problems, because we have, at best, only a very foggy idea how the mind is organized. In the last few years, paychologists have argued, for example, that there may be, as Howard Gardner has put it, "multiple intelligences"—very different faculties for different functions.[3] Even if we can learn quite a lot about the individual faculties, we are far from understanding how they are integrated. As Jerry Fodor has said:

> While some interesting things have been learned about the psychology of input analysis—primarily about language and vision—the psychology of thought has proved quite intractable.
>
> In particular, on my view, the attempt to develop general models of intelligent problem-solving—which one associates most closely with work in artificial intelligence by such figures as as Schank, Winograd and others—has produced surprisingly little insight despite the ingenuity and seriousness with which it has often been pursued.[4]

We are accustomed to understanding language, within the limits of our hermeneutic methods, but we are not accustomed to interpreting other aspects of thinking, much less the system, whatever it may be, that coordinates them. We cannot program a machine to think because we cannot specify what it is to think. It is in the nature of our understanding of the word "think," even more than of most words, that it must differ depending on the context in which it is used and the person who uses it.

These thought-experiments upon attempts to simulate thinking or language interpretation illustrate several aspects of the rationale for rights of dialogue. We do not suppose that human beings, taken individually or in groups, are especially

"good" at solving problems. Indeed, our prejudices and idiosyncracies make it difficult for us to evaluate alternatives even
as we rely on our prejudices as heuristics to search for alternatives. We don't have a fixed standard, however, for what it is to
be good at solving problems; if we had, we might, for example, be able to come closer to saying what it is to think. What
we do know is that we are bound to solve problems by some
method and that we are less likely to miss a viable alternative if
we can keep our methods open to criticism.

There is a cliché among critics of artificial intelligence to
the effect that a machine has no "history" in the sense that a
person has.[5] The first few times I encountered that criticism, I
thought it was empty romantic rhetoric; it did not seem to
me, as it certainly does not to supporters of artificial intelligence, squarely to answer the question whether a machine can
be programmed to "think." Yet finally I have come to believe
that, in an inarticulate way, it does imply the answer. A programmed machine does not think, insofar as we understand
the term, because it has no body that has taken in impressions
through its various faculties and integrated them through
growth, physical operation and discourse. It does not share
the juncture between the common and the idiosyncratic that is
the result of such a personal and general "history" and that is
the source of solutions for the sort of "open world" problems
that are the ones that matter most to us. The possibility of
disagreement is what makes meanings interesting and supplies
the opening for original solutions to problems. No matter how
large a body of public meanings could be specified to be fed
into Schank and Abelson's Script Applier Mechanism, its interpretations would remain wooden to the rest of us simply
because they had been specified. What is new for us comes
from another mind in dialogic response to a situation, and it is
new because that mind has a history that is different from our
own.

These conclusions suggest an oblique approach to some
tenets of liberal individualism. The individual is essential to
rights rooted in dialogue because the ultimate interpretive
agent is a human individual. Groups may reach a collective
decision rather different from what the individual members
would have reached, but the individuals must of course discuss

and reach that decision through their own thinking. There is, as the discussion of artificial intelligence shows, no more formal "method"; the only interpretive participant, and the only bearer of rights, is a human participant, either acting alone or with others.

If the government allows liberty of expression in order to ensure maximum rationality for its own decisions and to preserve its legitimacy, as I argued back in the fourth chapter, it will place a special value upon the opinions of individual persons and groups of persons because they are the only source of original decisions on matters that affect the government. It is in this way that a society that values dialogue will come to share some of the values of individualism.

Political ideologies that postulate the organization of society as the sum of the interests of separate individuals, on the one hand, or as the result of class or collective interests, on the other, are to some extent always in error. It is impossible, for example, to imagine any manner of satisfying collective needs that does not involve the thinking of individuals and groups. The solutions that those individuals or groups may conceive are not predictable, and the appropriateness of any solution cannot be understood without discussion the limits of which cannot be foreseen.

It is nearly as difficult to conceive any manner of social life that merely "aggregates" the needs or the decisions of individuals, viewed in isolation. While such aggregative modes of decision-making do occur, in situations as diverse as traffic jams and markets, in most important decisions the individual does not act alone, but rather through his dialogue with society.[6] Even a secret ballot, although it is carried out by each voter acting alone, is always used after a campaign of discussion in a context of common beliefs and customs. The "rights" of the individual, in some abstract sense divorced from the needs and the influences of society, are as blank as the concept of the individual from which they derive. An individual may, of course, be consistently in conflict with society, convinced that its decisions are destructive; but in the broader sense, society is as necessary to her understanding as she may suppose herself to be to society's understanding.

Human beings, as individuals or groups, have the rights

of method I have described in this book not just on their own account, but because they are the interpreters of and for society. They never lose those rights because they never stop interpreting language and the world, and because society never stops depending on their interpretations.

Appendices

APPENDIX I:

RELATIVISM

In the first chapter, I have taken a relativistic approach to knowledge, linking it to the indeterminacy of language. In the passage at the close of that chapter that refers to this appendix, I draw back somewhat from that relativism. Although the controversy concerning the relativity of knowledge is not central to this book, I do not want to seem to waffle on it. Philosophers have argued cogently that cognitive relativism is untenable because it points toward the paradox that the acceptance of the position of relativism must itself have some ground, or else it may turn out not to be true, to be rooted in some absolute.[1] Put more simply, it is hard to know how anyone could have a conviction that knowledge is relative without some place from which to make that conviction firm.

So far from thinking that this objection is fatal, I think it can be understoood rather as a source for a creative approach to knowledge. We treat the two halves of the paradox, in which on the one hand I feel a conviction that I am certain of some knowledge and on the other I feel that I might find a ground upon which to criticize any such certain knowledge, as the parts of a dialogue by which we try to understand. It is part of the modern method to go back and forth between the poles of the dilemma. We don't know, as a practical matter, whether our knowledge has a positive ground or not. If we argue that all knowledge is relative, then we seem to rest that conclusion on some ground; but if we pick such a ground, we immediately criticize it. In short we choose temporary positive grounds, *as if* they are final, and then we subject them to critique *as if* they are relative.

We know that we are going to act upon our understanding, either by changing something, or simply by accepting something as understood, interpreted for the purpose that confronts us. Because we are bound to engage in these acts, even if only that of understanding, we establish frameworks that make it possible for us to do so.[2] They are, as described in more detail in the second chapter, scenarios of past social relations as we have seen them, disciplines, procedures, customs, and the like. We may take them as final definitions of the limits of knowledge if we choose, but it is not, in the sense used in this book, consistent with modern rationality to do so. It is, nevertheless, rational for us to recognize that we must act on them.

Thus we tack back and forth between treating knowledge as relative and treating it as positive. We treat it as positive for purposes of acting upon it and questioning it. It is important that we be able to do so, in order to give a ground both for understanding and for action. But after we have made the decision, it is equally important that we ourselves or someone else should be able to see that that is what we have done, so the action or the decision can be subjected to criticism.

APPENDIX II: THE PROBLEM OF PSYCHOLOGICAL INQUIRY

In 1982, in a controversy with developmental psychologists, the behaviorist J. P. Rushton wrote:

> At that time [i.e., 1913] . . . Watson changed the direction of psychology from the study of the contents of consciousness to the study of behavior. It will be well to remind ourselves of why he was able to do so. There was a general revulsion among scientifically minded psychologists that the unresolvable controversies of the day over such issues as whether it was possible to have a thought without having an image (the famous imageless-thought controversy) were not even controversies about facts. There were no "facts" involved. The data were all subjective. This desire for the primary data of psychology to be "objective" (i.e., susceptible to being measured by more than one person at a time) led to the suggestion that behavior be the primary data of psychology, not consciousness. By focusing on behavior, the discipline of psychology could truly become a natural science.[1]

Behaviorists inspired by J. B. Watson were determined, if they could, to get everything intentional and "mental" out of psychology.[2] They were after a "correspondence theory" for psychology, in which something externally measurable—physical behavior—could be matched unambiguously with something else externally measurable, such as a stimulus.

The behaviorist approach was strategically designed to avoid two problems that have pernennially plagued psychology. The first was the involvement of the investigator in the experiment. If the psychologist uses reports of his internal workings and feelings as evidence, he is pulled into his own experiment in an obvious way; but the situation is not much improved if he takes reports from subjects other than himself about their interiors. Because he cannot go behind what they tell him, he simply adopts whatever errors the subjects may make in perception or reporting.

The second problem was the use of question-begging "explanations" for the material that subjects reported from their interiors. The use of mentalistic labels such as personality, concept, or mind, as part of the explanation of behavior simply gave problems a new name and shifted them to new places. The Mind was a homunculus that rewrote the mystery of human behavior in a different key.[3] In short, unless the facts to be explained could be referred to a framework, such as the mechanism of the nervous system, that was qualitatively different from the phenomena that were being studied, it was difficult to say how anything was really being explained.

Behaviorism, then, is a serious effort to grapple with problems of method; if its hegemony has faded, it is not because those problems have been solved but because they have been put to one side for a number of interrelated reasons. A dominant school of linguists led by Noam Chomsky has come to accept the argument that humans have an innate ability to construct and learn syntactical structures, even that there is a "universal grammer" that sets natural limits on the diversity of languages. Such an ability, Chomsky thought, implied a mental structure fatal to the view that all learning might be explained through stimulus and response.[4] Psychologists saw that the cognitive abilities of humans, perceptual as well as linguistic, might have a structure that was not of the mechanical-neurological sort that the radical behaviorists imagined. To try to understand behavior through the neurological make-up of the brain, some psychologists thought, was like trying to understand a computer by the electrical equipment that is put into it.[5]

I might have developed an account of modern cognitive psychology similar to the account of language philosophy in the first chapter, with a simple theory of behaviorism as the working model to be criticized in place of a correspondence theory of meaning. It is not necessary to begin from the ground up, however, because Chapter I has implied the critique of this sort of behaviorism. Reductionism is exploded; there is no independent theoretical language in which the correspondences between behavior and stimulus can be stated. The "meaning" of behavior, in fact the definition of what is behavior and what is not, always depends on other parts of the theory of psychology.[6]

Behaviorism is a theory-laden approach to psychology; that in itself is no objection to it any more than to any other approach. The difficulty is that the theory is often inadequate to a large part of the evidence, so much so that when it has been applied to complex phenomena such as speech it becomes oddly anti-empirical. B. F. Skinner's description of the use of language through stimulus-response mechanisms, for example, is not an empirical investigation of language; it is an attempt to show that a reductionist account of such a complex activity is plausible. About the learning of abstract words, for example, he writes:

> If metaphor is often taken to be, not the natural result of stimulus induction, but an achievement attributed to some special faculty or power of the gifted speaker, even more extensive claims are made for a faculty of abstraction. Nevertheless, the process is easily demonstrated in animals other than man. The formula is surprisingly simple when we recall how complicated classical treatments of the subject have been. Pavlov studied the process in his conditioned-reflex experiments. He found that the salivary response of his dog could be brought under the control of a single property of a stimulus, or a given combination of properties, if responses to other properties or combinations of properties were not reinforced.[7]

But Skinner does not show here or elsewhere that language is actually learned or used through stimulus-response, reinforcement, and association; indeed he is disabled by his own theoretical strictures from making such a demonstration. Since his theory contains nothing about the internal operations of the speech-faculty (if that is what it is), he cannot "prove" that speech is explained by the theory; he must make the connection by fiat.

In the effort to get the experimenter out of the experiment, radical behaviorists had refused to accept as facts worthy of investigation a large part of the phenomena that were most interesting to psychologists, including emotions, ways of reasoning about problems, and specialized modes of cognition, as well as the ability to acquire language. Once they were again convinced that there was a mental structure, however complex, psychologists were ready to go back to subjective facts to look for the structure.

Psychology has thus undertaken the experimental study of cognition (roughly, perception combined with knowledge) and development, without blinking the fact that its field is "mental" and intentional, yet without quite confronting the consequences. Psychology has continued to use the experimental method almost as if the objectivity sought by behaviorism were possible. Experiments are frequently designed in such a way that they can be repeated by another investigator, using other subjects, as if the results were to be totally "neutral," although they never escape the involvement of the experimenter (both the subject and the psychologist) in the experiment. In research intended to determine whether people can represent and manipulate images in a concrete way, for example, Roger Shepard and Jacqueline Metzler asked subjects to picture specified three-dimensional shapes to themselves and then to rotate the shapes through a certain angle. The psychologists found that the reaction time varied directly and reliably (from subject to subject) with the size of the angle of rotation. Now this experiment does suggest, as the experimenters inferred, that people really do picture an image to themselves and rotate it; but it does not do so in a way that is free from theory. The subjects are doing what they are asked to do in an experimental situation; it is not clear that they would behave the same way outside the situation. It is not even clear that they actually had images in their minds; they might be doing something complex and unconscious to accommodate the investigators.[8] In a social science like psychology there is no escape from the attempt to understand what the subjects themselves believe about their actions. The hermeneutic method of interpretation, in which the investigator is pulled into the experiment, but knows he is pulled in, is unavoidable. The requirements of experimentation, applied to mental operations, must be seen as a controlled hermeneutic, in which the assumptions and results of inquiry are at least stated clearly enough so they can be subjected to criticism and, if necessary, other experiments devised to embody the criticism.

In the last thirty years some psychologists have sought to model the mind through computer programs in an effort to escape the confines of experiment.[9] The catch is that all the models are based on some sort of "experiment" supposed to exhibit a characteristic of the mind, even if it be only the introspection of the psychologist. Computer programs are wonderful tools for thought; they expand the hermeneutic process by presenting results in a concrete and accountable form that can be compared with still other evidence. But the computer model does not escape from the experimental evidence; on the contrary, it reflects that evidence in a way that mercilessly clarifies its implications.

The methods of psychology, whether simulative or experimental, do not permit us to be "certain" about the properties of mind and language. Within the confines of the knowledge afforded by the controlled hermeneutic of experiment, as I show in the second chapter, psychology confirms the image of human problem-solving and of the interpretation of language in particular as multi-centered, unpredictable, and dependent on communication with others.

APPENDIX III: FALSE CONSCIOUSNESS, THE UNCONSCIOUS, AND THE IRRATIONAL

The argument for the inevitable irrationality of much of society's efforts at problem-solving, summarized in Chapters I and II, involves a claim that the psychological and cultural distortion created by internalized or unconscious patterns of authority is so great that it is impossible for us to break out of them. One version of the claim, found in Freud's *Civilization and Its Discontents*, argues that the repression identified with authority is essential to civilization. Some modern Marxist and psychoanalytical theorists, on the other hand, have hoped to break out of the circle of authority and culture to a more emancipated stance toward life. On its surface, either one of these views might suggest that the value given in this book to problem-solving through dialogue is misplaced—on the one hand, because the endemic problems of society cannot be much changed by this or any other means or, on the other hand, because a much more radical attack upon existing habits of discourse is required.

Without confronting these views head on, I seek here to advance three propositions that help to establish the relation between the understanding of the unconscious and linguistic understanding and problem-solving generally. I think these three points will make it clear that, however distorted our thinking may be by unconscious drives, such distortion does not justify a curtailment of dialogue.

1. The approach to language and inquiry essential to dialogue rights is consistent with and in fact illuminates Freudian methods of interpretation and treatment.

2. There is no conflict between the social dilemmas sketched in *Civilization and Its Discontents* and the claims in Chapters I and II of this book about the need for dialogue.

3. Projects for emancipatory discourse become contradictory if they are viewed as inconsistent with the claims made in Chapters I and II of this book about the need for dialogue.

The psychoanalytic technique of inquiry, rooted as it is in the verbal flow of the subject's thoughts, uses a double hermeneutic structurally similar to that of other social sciences. The analyst seeks to understand the subject's discourse at the level of usage and to interpret the symptoms through unconscious patterns as they intrude through metaphors, slips of the tongue, descriptions of emotions, recollections of dreams, and other actions.

The unconscious, which retains fragments of the subject's consciousness that have been censored because they are too painful, affords a discourse in part accessible to the conscious mind through the dream process as well as other means. Even though some of its rules of usage are different from those of the conscious mind, the discourse of dreams is recognizable as language. Its propositions, as presented to the conscious mind, have the form of a rebus, with repressed thoughts replaced by images or other words; the meanings of the puzzle can be understood through a dialogue in which the subject searches for the context of the meanings through their associations.[1]

Language, then, is the medium in which psychoanalysis is cast. Jacques Lacan has placed the lens of one version of modern language philosophy, derived from French structuralism, over Freud's theory and practice to read them anew; he would say that if that philosophy of language is to be believed, then there is in fact no other way to read Freud correctly.

In the view of language familiar to us in this book, some of which is shared by Lacan, words do not simply signal or "stand for" things; they have flexible symbolic value within the language depending on the context. And our understanding of the world is mediated through and dependent upon the meanings of the sentences we use. For Lacan, the discourse the subject uses must share these characteristics.

The results are complex, in part because two interrelated realms of meanings, both mediated through language, although with somewhat different usages, have to be understood. Lacan tells us, using the Saussurean terminology, that the words in which the dreamer recounts his dream are the signifiers for the repressed thoughts that ostensibly are the signified. The signified, however, is not a "thing" but another signifier that is subject to reinterpretation. Lacan understands all the contents of the unconscious to be mediated through language, at least insofar as they can be interpreted by the subject. All the objects of desire, including the .phallus, for example, as well as the love-objects derived from the family, are presented to the mind through language. Desire itself is not some sort of naked physical "need," but is mediated through language. The unconscious does not "perceive" things, including its own drives and obects of desire, directly and without mediation; rather the subject perceives them through linguistic constructs.[2]

As we know from the philosophy and psychology of language in Chapters I and II, people ordinarily make use of the flexibility of meanings through metaphor and reinterpretation to understand sentences in new ways; they do substantially the same thing with the meanings in their unconscious discourse. This characteristic of usage, at once so familiar and so difficult to understand, is essential to the "talking cure." Obviously, the process of interpreting the unconscious meanings concealed in the subject's talk depends upon her acceptance of a universe of alternative meanings; otherwise, the subject could not begin to see even that her conscious utterances might have unconscious meanings. But the subject must go farther and see that no one alternative meaning is the "right" one, except in the context where she applies it. The cure cannot take place unless meanings can shift, and the subject can sense that they shift at the unconscious level. The subject must be able to transfer to the analyst some of the emotions of love and aggression that she has felt toward others; she must change some of the objects of her fear and desire for other objects. Patterns in the unconscious that had a particular configuration must come to have another.

In a profound sense, in order to be cured the subject must become aware, at least implicitly, of the hermeneutic nature of understanding. She must realize that emotions can be transferred to another object, and that the meanings within the unconscious world can be changed. The route through dialogue to those realizations is not predictable because the meanings that the individual gives to concepts, whether conscious or not, and the way he relates one to another, are like any other language rooted in her history.

Some empirical insights in Freud's work confirm in dramatic ways the connection between the treatment and the hermeneutic character of discourse. In the essay *The Unconscious* of 1915, Freud argued that some of those who cannot be reached by the talking cure are inaccessible because of the way they use language. They bring the signifiers of unconscious fantasies into everyday speech, and treat them as though they were not symbolic but "real" in the most literal sense. Thus in the thinking of some schizophrenics, the metaphoric or symbolic becomes concrete; Freud gave the example of a woman who believed that her lover had "twisted her eyes" because she suspected that he was a deceiver (in German, *Augenverdreher,* or "eye-twister").[3] Such subjects are incurable by psychoanalysis in part because they are inaccessible to the changing world of meanings that is essential to a dialogue; they cannot make a transference to the therapist nor make changes in their objects of fear and desire.

Uncensored inquiry is essential to the talking cure for the same reason that it is essential to any other hermeneutic inquiry conducted through language; the therapist and the subject cannot predict where the "best" interpretation—the one finally taken as true by the subject—will come from or how the subject will reach it. But it is essential also for reasons that are peculiar to the problems of repression in the unconscious. In the talking cure, the experience of a subject with censorship will never have been good; because of the pressure of guilt, the subject has suppressed some understanding that is true for him. When he senses pressure again from someone in authority such as the therapist to select an interpretation, he will tend again to select an interpretation that will avoid confronting the idea that he has suppressed; the guilt that is attendant upon censorship does not leave him free to find the best alternative. The confidence that he is not being asked to censor his thoughts is precisely one of the elements of the talking cure that he is trying to acquire. The full acceptance of the hermeneutic character of meanings, including the possibility of changing the meanings of his own unconscious concepts, is not possible if the subject feels that some meanings are forbidden to him.

Although his methods for the therapeutic process imply absolute oppenness of inquiry, Freud nevertheless thought that the range of possible alternatives for patterns of love and aggression in modern society were limited. The contradiction, puzzling at first glance, is only apparent. Language allows for more interpretations, and the mind allows for more desires and fantasies, than society or even individual life can afford to put into practice. Murderous aggression can have a play in fantasy that it cannot have in life, and therapy may tell us what that fantasy is. In *Civilization and Its Discontents* Freud claimed that, because of the severity of the instinctual drives to aggression, the accomplishments of civilization are possible only through guilty repression, in effect through choices that hark back to parental authority and deny freedom. When he wrote the startling words, "Liberty of the individual is not a benefit of culture,"[4] he was thinking of the freedom found in fantasy, the infantile liberty of instinctual gratification.

The freedom of expression that I write about in this book, however, is not only a benefit of but is inconceivable without culture. The dialogue is a social act, which may suggest new ideas; it cannot take us to an instinctual utopia, although because of the variety of language and fantasy it can give us a vision of what that utopia might be like. And with this sort of liberty, I take it Freud has no quarrel. He would suppose it to be one of the means by which civilization continues and changes, always within the rigid shell of authority necessary to prevent the war of all against all.

Many later thinkers who have grappled with the same problems as Freud have found both of these positions inadequate. While they may agree that a repressive structure of authority has been essential to modern society, whether they think it originates from unconscious drives in the Freudian sense or from false consciousness in the Marxist sense, they are still determined to find a way to alter that structure in the interests of affording a little more instinctual gratification, or anyhow a more equal distribution of such gratification as there is. Because they believe that it has no chance of changing the structure of authority, the interpretive dialogue of which I write is of little interest to them except insofar as it may embody the memory of and aspiration to freedom from the bonds of authority and false consciousness.[5]

It is not necessary here to try to refute or support the arguments of Freud or of his Freudian-Marxist critics. I shall show instead that any program for an emancipatory psychology must take account of and provide for an unfettered hermeneutic dialogue.

We may believe, for example, that the present system of child-rearing and social relations tends to perpetuate patriarchy and institutions of economic domination. Such a proposition can of course only be demonstrated through the hermeneutic methods of understanding by which social relations are interpreted and are compared with some alternative set of values. If the proposition is believed, then the way out of the perpetual reproduction of institutions of domination must lie either in the authoritative imposition of a new set of values, through which children will be raised in a new way and adults obliged to behave in a new way, or in some sort of communicative discourse through which people come to understand the nature of the domination and to decline to perpetuate it.

The authoritative solution presents the sort of problems that are described in Chapter II. Because the truth about the alleged system of domination cannot be known positively, but only through a context-dependent dialogue about society, we should not be more persuaded that the "solution" is reliable than we are that our knowledge is reliable. If we nevertheless act as though our knowledge were reliable, as we freqently do, it is inevitable, as argued in Chapter II, either that the "authoritative" solution will be tainted by the institutions of domination or at least that we will not be certain whether the authoritative solution is tainted or not. It is impossible to have positive knowledge that any alternative really is free of elements believed to be undesirable, and thus to exonerate it from criticism. We may accept a set of values as "authoritative" in the sense that we find reasons to abide by them, but we cannot make them immune to criticism.

There are many versions of the solution through comunicative discourse. Habermas has said, for example, that communicative competence may open the way to an emancipatory dialogue; Jessica Benjamin suggests that a change in patriarchal relations in families may break the authoritarian cycle; Joel Kovel has written of a "transcendental praxis" for therapy, which can point toward freedom.[6] Although each of these is a version of the hermeneutic dialogue that increases understanding, any of the authors would doubtless brand as inadequate the sort of dialogue I have described in the first two chapters. The dialogue they have in mind is more carefully channelled, with the intention of compensating for the skew in inquiry created by patterns of domination. One would expect them to say that a discussion that does not take account of those patterns may be worse than none, because it may tend to confirm and strengthen the domination.

As I have said, I have no difficulty accepting the premise of those arguments that our thinking is skewed by unconscious patterns. My problem with them lies rather in the specification of a method by which those patterns can be changed or avoided. Insofar as such a method is prescribed, it takes on the appearance of the authoritative method for which there is some positive and unvarying warrant. It then shares in the defects described above of all such authoritative solutions, that they cannot in fact be known positively and that they are likely to participate in the patterns of domination. In short, there is no way to be sure that such a specialized method of dialogue is more likely than any other to lead to an emancipatory discourse.

Does it follow that absolutely nothing can be done, that we are condemned to do exactly what we are now doing, to put up with our present habits, however banal they may be, and to make the same mistakes that we think we are now making? Perhaps not. If there are institutional changes or methods of inquiry by which, according to some standard, our thinking may become less skewed than it is thought to be at present, then there is no reason they ought not to be used. If non-patriarchal family relations can be approximated, or if "transcendental praxis" can be described (or performed without being described), then we should struggle to attain those practices. We cannot know in any positive way, however, but only through hermeneutic inquiry that our methods are successful. Accordingly they cannot be established as authoritative modes immune to criticism, revision, or replacement.

The conclusion of this lengthy appendix is this. Critical philosophers, lawyers, and psychologists may disagree with me about the importance of a right of dialogical inquiry; they may believe that nothing but an emancipatory program is worth fighting for. But they cannot eliminate the need for an open dialogical inquiry in the interest of pressing the emancipatory program, because open dialogue must always be constitutive of any such program. It will not do to claim that a "right" to open dialogue would not be needed in a world without false consciousness, alienation, and repressive authority, because we do not know what such a world would be like; the only way to find out what it might be like, supposing there is a way, is with the aid of an open dialogue.

Notes and Index

Notes

Introduction

1. Louis Henkin, "Rights: American and Human," *Columbia Law Review* 79 (1979): 409.
2. Mary Hawkesworth, "Ideological Immunity: The Soviet Response to Human Rights Criticism," *Universal Human Rights* 2, no. 1 (1980): 67.
3. U.S. State Department, *Country Reports on Human Rights Practices for 1981* (Washington, D.C.: GPO, 1982) pp. 4–6; U.S. State Department, *Country Reports on Human Rights Practices for 1982* (Washington, D.C.: GPO, 1983), pp. 3–5; Cynthia Brown, ed., *With Friends like These* (New York: Pantheon, 1985), pp. 6–9, 29–34.
4. *American Anthropologist* 49, no. 4 (1947): 542.
5. Marnia Lazreg, "Human Rights, State, and Ideology," in Adamantia Pollis and Peter Schwab, eds., *Human Rights* (New York: Praeger, 1980), pp. 32, 41; Lars Schoultz, review of Raymond Gastil, *Freedom in the World: Political and Civil Liberties, 1978, Universal Human Rights*, 2, no. 1 (1980): 96.
6. Frederich Schauer, *Free Speech: A Philosophical Inquiry* (Cambridge, Eng.: Cambridge University Press, 1982), summarizes these arguments.
7. J. S. Mill, *Utilitarianism, On Liberty, Essay on Bentham*, ed. Mary Warnock (New York: New American Library, 1962), pp. 193, 206, 136, respectively.

8. Ibid., p. 186. The romantic notion is there attributed to Wilhelm von Humboldt.

9. C. E. Baker, "Scope of the First Amendment Freedom of Speech," *UCLA Law Review* 25 (1978): 964–1039.

10. Thomas Scanlon, "A Theory of Freedom of Expression," *Philosophy and Public Affairs* 1 (1972): 204–226, reprinted in Ronald Dworkin, ed., *Philosophy of Law* (London: Oxford University Press, 1977); references are to the latter.

11. *Abrams v. U.S.*, 250 U.S. 616, 630 (1919).

12. Mill, *Utilitarianism, On Liberty, Essay on Bentham*, p. 166.

13. Baker, "Scope of the First Amendment Freedom of Speech," pp. 964–1039; Benjamin DuVal, "Free Communication of Ideas and the Quest for Truth," *George Washington Law Review* 41 (1972): 161–259. See also Chapter I of this book.

14. The intellectual history of the connection is traced in Guido de Ruggiero, *History of European Liberalism* (Boston: Beacon, 1959). The connection is used, e.g., in Milton Friedman, *Capitalism and Freedom* (Chicago: University Chicago Press, 1962). A literal market for ideas is advanced in Ronald Coase, "The Market for Goods and the Market for Ideas." *American Economic Review* 64, no. 2 (1974): 384–391.

15. Alexander Meiklejohn, *Political Freedom* (New York: Oxford University Press, 1965), pp. 23, 73–75 (which includes the earlier work of 1948).

16. Ibid., 79.

17. Scanlon, "A Theory of Freedom of Expression," pp. 154, 155.

18. Michael Sandel, *Liberalism and the Limits of Justice* (New York: Cambridge University Press, 1982), chap. 4. See also Richard Rorty, "Post-Modernist Bourgeois Liberalism," *Journal of Philosophy* 80 (1983): 583–589.

19. Hawkesworth, "Ideological Immunity," p. 70.

20. Ibid.; Richard Dean, "Beyond Helsinki: The Soviet View of Human Rights in International Law," *Virginia Journal of International Law* 21 (1980): 55–95; Howard Babb, ed., *Soviet Legal Philosophy* (Cambridge, Mass.: Harvard University Press, 1951).

21. Constitution of the Republic of Cuba, sec. 61; see also Louis Henkin, "Rights: Here and There," *Columbia Law Review* 81 (1981): 1598–1605.

22. Quoted in Dean, "Beyond Helsinki," p. 63.

23. John Tagliabue, "Yugoslav Official Attacks the Nation's Press," *New York Times*, March 1, 1983, p. A3.

24. These arguments, which have been fought over repeatedly, are

summarized in Hugh Collins, *Marxism and Law* (Oxford, Eng.: Oxford University Press, 1982), pp. 22–93.

25. Ibid.; Milton Fisk, *Ethics and Society* (New York: New York University Press, 1980); the arguments are summarized in Tom Campbell, *The Left and Rights* (London: Routledge and Kegan Paul, 1983), chap. 1. See also Duncan Kennedy and Peter Gabel, "Roll Over Beethoven," *Stanford Law Review* 36 (1984): 1–55. Very similar conclusions, but not from a Marxist point of view, are in R. M. Unger, *Knowledge and Politics* (New York: Free Press, 1975).

26. Recent examples are Campbell, *The Left and Rights*, chap. 1; Edward Sparer, "Fundamental Human Rights, Legal Entitlements, and the Social Struggle . . . ," *Stanford Law Review* 36 (1984): 509–574; Santiago Carrillo, *Eurocommunism and the State* (Westport, Conn.: Lawrence Hill, 1978). Herbert Gintis, "Communication and Politics," *Socialist Review* 50/51 (1980); 189–232, makes an argument that somewhat resembles the one made in Chapter I.

27. Sparer, "Fundamental Human Rights," pp. 512, 547.

28. Bertell Ollman, "Marx's Vision of Communism: A Reconstruction," *Critique* 8 (1977): 4, 32. See also D. F. B. Tucker, *Marxism and Individualism* (Oxford, Eng.: Basil Blackwell, 1980), pp. 65, 78.

29. Quoted in Robert Martin, *Personal Freedom and the Law in Tanzania* (Nairobi: Oxford University Press, 1974), pp. 2–3.

30. Adamantia Pollis and Peter Schwab, "Human Rights: A Western Construct with Limited Applicability," in Pollis and Schwab, eds., *Human Rights*, p. 13.

31. Thomas Emerson, *System of Freedom of Expression* (New York: Random House, 1970), p. 7.

32. Bruce Ackerman, *Social Justice in the Liberal State* (New Haven, Conn.: Yale University Press, 1980). Further discussion appears in note 34 of Chapter I, infra.

33. There is at least one passage in J. S. Mill's *On Liberty* in which he says that, when a false argument is suppressed, some of the "meaning" of the true argument is lost. As I noted above in connection with note 12, the phrase adumbrates some of the ideas in this book. *On Liberty* is such a rich and suggestive text that it might be interpreted to support substantially any of the modern arguments for individual liberty. The center of gravity of Mill's argument, however, concerns "truth" and the development of the individual. It would have been all but impossible for Mill to have made arguments very similar to the ones

that are made in succeeding chapters of this book, because the background philosophy about "meaning" and "understanding" of ordinary language had not yet been developed. The quoted passage, tantalizing though it is, thus does not have much support in the rest of the essay. John Gray, in his *Mill on Liberty: A Defence* (London: Routledge and Kegan Paul, 1983), pp. 107–108, has this to say:

> He may be suggesting that a form of dialectical reasoning is especially appropriate for some subject-matters, not just as a means to the adoption of well-grounded beliefs, but even as an indispensable condition of understanding. There is here, at least vestigially, a conception of inquiry as being internally related to certain imaginative and emotional as well as intellectual activities. . . . It would be idle to pretend that any of this is explicit in Mill, however; and it would be dishonest not admit that some of the things he says in *On Liberty* run counter to these interpretations.

Chapter I: Interpretation and Freedom

1. Ludwig Wittgenstein, *Philosophical Investigations* (New York: Macmillan, 1958), secs. 199, 202. The usage of the word "rule" is somewhat confusing in this context. Rules are often quite rigid and define results with some specificity; language, of course, is not like that. Accordingly, as I shall have more occasion to note in Chapter II, I try to use the term "regularity" to refer to the rule-bound properties of language.
2. Hans Aarsleff, *From Locke to Saussure* (Minneapolis: University of Minnesota Press, 1982), p. 24.
3. Bertrand Russell, "Descriptions" (from *Introduction to Mathematical Philosophy*, 1920), in Leonard Linsky, ed., *Semantics and the Philosophy of Language* (Urbana: University of Illinois Press, 1952), p. 169.
4. Ludwig Wittgenstein, *Tractatus Logico-Philosophicus* (Atlantic Highlands, N.J.: Humanities Press, 1974), secs. 4.121, 4.1212. The usage of the word "sense" is derived from Frege.
5. Ibid., secs. 6.54, 7. These are the last two sections of the book, which say:

> My propositions serve as elucidations in the following way: anyone who understands me inevitably recognizes them

as nonsensical, when he has used them—as steps—to climb
up beyond them. (He must, so to speak, throw away the
ladder after he has climbed up it.)

He must transcend these propositions, and then he will
see the world aright.

What we cannot speak about we must pass over in
silence.

6. Dudley Shapere, "Philosophy and the Analysis of Language"
    (1960), in Richard Rorty, ed., *Linguistic Turn* (Chicago: Uni-
    versity of Chicago Press, 1967), pp. 276, 278.
7. A. J. Ayer, *Language, Truth, and Logic* (New York: Dover, n.d.
    [1946]), p. 31.
8. The foregoing analysis is based on Ian Hacking, *Why Does Lan-
    guage Matter to Philosophy?* (Cambridge, Eng.: Cambridge Uni-
    versity Press, 1975), pp. 97–98; John Wisdom, "Metaphysics
    and Verification," *Mind* 47 (1938): 454–498.
9. W. V. Quine, "Two Dogmas of Empiricism" (1951), in W. V.
    Quine, *From a Logical Point of View* (New York: Harper,
    1963).
10. W. V. Quine, "Ontological Relativity," in W. V. Quine, *On-
    tological Relativity and Other Essays* (New York: Columbia Uni-
    versity Press, 1969); W. V. Quine, *Word and Object* (Cam-
    bridge, Mass.: MIT Press, 1960).
11. Wittgenstein, *Philosophical Investigations*, sec. 23.
12. Ibid., sec. 67.
13. Bertrand Russell, epigraph to Ernest Gellner, *Words and Things*
    (London: Gollancz, 1959), n.p.
14. P. F. Strawson, "Intention and Convention in Speech Acts," in
    P. F. Strawson, *Logico-Linguistic Papers* (London: Methuen,
    1971), pp. 149–169, describes and criticizes the Grice argu-
    ment along the lines set forth here. In later writings Grice has
    linked speaker's intention to the public aspect of language
    through a structure of cooperative principles that we expect a
    speaker to follow if his speech is to be comprehensible. These
    come close to making conventions for the attribution of inten-
    tions, whether they are in fact present or not. Cooperative
    principles, like the rest of the scheme of intentional meanings,
    work only in cases where there is already agreement (H. P.
    Grice, "Logic and Conversation," in Peter Cole and Jerry Mor-
    gan, eds., *Syntax and Semantics*, vol. 3: *Speech Acts* [New York:
    Academic, 1975]).
15. Donald Davidson, "Radical Interpretation," *Dialectica* 27

(1973): 324. Arguments similar to the one I have made here may be found in Steven Lukes, "Relativism in Its Place," in Martin Hollis and Steven Lukes, eds., "Rationality and Relativism (Cambridge, Mass.: MIT Press, 1982), pp. 262–264; Bernard Harrison, *Introduction to the Philosophy of Language* (New York: St. Martin's, 1979), pp. 134–141.

16. Richard Rorty, *Philosophy and the Mirror of Nature* (Princeton, N.J.: Princeton University Press, 1979), is a notable recent critique of much of the ordinary language tradition and a presentation of a version of the hermeneutic tradition. Somewhat more brief presentations can be found in Charles Taylor, *Philosophy and the Human Sciences* (Cambridge, Eng.: Cambridge University Press, 1985), vol. 1, chaps. 9 and 10.

17. Hans-Georg Gadamer, *Philosophical Hermeneutics* (Berkeley, Calif.: University of California Press, 1977), p. 62.

18. Hans-Georg Gadamer, *Truth and Method* (New York: Seabury, 1975), p. 422.

19. Paul Ricoeur, "The Model of the Text: Meaningful Action Considered as a Text," in Fred Dallmayr and Thomas McCarthy, eds., *Understanding and Social Inquiry* (Notre Dame, Ind.: University of Notre Dame Press, 1977), pp. 316–334.

20. Gadamer, *Truth and Method,* pp. 292–294.

21. The "double" hermeneutic of the human sciences is discussed in Anthony Giddens, *New Rules for Sociological Method* (New York: Basic Books, 1978), p. 158; Jürgen Habermas, *Theory of Communicative Action* (Boston: Beacon, 1984), vol. 1, pp. 109–120.

22. This is a subject of some dispute. Peter Winch, *The Idea of a Social Science in Its Relation to Philosophy* (London: Routledge and Kegan Paul, 1958), takes the view taken here, for which there is support in *Philosophical Investigations.* That view is disputed by David Rubinstein, *Marx and Wittgenstein* (Boston: Routledge and Kegan Paul, 1981), p. 149.

23. This example is constructed out of materials in Paul Chevigny, "Review Essay: The Paradox of Campaign Finance," *NYU Law Review* 56 (1981): 206–226.

24. Anthropologists may criticize the usage "deep waters" as culturally relative. It is next to impossible, I believe, to choose an example for this point that is entirely free from theoretical objection. This example is chosen because it involves the notion of "dark," which may have elements of a cognitive universal (Eleanor Rosch, "Structure of the Color Space in Naming and Memory for Two Languages," *Cognitive Psychology* 3

[1972]: 337–354; Roger Brown, "Reference: In Memorial Tribute to Eric Lenneberg," *Cognition* 4 [1976]: 1125–1153).

25. Norwood Hanson, quoted in Frederick Suppe, *Structure of Scientific Theories* (Urbana: University of Illinois Press, 1977), p. 635.

26. Heinz Pagels, *Cosmic Code* (New York: Simon and Schuster, 1982), pp. 23–24.

27. Imre Lakatos, "Falsification and the Methodology of Scientific Research Programmes," in Imre Lakatos and Alan Musgrave, eds., *Criticism and the Growth of Knowledge* (Cambridge, Eng.: Cambridge University Press, 1970), p. 119; the same point is made by Thomas Kuhn, *Structure of Scientific Revolutions* (Chicago: University of Chicago Press, 1970), p. 77.

28. Rubinstein, *Marx and Wittgenstein,* chap. 9.

29. V. N. Volosinov, *Marxism and the Philosophy of Language* (New York: Seminar, 1973), pp. 12, 86, 102, respectively. It is widely accepted that Mikhail Bakhtin had a major hand in the writing of this book.

30. Karl Marx, *Eighteenth Brumaire of Louis Bonaparte* (New York: International, 1963), p. 15.

31. Adam Schaff, *Language and Cognition* (New York: McGraw-Hill, 1973).

32. Alvin Gouldner, *Dialectic of Ideology and Technology* (New York: Seabury, 1976); Leszek Kolakowski, "Karl Marx and the Classical Definition of Truth," in Leszek Kolakowski, *Toward a Marxist Humanism* (New York: Grove, 1968); Jürgen Habermas, *Knowledge and Human Interests* (Boston: Beacon, 1971), pp. 62–63; Karl Korsch, *Marxism and Philosophy* (London: NLB, 1970).

33. This can be shown in a somewhat more formal way within the analytic tradition characteristic of anglo-American philosophy. In his discussion of "truth" as it is applied in language, the logician Alfred Tarski went back to the intuitive notion of truth, for which we imagine, roughly, a correspondence. We say:

The sentence "snow is white" is true only if snow is white.

We already know from Quine and Wittgenstein that there is no "automatic" way of signalling the relation between facts and sentences such as the one in quotation marks. Tarski went on to say that the "truth"of such a sentence could be made viable ina formalized language for which the "correspondence"

between terms and facts is established, as it were, ax-
iomatically, in another language, the meta-language.
    But one characteristic of natural languages is precisely
that they have no meta-languages. In such "semantically
closed" languages, as Tarski called them, what is true can only
be defined by referring round to other sentences within the
language. Donald Davidson found, when he applied Tarski's
definition of truth to the understanding of an ordinary language, that it would lead to a maze of meanings, in the style of
Quine, the truth of which could only be known through the
holistic understanding of all the meanings. As we know, this
pulls us into a hermeneutic method, because those meanings,
unless implicitly recognized, can be found only through dialogue, and are never final, but only interpreted for us. Tarski
and Davidson elaborate a basic insight: The circular nature of
definition in language implies that there is no end to definition (Alfred Tarski, "Semantic Conception of Truth," in
Linsky, ed., *Semantics and the Philosophy of Language*; Donald
Davidson, "Truth and Meaning," *Synthese* 17 [1967]: 304–
323).

34. The most straightforward presentation is Herbert Marcuse, "Repressive Tolerance," in R. P. Wolff et al., *Critique of Pure
Tolerance* (Boston: Beacon, 1965). Habermas has been more
ambivalent concerning liberal rights (Jürgen Habermas, *Theory and Practice* [Boston: Beacon, 1973], pp. 3–4).
    In *Social Justice in the Liberal State* (New Haven, Conn.:
Yale University Press, 1980), Bruce Ackerman presents a special version of the problem. Ackerman's book, of course, is not
primarily concerned with a theory of such rights as freedom of
expression, but rather with a political theory of the liberal
state. He bases his theory in part, however, on the existence of
a "neutral dialogue" among the participants in his imaginary
society. Dialogue is kept "neutral" by constraints that prevent
each of the discussants from asserting that her conception of
the good is better than that of others or that she is a superior
person; the constraints are enforced by a "commander." Ackerman has, I take it, introduced these conditions precisely in
order to avoid the distortion that may otherwise interfere with
the effectiveness of the dialogue. The existence of such constraints has caused one commentator to say that Ackerman's
"neutral dialogue" is "diametrically opposite" to "emancipatory discourse" as conceived by Habermas (Alan Hyde, "Is
Liberalism Possible?" [book review], *New York University Law*

Review 57 [1982]: 1035). It seems to me, however, that Ackerman has simply chosen one horn of the dilemma that is presented by such a notion. As I argue in the text in this and the next chapter, for philosophical and psychological reasons I do not think such strictures are viable. See also Apendix III to this book and the discussion at the end of Chapter II.

Chapter II: Cognition and Rationality

1. Melissa Bowerman, "The Acquisition of Word-Meaning: An Investigation of Some Current Concepts," in P. N. Johnson-Laird and P. C. Wason, eds., *Thinking* (Cambridge, Eng.: Cambridge University Press, 1977), p. 241. I have taken out of the text some numbers used by Bowerman for technical reference. I use the term "regularity" rather than "rule" in identifying the organization the child brings to meaning, because "rule" may be understood in the strong sense of a universe of applicable law that is consistent, as in the phrase "rules of chess." It has been persuasively argued that rules in that sense are not used for meanings (Paul Ziff, *Semantic Analysis* [Ithaca, N.Y.: Cornell University Press, 1960]). It is not necessary to assume more than "regularity" for purposes of the argument here or in Chapter I.

2. Lev Vygotsky, *Thought and Language* (Cambridge, Mass.: MIT Press, 1962), pp. 72–75; George Lakoff and Mark Johnson, "Metaphorical Structure of the Human Conceptual System," *Cognitive Science* 4 (1980): 195–208; Roman Jakobson, "Two Aspects of Language and Two Types of Aphasic Disturbances," in Roman Jakobson and Morris Halle, *Fundamentals of Language* (Hague: Mouton, 1971).

3. The Bowerman child's collection of meanings for the word "moon," although idiosyncratic, is typical of the speech of young children in the sense that it does not much resemble the way adults use the word. Chomsky and other psycholinguists have drawn upon this characteristic of language acquisition as evidence that the child's language abilities are innate; the regularities in the child's usages, they argue, if learned rather than devised, should correspond more closely with those of adults. General acceptance of the view that the talent for creating such regularities is inborn has not, however, resulted in any master-system for understanding the sentences of either children or adults. Although psycholinguists have found some

predictable patterns in the way the child brings its usages into accord with those of society, they have not been able to find any universal method of interpreting meanings. Concerning the use by children of regularities not used by adults, see Herbert Clark and Eve Clark, *Psychology and Language* (New York: Harcourt, Brace, 1977), chap. 13; Neil Smith and Deirdre Wilson, *Modern Linguistics* (Bloomington: Indiana University Press, 1979), pp. 210–212; Alison Gopnik and Andrew Meltzoff, "Semantic and Cognitive Development in 15- to 21-Month-Old Children," *Journal of Child Language* 12 (1984): 495–513.

Chomsky has said (Noam Chomsky, *Language and Responsibility* [New York: Pantheon, 1977], p. 142):

Why, then, raise a question about the possibility of a universal semantics, which would provide an exact representation of the full meaning of each lexical item, and the meaning of expressions in which these items appear? There are, I believe, good reasons for being skeptical about such a program. It seems that other cognitive systems—in particular, our system of beliefs concerning things in the world and their behavior—play an essential part in our judgments of meaning and reference, in an extremely intricate manner, and it is not at all clear that much will remain if we try to separate the purely linguistic components of what in informal usage or even in technical discussion we call "the meaning of linguistic expression."

Chomsky has repeatedly made the point that the innate language ability enables the speaker freely to express his meanings, but does not give a key to pragmatic usage. See, e.g., Noam Chomsky, *Cartesian Linguistics* (New York: Harper and Row, 1966). See also Jerry Fodor, Thomas Bever, and M. F. Garrett, *Psychology of Language* (New York: McGraw-Hill, 1974), pp. 505–515.

I am not treating here a large body of research concerning cognitive universals: e.g., Michael Cole and Susan Scribner, *Culture and Thought* (New York: Wiley, 1974); Clark and Clark, *Psychology and Language,* chap. 14; Roger Brown, "Reference: In Memorial Tribute to Eric Lenneberg," *Cognition* 4 (1976): 1125–1153. Such universals lead to cross-cultural similarities in the meaning of words, but do very little to solve the meaning of sentences. See, e.g., Eleanor Rosch, "Principles of Categorization," in Eleanor Rosch and Barbara Lloyd, eds., *Cognition and Categorization* (Hillsdale, N.J.: L. Erlbaum, 1978).

4. Daniel Stern, *The First Relationship* (Cambridge, Mass.: Harvard University Press, 1977); Colwyn Trevarthen, "The Primary Motives for Cooperative Understanding," in George Butterworth and Paul Light, eds., *Social Cognition* (Chicago: University of Chicago Press, 1982); Alexander Thomas, "Current Trends in Developmental Theory," *American Journal of Orthopsychiatry* 51 (1981): 580–609.

5. Jerome Bruner, "Ontogenesis of Speech Acts," *Journal of Child Language* 2 (1975): 4, 7; Clark and Clark, *Psychology and Language*, pp. 31–35. The general point has been made repeatedly: e.g., Lois Tamir, "Language Development: New Directions," *Human Development* 22 (1979): 263–269.

6. Jean Piaget, "Piaget's Theory," in Bärbel Inhelder and Harold Chipman, eds., *Piaget and His School* (New York: Springer, 1976), p. 12. The chief source for the point is Jean Piaget, *Origins of Intelligence in Children* (New York: International University Press, 1965), pt. 2.

7. Annette Karmiloff-Smith and Bärbel Inhelder, "If You Want to Get Ahead, Get a Theory," *Cognition* 3 (1974/5): 195–212; Gabriel Mugny and Willem Doise, "Socio-Cognitive Conflict and Structure of Individual and Collective Performances," *European Journal of Social Psychology* 8 (1978): 181–192; A. N. Perret-Clermont, *Social Interaction and Cognition in Children* (New York: Academic, 1980); Marvin Berkowitz and John Gibbs, "Measuring the Developmental Features of Moral Discussion," *Merrill-Palmer Quarterly* 29 (1983): 399–410; William Damon and Melanie Killen, "Peer Interaction and the Process of Change in Children's Moral Reasoning," *Merrill-Palmer Quarterly* 28 (1982): 347–367. The uncertainty of the process of social-science experiment is at its most noticeable in the attempt to evaluate the dialogues contributing to "moral development," and more especially in estimating the "transactive" nature of discussion. The assumptions of such experiments are criticized in John Broughton, "Cognitive Interaction and the Development of Sociality: a Comment on Damon and Killen," *Merrill-Palmer Quarterly* 28 (1982): 369–378. See also note 13 infra.

8. Jean Piaget, "Intellectual Evolution from Adolescence to Adulthood," *Human Development* 15 (1972): 3. At the preoperational level, generally before eight years of age, the child is able to represent the functions of objects to himself, but he does not

grasp notions such as that of the conservation of fluid in trans-
fers between containers. At the operational level, the child
understands conservation and other general properties of physical operations, such as reversibility, but cannot think about
those operations apart from the concrete problems in which
they are found.

9. John Broughton, "Piaget's Structural Developmental Psychology
    II: Logic and Psychology," *Human Development* 24 (1981): 202.

10. Lawrence Kohlberg, "The Claim to Moral Adequacy of a High-
    est Stage of Moral Development," *Journal of Philosophy* 70
    (1973): 630–646. The three levels were subdivided into six
    stages. Kohlberg and his students conducted cross-cultural
    experiments to show that the levels and stages, like the Piage-
    tian levels to which they were linked, were universal in se-
    quence (Lawrence Kohlberg, "From Is to Ought: How to
    Commit the Naturalistic Fallacy and Get Away with It," in
    Theodore Mischel, ed., *Cognitive Development and Epistemology*
    [New York: Academic, 1971], pp. 151–235). The issue of
    cultural bias in Kohlberg's work has been extensively argued:
    e.g., E. L. Simpson, "Moral Development Research: A Case
    Study of Scientific Cultural Bias," *Human Development* 17
    (1974): 81–106. Similar criticisms have been made of Piaget:
    Susan Buck-Morss, "Socio-Economic Bias in Piaget's Theory,"
    Human Development 18 (1975): 35–49; Cole and Scribner, *Cul-
    ture and Thought*. In his most recent writings, Kohlberg was
    himself apparently persuaded that the sixth stage does not have
    cross-cultural application (Lawrence Kohlberg et al., *Moral
    Stages: A Current Formulation and a Response to Critics* [Basel:
    Karger, 1983]).

11. The evidence is collected in John Broughton, "Women's Ra-
    tionality and Men's Virtues: A Critique of Gender Dualism in
    Gilligan's Theory of Moral Development," *Social Research* 50
    (1983): 597–642.

12. John Murphy and Carol Gilligan, "Moral Development in Late
    Adolescence and Adulthood: A Critique and Reconstruction of
    Kohlberg's Theory," *Human Development* 23 (1980): 98; gener-
    ally, Carol Gilligan, *In a Different Voice* (Cambridge, Mass.:
    Harvard University Press, 1982).

13. Norma Haan, "Two Moralities in Action Contexts," *Journal of
    Personality and Social Psychology* 36 (1978): 286–305. John
    Broughton reexamined interviews used by Gilligan to ex-
    emplify the "post-conventional contextual" and found that
    some of them could have been scored at the upper end of the

scale according to the standards established by Kohlberg. To me, that result suggests that the understanding of Kohlberg's notion of the "universal," and of whether a given text fits that understanding, itself varies depending on the context (Broughton, "Women's Rationality and Men's Virtues," pp. 597–642). On the issue of the relativism of Kohlberg's standards, see generally Simpson, "Moral Development Research," pp. 81–106; Buck-Morss, "Socio-Economic Bias," pp. 35–49. The issue is rendered still more puzzling by Kohlberg's argument that universal principles are to be interpreted in a "contextualized" way (Lawrence Kohlberg, "Reply to Owen Flanagan and Some Comments on the Puka-Goodpaster Exchange," *Ethics* 92 [1982]: 513–528). The bearing of this position on Kohlberg's other views is not clear to me. See also note 10 supra.

14. John Bransford and Jeffrey Franks, "Abstraction of Linguistic Ideas," *Cognitive Psychology* 2 (1971): 331–350. See also the discussion in Fodor, Bever, and Garrett, *Psychology of Language*, pp. 271–273; Marvin Minsky, "Frame-System Theory," in Johnson-Laird and Wason, eds., *Thinking*, pp. 355–376.

15. Roger Schank and R. P. Abelson, *Scripts, Plans, Goals, and Understanding* (Hillsdale, N.J.: L. Erlbaum, 1977).

16. Terry Winograd, "What Does It Mean to Understand Language?" *Cognitive Science* 4 (1980): 224.

17. Part of the reason lies in the fact that the body of prior belief and knowledge that a person draws upon in thinking is to some extent organized both by language and on the model of language. The word "memory" is itself only an heuristic, perhaps a "family resemblance" word; we have an ill-defined notion of what it is we bring to bear when we call upon our background knowledge. It is a bare fifteen years since Tulving pointed out one major division, between memory for specific episodes (perhaps closest to the prototype notion of "memory") and the enormous structure of retrievable material organized as "semantic memory." Semantic memory might better be called "semiotic memory," memory for symbols drawn from all our faculties, including visual images as well as words. See Endel Tulving, "Episodic and Semantic Memory," in Endel Tulving and Wayne Donaldson, eds., *Organization of Memory* (New York: Academic, 1972). More generally, see Allan Collins and R. Quillian, "How to Make a Language-User," in the same volume; Phillip Shaver et al., "Converging Evidence for the

Functional Significance of Imagery in Problem-Solving," *Cognition* 3 (1975): 359–375. All of these, episodic memory, verbal memory, and memory for other symbols, interpenetrate and affect one another. The schemas or frames connected to verbal meanings are affected by episodes in the life of the subject; speakers assign variant senses to words depending on their experience. Conversely, words and sentences affect the memory for episodes. Elizabeth Loftus found, for example, that subjects who had viewed a film of a traffic accident gave a higher estimate of the speed of the automobiles involved when they were asked "About how fast were the cars going when they smashed into each other?" than they did when the word "hit" was used in place of "smashed into." The question poses a verbal schema or frame to the subject, and invites him to use it, thus infusing the episodic memory with the meaning of the words in the question. Yet the verbal memory may be essential to the recall of an episode or an image, at the same time that it distorts it. In the classic study, conducted over fifty years ago, subjects were shown shapes and subsequently asked to reproduce them in a drawing. Those who were given verbal names for the shapes were able to recall more of the shapes than those who had no labels to work with, but their drawings tended to look more like the object named than like the original image (Elizabeth Loftus, *Eyewitness Testimony* [Cambridge, Mass.: Harvard University Press, 1979], pp. 77–79; L. Carmichagel et al., "An Experimental Study of the Effect of Language on the Reproduction of Visually Perceived Form," *Journal of Experimental Psychology* 15 [1932]: 73–86). Thus two small circles connected by a single line were remembered differently depending on whether they were called "dumbbells" or "eyeglasses."

The process of the use of images, episodes, propositions, or other sorts of memory (olfactory, for example) in the course of thinking is rendered still more puzzling and unpredictable by factors I do not discuss here, including the fact that different sorts of knowledge are organized in the left and right halves of the brain and are integrated in use (Sally Springer and George Deutsch, *Left Brain, Right Brain* [San Francisco: Freeman, 1981]). There is strong evidence that there are different "faculties" of perception and knowledge, the integration of which is not understood (Jerry Fodor, *Modularity of Mind* [Cambridge, Mass.: MIT Press, 1983]; Howard Gardner, *Frames of Mind: The Theory of Multiple Intelligences* [New York: Basic Books, 1983]). See also the Conclusion to this book.

18. The foregoing is distilled from Amos Tversky, Paul Slovic, and Daniel Kahneman, *Judgment Under Uncertainty: Heuristics and Biases* (Cambridge, Eng.: Cambridge University Press, 1982), and Richard Nisbett and Lee Ross, *Human Inference: Strategies and Shortcomings of Social Judgment* (Englewood Cliffs, N.J.: Prentice-Hall, 1980).

19. Comparing anchoring in children and adults, Karmiloff-Smith and Inhelder write ("If You Want to Get Ahead," p. 209):

> The tendency to explain phenomena by a unified theory, the most general or the simplest one possible, appears to be a natural aspect of the creative process, both for the child and the scientist. The construction of false theories or the overgeneralization of limited ones are in effect productive processess. . . .
>
> Overgeneralization is not only a means to simplify but also to unify; it is thus not surprising that the child and the scientist often refuse counter-examples since they complicate the unification process.

20. This argument is made in L. J. Cohen, "Can Human Irrationality Be Experimentally Demonstrated?" *Brain and Behavioral Science* 4 (1981): 328. There is an attempt to refute Cohen in the comments in the same volume (p. 331), which serves only, I think, to show that the issue cannot be settled by logic.

21. Herbert Simon, *Administrative Behavior* (3d ed.; New York: Free Press, 1976), pp. xx–xxi, chap. 5. The Collins quotation is from Allan Collins et al., "Reasoning from Incomplete Knowlege," in Daniel Bobrow and Allan Collins, eds., *Representation and Understanding* (New York: Academic, 1975), p. 414. The "open world" phrase also comes from this source.

22. Craig Anderson et al., "Perseverance of Social Theories: The Role of Explanation in the Persistence of Discredited Information," *Journal of Personality and Psychology* 39 (1980): 1037–1049; Craig Anderson et al., "Inoculation and Counterexplanation: Debiasing Techniques in the Perseverance of Social Theories," *Social Cognition* 1 (1982): 126–139 This evidence is consistent with that drawn from older theories of attitude change, rooted in the notions of consistency and incongruity (Roger Brown, *Social Psychology* [New York: Free Press, 1965], chap. 11; Chester Insko, *Theories of Attitude Change* [New York: Appleton-Century, 1967]). In older studies, Irving Janis reached somewhat similar conclusions, finding that challenges to outworn decisions and changes in in-

grained habits and beliefs were accessible through role-
playing. If the subjects could act out the consequences of their
present positions and of projected changes, their imagination
of alternative scenarios became strong enough to support a
change of attitude (Irving Janis and Leon Mann, *Decision-
Making* [New York: Free Press, 1977], pt. 4).

23. Janis and Mann, *Decision-Making*; Irving Janis, *Victims of Groupthink* (Boston: Houghton Mifflin, 1972); Willem Doise,
Groups and Individuals (Cambridge, Eng.: Cambridge University Press, 1978), pp. 69–72.

24. Jürgen Habermas, *Theory of Communicative Action* (Boston: Beacon, 1984), vol. 1, p. 9. Jon Elster, *Sour Grapes* (Cambridge,
Eng.: Cambridge University Press, 1983), chap. 1, isolates
various usages of the term "rationality."

25. Stanley Cavell, *Must We Mean What We Say?* (Cambridge, Eng.:
Cambridge University Press, 1976), p. xxii.

26. This passage draws upon Stephen Toulmin, *Human Understanding* (Princeton, N.J.: Princeton University Press, 1972), vol.
I, pp. 42–52; Jack Goody, *The Domestication of the Savage Mind*
(Cambridge, Eng.: Cambridge University Press, 1977); Elizabeth Eisenstein, *The Printing Press as an Agent of Change* (Cambridge, Eng.: Cambridge University Press, 1979).

27. Edward Evans-Pritchard, *Witchcraft, Oracles, and Magic Among
the Azande* (Oxford, Eng.: Oxford University Press, 1936), p.
194.

28. The contrast between the modern and the mythical approaches
to understanding has presented a dilemma for anthropology.
On the one hand, the anthropologist assumes that explanations
of the world used in "primitive" societies are rational, at least
in the narrow sense that they are interconnected in some consistent way, or that arguments can be made for them; such an
assumption is basic to the anthropological project of interpreting mythical thought. On the other hand, the anthropologist, openly or implicitly through his practice, assumes that he
is "more rational" than his subjects, in the sense that his
interpretations have greater explanatory power. To that extent, although cultural relativism may be part of his anthropological creed, he is not functionally relativist. The difference is that the approach of the social scientist is made
modern through his recognition that no explanatory framework is immune to criticism. His stance arguably does have
broader explanatory power. This debate is carried out in Bryan
Wilson, ed., *Rationality* (Oxford, Eng.: Basil Blackwell,

1970); Martin Hollis and Steven Lukes, eds., *Rationality and Relativism* (Cambridge, Mass.: MIT Press, 1982).

29. Charles Taylor, "Rationality," in Hollis and Lukes, eds., *Rationality and Relativism*; Habermas, *Theory of Communicative Action*, vol. 1, pp. 68–74.

30. Deanna Kuhn et al., "Adult Reasoning in Developmental Perspective: The Sample Case of Juror Reasoning," in Paul Baltes and Orville Brim, eds., *Life Span Development and Behavior*, vol. 5 (New York: Academic, 1983).

31. Loosely identified with Adorno and Marcuse respectively. See, e.g., Max Horkheimer and Theodor Adorno, *Dialectic of Enlightenment* (New York: Seabury, 1972); Herbert Marcuse, "Repressive Tolerance," in R. P. Wolff et al., *Critique of Pure Tolerance* (Boston: Beacon, 1965). See also Jürgen Habermas, *Theory and Practice* (Boston: Beacon, 1973), pp. 3–4.

32. Herbert Marcuse, *Eros and Civilization* (New York: Random House, 1962), p. 82.

Interlude: Sketch of a Dialogical Freedom of Expression

1. Alan Gewirth, *Reason and Morality* (Chicago: University of Chicago Press, 1978); Paul Allen III, "Critique of Gewirth's 'Is–Ought' Derivation," *Ethics* 92 (1982): 211–226; E. J. Bond, "Gewirth on Reason and Morality," *Metaphilosophy* 11 (1980): 36–53. See also Gewirth's and Bond's rejoinders in *Metaphilosophy* 11 (1980): 54–59, 70–75.

2. Thomas Scanlon, "A Theory of Freedom of Expression," in Ronald Dworkin, ed., *Philosophy of Law* (London: Oxford University Press, 1977).

3. Although it is always risky to generalize about the "critical legal studies movement" as though its members substantially agreed, the tendency described in the text appears in a number of places, many of which are collected in Sanford Levinson, "Escaping Liberalism: Easier Said Than Done" (book review), *Harvard Law Review* 96 (1983): 1466–1488, and in Allan Hutchinson and Patrick Monahan, "The 'Rights' Stuff: Roberto Unger and Beyond," *Texas Law Review* 62 (1984): 1477–1539. The deconstructionist position is illuminated in the dispute between ordinary language philosophy and deconstruction. See, e.g., Jacques Derrida, "Signature, Event, Con-

text," *Glyph* 1 (1977): 172–197; John Searle, "Reiterating the Differences: A Reply to Derrida," *Glyph* 1 (1977): 198–208; Jacques Derrida, "Limited Inc. abc," *Glyph* 2 (1977): 162–254.

4. Andrew Altman, "Legal Realism, Critical Legal Studies, and Dworkin," *Philosophy and Public Affairs* 15 (1986): 205–235.

5. Roberto Unger, for example, has made use of rights concepts in trying to construct new possibilities for law (Roberto Unger, "The Critical Legal Studies Movement," *Harvard Law Review* 96 [1983]: 561–675).

6. Willem Doise, *Groups and Individuals* (Cambridge, Eng.: Cambridge University Press, 1978); Irving Janis and Leon Mann, *Decision-Making* (New York: Free Press, 1977). Michael Saks, *Small Group Decision-Making and Complex Information Tasks* (Washington, D.C.: Federal Judicial Center, 1981), shows that for certain types of tasks groups do reach correct conclusions more often than individuals. See also Bernard Grofman, "Judgmental Competence of Individuals and Groups in a Dichotomous Choice Situation," *Journal of Mathematical Sociology* 6 (1978): 47–60.

Chapter III: Three Irrational Government Decisions

1. I have drawn upon the following works by authors outside Poland: T. G. Ash, *The Polish Revolution: Solidarity* (New York: Scribner's, 1983); George Blazyca, "The Degeneration of Central Planning in Poland," in Jean Woodall, ed., *Policy and Politics in Contemporary Poland* (New York: St. Martin's, 1982); Z. A. Pelczynski, chaps. 12–17 in R. F. Leslie, ed., *History of Poland since 1863* (Cambridge, Eng.: Cambridge University Press, 1980); George Blazynski, *Flashpoint Poland* (New York: Pergamon, 1979); Jeffrey Goldfarb, *On Cultural Freedom: An Exploration of Public Life in Poland and America* (Chicago: University of Chicago Press, 1982). For opinion from within Poland, see Experience and Future Discussion Group, *Poland: The State of the Republic* (London: Pluto, 1981), hereafter referred to as "DiP Report."

2. Pelczynski, in Leslie, ed., *History of Poland*, p. 406; J. L. Curry, "Media Control in Eastern Europe," in Jane L. Curry and Joan Dassin, *Press Control Around the World* (New York: Praeger, 1982).

3. Pelczynski, in Leslie, ed., *History of Poland*, pp. 397–398.

4. DiP Report, p. 153.
5. Ibid., pp. 25–26.
6. Ibid., pp. 147–148. It should be noted that the respondents are as frank as they are in part because they are anonymous. A typical opinion in the Report, one of a dozen similar passages is (p. 118):

> At the first plenary meeting of the "Experience and the Future" group, a specialist in social policy described the current political and economic needs as follows:
> "The most important task today must be to halt negative processes and restore proportion to development. However, this must necessarily take several years, and no authorities, of whatever kind, could manage such a policy without the far-ranging cooperation, patience, and understanding of society. That is why the question of dialogue and participation is so relevant. It is our greatest noncapital reserve, one that with a great deal of effort we may be able to mobilize."
> "Society must believe," wrote a journalist specializing in problems of organization and management and a member of the party, "that it will be treated seriously. If it does not believe this, then nothing will change. There is no place today for any attempt to manipulate—give a little here, take a little there. Without a society ready and willing to cooperate there is no chance of reviving the economy and the state."

7. Ash, *The Polish Revolution*, p. 43.
8. Ibid., p. 137.
9. Max Weber, *Theory of Social and Economic Organization* (New York: Free Press, 1964), pp. 358–373. Weber distinguished three types of legitimation: traditional or customary, charismatic, and bureaucratic-rational. Weber's "charismatic leader" concept is applied to Cuba in Edward Gonzalez, *Cuba Under Castro: The Limits of Charisma* (Boston: Houghton Mifflin, 1974). It is discussed in Jorge Dominguez, *Cuba: Order and Revolution* (Cambridge, Mass.: Harvard University Press, 1978); Max Azicri, "Institutionalization of the Cuban State," *Journal of Interamerican Studies and World Affairs* 22 (1980): 315–344. In what follows, I have drawn generally upon the latter two works, in addition to K. S. Karol, *Guerillas in Power* (New York: Hill and Wang, 1970); Carmelo Mesa-Lago, *Cuba in the 1970s: Pragmatism and Institutionalization* (Albuquerque: University of New Mexico Press, 1978); Marta Harnecker, *Cuba: Dictatorship or Democracy?* (Westport, Conn.: Lawrence

Hill, 1979); Max Azicri, "Institutionalization of the Cuban Revolution: A Review of the Literature," *Cuban Studies* 9 (July, 1979): 63–90.

10. Carlos Rafael Rodriguez, quoted in Karol, *Guerillas in Power*, p. 418.

11. Leo Huberman and Paul Sweezy, *Socialism in Cuba* (New York: Monthly Review, 1969), pp. 173–180; Karol, *Guerillas in Power*, pp. 410–420. Karol was subsequently criticized in Cuba as biased against the revolution; the internal evidence of the book indicates otherwise.

12. According to reporter Lee Lockwood, Castro said in 1965 that he knew of no major errors by the Cuban leadership, nor of any occasion when the people had informed him of any (Dominguez, *Cuba*, p. 281). Such a statement should, however, be taken with a grain of salt; a statement made to a U.S. reporter may be much different from a statement made to another person.

13. Dominguez, *Cuba*, pp. 275–276.

14. *Granma* (weekly review), English ed., Aug. 2, 1970.

15. Fidel Castro, "Democratization of the Revolutionary Process," Sept. 28, 1970, in Fidel Castro, *Speeches* (New York: Pathfinder, 1983), vol. 2, pp. 141–142.

16. Fidel Castro, "Need for a Democratic Labor Movement," Sept. 2–3, 1970 in Castro, *Speeches*, p. 129.

17. Dominguez, *Cuba*, pp. 383–384. The causative relation between the harvest of 1970 and the development of Poder Popular is generally accepted, although Azicri, in the works cited in note 9 supra, indicates that existing plans were merely expedited. The effectiveness of the institutions is described by Harnecker, *Cuba*, from a strongly pro-Cuban point of view. My description receives support from a more neutral point of view in Dominguez, *Cuba*, pp. 282–286, 299–305.

18. L. M. Werner, "High Cuban Defector Speaks Out, Denouncing Castro as 'Impulsive,'" *New York Times*, Nov. 19, 1984, p. A1.

19. Irving Janis, *Victims of Groupthink* (Boston: Houghton Mifflin, 1972), chap. 2. In what follows, I draw on this as well as Peter Wyden, *Bay of Pigs* (New York: Simon and Schuster, 1979); Theodore Sorensen, *Kennedy* (New York: Harper and Row, 1965), chaps. 11–12; Arthur Schlesinger, Jr., *A Thousand Days* (Boston: Houghton Mifflin, 1965), chaps. 9–11.

20. Stephen Schlesinger and Stephen Kinzer, *Bitter Fruit* (New York: Doubleday, 1982).

21. Sorensen, *Kennedy*, pp. 304–305.
22. Quoted in Schlesinger, *A Thousand Days*, p. 247.
23. Wyden, *Bay of Pigs*, p. 155; Schlesinger, *A Thousand Days*, p. 247.
24. Leslie Gelb and R. Betts, *Irony of Vietnam: The System Worked* (Washington, D.C.: Brookings, 1979), p. 2. Supporting the rationality view is Daniel Ellsberg, *Papers on the War* (New York: Simon and Schuster, 1972). A different view is expressed in David Curzon, "Generic Secrets of Government Decision-Making," in Itzhak Galnoor, ed., *Government Secrecy in Democracies* (New York: Harper, 1977). See also the essays in Sen. Gravel, ed., *Pentagon Papers* (Boston: Beacon, 1972), vol. 5.
25. Gelb and Betts, *Irony of Vietnam*, p. 237.
26. Thomas Hughes, "The Power to Speak and the Power to Listen: Reflections on Bureaucratic Politics and a Recommendation on Information Flows," in Thomas Franck and Edward Weisband, eds., *Secrecy and Foreign Policy* (New York: Oxford University Press, 1974), p. 37.
27. Ibid., pp. 34, 40.
28. The War Powers Act is 50 U.S.C. § 1451. The Oversight Committees are discussed, e.g., in Thomas Franck and Edward Weisband, *Foreign Policy by Congress* (New York: Oxford University Press, 1979), chap. 5.

Chapter IV: Political Protection for Free Expression

1. John Rawls, *Theory of Justice* (Cambridge, Mass.: Harvard University Press, 1971), p. 207; Thomas Scanlon, "A Theory of Freedom of Expression," in Ronald Dworkin, ed., *Philosophy of Law* (London: Oxford University Press, 1977), p. 164. See also David Richards, *Moral Criticism of Law* (Encino, Calif.: Dickenson, 1977), pp. 44–77.
2. Thomas Emerson, *Theory of Freedom of Expression* (New York: Random House, 1972), p. 8.
3. Scanlon, "A Theory of Freedom of Expression," p. 159.
4. *Whitney v. State of California*, 274 U.S. 357, 377 (1927).
5. Clement Eaton, *Freedom of Thought in the Old South* (Durham, N.C.: Duke University Press, 1940), pp. 292–293, 306–310.
6. Stephen Kinzer, "Nicaragua Loosens the Reins on Opposition Paper," *New York Times*, Nov. 21, 1983, p. A8; *La Prensa*

(censurada, Managua), May 19, 1984. *La Prensa,* which as of this writing had been closed down, kept copies of what was censored and would give copies to persons who came to its offices to request them.

7. Compare rules of Israeli military censor, Fund for Free Expression, *Israeli Censorship of Arab Publications* (New York: Fund for Free Expression, 1983), p. 19; Internal Security Act of South Africa, sec. 6, cited in K. W. Stewart, *Newspaperman's Guide to the Law* (Durban: Butterworth, 1982), p. 9.

8. "Black Book of Polish Censorship," in George Schoepflin, ed., *Censorship and Political Communication in Eastern Europe* (New York: St. Martin's, 1983), pp. 81–82,87.

9. Ibid., p. 113.

10. See Alexander Meiklejohn, *Political Freedom* (New York: Oxford University Press, 1965), pp. 78–83; Robert Bork, "Neutral Principles and Some First Amendment Problems," *Indiana Law Journal* 47 (1971): 1–35.

11. *American Booksellers Association v. Hudnut,* 598 F. Supp. 1316 (S.D. Ind. 1984), aff'd 771 F.2d 323 (7th Cir.), aff'd 107 S. Ct. 1172 (1986).

12. See, e.g., *Cox v. Louisiana,* 379 U.S. 536 (1965).

13. *Schneider v. State,* 308 U.S. 147 (1939). *Schneider* does not fully articulate this doctrinal point, but is usually so interpreted—e.g., in *Metromedia, Inc. v. San Diego,* 453 U.S. 490, 520, 527 (1981).

14. A British law pursuant to which comments in the press on a case that is under consideration but not yet decided by the courts could be treated as a contempt of court was held by the European Court on Human Rights to violate the European Convention on Human Rights (W-W. M. Wong. "*The Sunday Times Case:* Freedom of Expression versus English Contempt-of-Court Law in the European Court of Human Rights," *NYU Journal of International Law and Politics* 17 [1984]: 35–75).

15. Irving Janis, *Victims of Groupthink* (Boston: Houghton Mifflin, 1972), pp. 209–218.

16. See also Alexis de Tocqueville, *The Old Regime and the French Revolution* (New York: Doubleday, 1959); another example, that of Ethiopia, is recounted in Ryszard Kapuscinski, *The Emperor* (New York: Random House, 1983).

17. See the discussion in Chapter II.

18. This view is consistent with, e.g., Frederick Frey, "Communications and Development," in Ithiel Pool et al., eds., *Handbook of Communications* (Chicago: Rand, McNally, 1973), p. 403.

19. Quoted in T. G. Ash, *The Polish Revolution: Solidarity* (New York: Scribner's, 1983), p. 37. A similar point is made in Jeffrey Goldfarb, *On Cultural Freedom: An Exploration of Public Life in Poland and America* (Chicago: University of Chicago Press, 1982), pp. 57–58; Experience and Future Discussion Group, *Poland: The State of the Republic* (London: Pluto, 1981), p. 32. Of course, if the government claims ,to act in the interest of all the people, as western democracies do, then it will have no way of explaining why any citizen or any subject should not be heard.

Chapter V: Access to the Dialogue

1. *Zemel v. Rusk,* 381 U.S. 1, 16–17 (1965). See Note, "First Amendment Right to Gather State-Held Information," *Yale Law Journal* 89 (1980): 923–939.
2. *Houchins v. KQED,* 438 U.S. 1, 12 (1978). The passage is quoted from *Zemel v. Rusk.*
3. *Richmond Newspapers v. Virginia,* 448 U.S. 555 (1980).
4. Ibid.,p. 595; cf. p. 571.
5. The Court relied on the precedent in *Press Enterprise v. Superior Court,* 464 U.S. 501 (1984) (access to jury selection); *Globe Newspaper Co. v. Superior Court,* 457 U.S. 596 (1982) (access to sex crime trial). The explanation offered by the Court in *Richmond Newspapers,* 448 U.S. at 576 n. 11, for not affording access to prisons, that they are closed whereas courts are not, simply begs the question; cf. comments of Justice Stevens, 448 U.S. at 583–584.
6. The quoted phrase is from James Goodale, "Legal Pitfalls in the Right to Know," *Washington University Law Quarterly,* 1976, p. 29, a reply in part to Thomas Emerson, "Legal Foundations of the Right to Know," *Washington University Law Quarterly* (1976): 1–24. The arguments on the issue tend to be reiterated. Supporting a constitutional right of access at least to government information are Emerson, "Legal Foundations"; Wallace Parks, "The Open Government Principle: Applying the Right to Know Under the Constitution," *George Washington Law Review* 26 (1957): 1–22; Note, "First Amendment Right," 923–939. Among those opposed are Ronald Dworkin, "Is the Press Losing the First Amendment?" *New York Review of Books,* Dec. 4, 1980, p. 49; Gerald Baldasty and Roger Simpson, "The Deceptive Right to Know: How Pessimism Rewrote the First Amendment," *Washington Law Review*

56 (1981): 365–395; David O'Brien, *The Public's Right to Know* (New York: Praeger, 1981).

7. One of the recent articles opposing a right of access, for example in the course of criticizing "pessimism" about the media, took the position that, "although there are these two direct interests [i.e., speaker and listener], *only one of them, in simple conditions, needs protection.* To protect the freedom of the issuer is to protect the interest of the consumer and in general that of the community also" (Baldasty and Simpson, "The Deceptive Right to Know," p. 369).

8. Zechariah Chaffee, *Government and Mass Communications* (Hamden, Conn.: Archon, 1965); Commission on Freedom of the Press, *A Free and Responsible Press* (University of Chicago Press, 1947); Claus Mueller, *Politics of Communication* (New York: Oxford University Press, 1973); Charles Lindblom, *Politics and Markets* (New York: Basic Books, 1977), pt. 5.

9. On influence over the media generally, Ben Bagdikian, *Media Monopoly* (Boston: Beacon, 1983); on concentration in the print media, see Bruce Owen, *Economics and Freedom of Expression* (Cambridge, Mass.: Ballinger, 1975); S. Hoyer et al. *Politics and Economics of the Press: A Developmental Perspective* (Beverly Hills, Calif.: Sage, 1975). For Canada, Arthur Siegel, *Politics and the Media in Canada* (Toronto: McGraw-Hill Ryerson, 1983), pp. 108–124. For limitation and caution in press opinion, see Lindblom, *Politics and Markets,* and Mueller, *Politics of Communication.* Concerning television and cable, see Ithiel Pool, *Technologies of Freedom* (Cambridge, Mass.: Harvard University Press, 1983); Donald Pember, *Mass Media in America* (Chicago: Science Research Association, 1977), pp. 19–22 and chap. 8. On the alternative media, see David Armstrong, *Trumpet to Arms* (Los Angeles: Tarcher, 1981). Concerning restraints on campaigning, see Paul Chevigny, "Paradox of Campaign Finance," *NYU Law Review* 56 (1981): 206–226, reviewing Gary Jacobson, *Money in Congressional Elections* (New Haven, Conn.: Yale Univeristy Press, 1980); Harvard Institute of Politics, Campaign Finance Study Group, *Analysis of the Impact of FECA, 1972–78* (Cambridge, Mass.: The Institute, 1979); Elizabeth Drew, *Politics and Money* (New York: Macmillan, 1983).

10. Aaron Wildavsky, review, *Yale Law Journal* 88 (1979): 226; Lindblom, *Politics and Markets,* pp. 167–169, 179. The dispute concerning Lindblom's views is described well in Mark Yudof, *When Government Speaks* (Berkeley and Los Angeles: University of California Press, 1983), pp. 95–103.

11. My memory is buttressed by a survey of editorial material in the *New York Times* from the beginning of 1972 to the end of 1976, conducted by my research assistant, Robert Deyling.

12. See, generally, Itzhak Galnoor, ed., *Government Secrecy in Democracies* (New York: Harper, 1977); Donald Rowat, "Comparative Perspective on the Right of Access," in Donald Rowat, ed., *Right to Know* (Ottawa: Carleton University Press, 1980). For whistleblowers, see Thomas Franck and Edward Weisband, *Resignation in Protest* (New York: Viking, 1975). For England, see Thomas Franck and Edward Weisband, eds., *Secrecy and Foreign Policy* (New York: Oxford University Press, 1974); R. W. Apple, "Secrets Case Won, Briton Quits Post," *New York Times*, Feb. 18, 1985, p. A3. For France, see C. R. Eisendrath, "Press Freedom in France: Private Ownership and State Controls," in J. L. Curry and Joan Dassin, eds., *Press Control Around the World* (New York: Praeger, 1982). The French Freedom of Information Act is Loi no. 78-753 (July 17, 1978). The Council of Europe recommendation is R(81)19, in Herbert Miehsler and Herbert Petzold, eds., *European Convention on Human Rights* (Cologne: C. Heymanns, 1982), vol. 2.

13. *Houchins v. KQED,* 438 U.S. at 12. The FOIA statute is 5 U.S.C. § 552. It contains exemptions to protect the security interests discussed in the text.

14. See Note, "Constitutionality of Municipal Advocacy in Statewide Referendum Campaigns," *Harvard Law Review* 93 (1980): 535–563; *Anderson v. Boston,* 30 N.E.2d 628 (Mass. 1978), app. dism. 439 U.S. 1060 (1979). See also generally Yudof, *When Government Speaks.*

15. For Tanzania, see Dennis Wilcox, "Black African States," in Curry and Dassin, eds., *Press Control Around the World,* p. 216. For U.S., see *Hannegan v. Esquire,* 327 U.S. 146 (1946); William Preston, Jr., *Aliens and Dissenters* (New York: Harpers, 1966), pp. 144–149.

16. The Indian case is *B. Coleman & Co. et al. v. Union of India,* AIR 1973 Supreme Court 106. For Africa, see Wilcox, "Black African States," p. 217.

17. In capitalist countries, some potentially public communication services get passed back to the private sector for development. Cable television, for example, has been franchised by municipalities to private cable companies in the United States. It was theoretically possible to treat those cables as "common carriers," which would in effect make them the private equivalent of public forums, obliged to lease time to anyone who could

pay the fee. In order to make the franchises more attractive as profit-making ventures the cable companies have been given a great deal of discretion to lease time and dictate programming. The U.S. Federal Communications Act forbids making broadcasters into common carriers (47 U.S.C. § 153h). FCC regulations mandating the reservation of cable channels for public use were struck down in *FCC v. Midwest Video Corp.*, 440 U.S. 689 (1979). In many communities, nevertheless, some of the channels have been reserved to the municipality by contract, to be used by the government or leased to others. Boston, for example, has established a corporation with a board independent of direct control by the municipality to manage its cable channels reserved for public use. See Pool, *Technologies of Freedom*, Chap. 7.

18. Arthur Williams, *Broadcasting and Democracy in West Germany* (London: Grenada, 1976); Ruth Thomas, *Broadcasting and Democracy in France* (Philadelphia: Temple University Press, 1976); Committee of Inquiry on the Future of Broadcasting, *Report* (London: HMSO, 1977), hereafter cited as Annan Report; for U.S. 47 U.S.C. §§ 151 et seq., 396 et seq.

19. Wilcox, "Black African States," pp. 210–211; Committee to Protect Journalists, *South Africa and Zimbabwe: The Freest Press in Africa?* (New York: CPJ, 1983); Elihu Katz and George Wedell, *Broadcasting in the Third World* (Cambridge, Mass.: Harvard University Press, 1977), chap. 2. Cf. Robert Pozen, *Legal Theories for State Enterprises in the Third World* (New York: New York University Press, 1976).

20. Katz and Wedell, *Broadcasting in the Third World,* p. 42. See citations in previous two notes and Oscar Chase, "Public Broadcasting and the Problem of Government Influence: Towards a Legislative Solution," *Univeristy of Michigan Journal of Legal Reform* 9 (1975): 62–112; William Canby, Jr., "First Amendment and the State as Editor: Implications for Public Broadcasting," *Texas Law Review* 52 (1974): 1123–1165.

21. *FCC v. League of Women Voters,* 468 U.S. 364 (1984). It would be an exaggeration to pretend that U.S. courts have reached any general conclusion that government-aided bodies have full constitutional rights of free speech, an issue that must depend on the character of the body. The controversy is aired in *Muir v. Alabama Educational TV,* 688 F.2d 1033 (5th Cir. 1982), which upholds the decision of publicly funded stations to refuse to screen the politically controversial film "Death of a Princess."

22. This is not as impossible as it seems at first glance. Western television monopolies have long worked within directives to balance their presentations (see citations in note 24). During the election campaign of 1984 in Nicaragua the official Sandinista paper *Barricada* (which was not a monopoly) printed sketches of opposition candidates and their platforms.

23. This is one significance, I think, of the *Pico* case, in which the United States Supreme Court recognized that an intent to interfere with free expression could be inferred from the fact that a school board had failed to follow its own procedures in removing books from a school library (*Board of Education v. Pico*, 457 U.S. 853 [1982]). For references to broadcasting law in France, Germany, and the United States, see notes 18 and 20. It is doubtful that a franchise fee imposed on television receivers could be used to finance public television alone under present U.S. constitutional law, since many viewers might not choose to watch public TV.

24. For U.S. fairness doctrine, see *Red Lion v. FCC*, 395 U.S. 367 (1965); for public broadcasting, 47 U.S.C. § 369(g)(1)(a). For Britain, see Annan Report, secs. 6.12–13, 17.6. For France and Germany, see note 18 supra.

25. Mark Fowler and Daniel Brenner, "Marketplace Approach to Broadcast Regulation," *Texas Law Review* 60 (1982): 207–257; Note, "Access to the Press, A Teleological Analysis of a Double Standard," *George Washington Law Review* 50 (1982): 430–464. The argument that comes closest to the one made here is Lee Bollinger, "Freedom of the Press and Public Access: Toward a Theory of Partial Regulation of the Mass Media," *Michigan Law Review* 75 (1976): 1–42.

26. Select Committee to Study Government Operations with respect to Intelligence Activities, U.S. Senate, 94th Cong., 1st Sess., *Staff Report on Covert Action in Chile* (Washington, D.C.: GPO, 1975), pp. 8, 22, 25, 29. It has been reported that during the coup of 1954 in Guatemala against the government of Jacobo Arbenz Guzmán, influential forces including military representatives abandoned Arbenz because of disinformation in local media sponsored by the CIA (Stephen Schlesinger and Stephen Kinzer, *Bitter Fruit* [New York: Doubleday, 1982], pp. 189, 194). For Canada, see Anthony Smith, *Geopolitics of Information* (New York: Oxford University Press, 1980), pp. 52–54; Dallas Smythe, *Dependency Road* (Norwood, N.J.: Albex, 1981), chap. 6.

27. Katz and Wedell, *Broadcasting in the Third World*, p. 156; Tapio

Varis, "Global Traffic in Television Programming," in George
Gerbner and Marsha Siefert, eds., *World Communications* (New
York: Longman, 1984), pp. 144–152,
28. Smith, *Geopolitics of Information,* pp. 73, 91–92; Biola Olasope,
"Nonaligned News Agencies Pool and the Free Flow of Meaningful News: An African Viewpoint," in Philip Horton, ed.,
Third World and Press Freedom (New York: Praeger, 1978), pp.
162–172. The evidence that the transnational news agencies
pay relatively little attention to the third world except in times
of conflict is very strong. The evidence of prejudice or distortion is much more ambiguous, as is natural, since such evidence is largely subjective. See studies described in Smith,
Geopolitics of Information, chap. 3; Roger Tatarian, "News Flow
in the Third World," in Horton, ed., *Third World,* pp. 1–54;
W. Fitzmaurice, "New World Information and Communication Order: Is the International Programme for the Development of Communication the Answer?" *NYU Journal of International Law and Politics* 15 (1983): 965 n. 46.
29. UNESCO General Conference Resolution 4/19 (21st Sess.,
1980, Belgrade), quoted in Fitzmaurice, "New World Information and Communication Order," p. 962 n. 32.
30. Tatarian, "News Flow," p. 11. On the issue of requiring "objectivity and accuracy," see Mustapha Masmoudi, "New World
Information Order," pp. 14–27, and Kaarle Nordenstreng,
"Defining the New International Information Order," pp. 28–
36, in Gerbner and Siefert, eds., *World Communications.*
31. Paul Fisher, U.S. observer at Costa Rica UNESCO conference,
quoted in Sean Kelly, *Access Denied* (Washington Papers, vol.
6, no. 55; Beverly Hills, Calif.: Sage, 1978), p. 31; U.S.
statement of withdrawal from UNESCO, *New York Times,*
Dec. 20, 1984, p. A10.
32. For the Non-Aligned News Pool see Horton, ed., *Third World,*
passim, especially Olasope "Nonaligned News Agencies Pool."
Similar problems seem to have arisen in the case of other
attempts, such as Depthnews, an agency that was supposed to
emphasize reports of economic and social projects (S. M. Ali,
"Depthnews: A Model for a Third-World Feature Agency,"
pp. 187–196, and Narinder Aggarwala, "News in Third
World Perspective," pp. 197–209, both in Horton, ed.,
Third World). For the IPDC see Fitzmaurice, "New World
Information and Communication Order."
33. Peter Hajnal, *Guide to UNESCO* (New York: Oceana, 1983),
pp. 60–61, 91. It is implied there that UNESCO would not

have the funds for such a project. The supply or the lack of funds is of course partly a function of the willingness on the part of members to carry out a large project. Apart from that, it is unclear what funds UNESCO could have made available; its accounting is said to be snarled. In its statement withdrawing from UNESCO (*New York Times*, Dec. 20, 1984, p. A10), the United States asserted that 80 percent of the biennial budget of $374 million is spent at headquarters.

The measures advocated in my text are supported by Twentieth Century Fund Task Force on International Flow of News, *Report* (Lexington, Mass.: Heath, 1978).

34. Rita Atwood and Sergio Mattos, "Mass Media Reform and Social Change: The Peruvian Experience," in Gerbner and Siefert, eds., *World Communications*, pp. 309–321; Katz and Wedell, *Broadcasting in the Third World*, pp. 219–221, chap. 4; Mario Vargas Llosa, *Aunt Julia and the Scriptwriter* (New York: Farrar, Straus, 1982).

35. A non-citizen may not have more than a one-fifth interest in a broadcast facility in the United States (47 U.S.C. § 310), a measure that affected the attempt of Rupert Murdoch, an Australian national, to acquire a television network in the United States (William Safire, "Citizen of the World," *New York Times*, May 16, 1985, p. A31).

Interlude: Dialogues and Disputes

1. For a trial about death by sorcery, see Paul Bohannon, *Justice and Judgment Among the Tiv* (Oxford University Press, 1957), pp. 196–203. Examples of trials by ordeal appear, e.g., in Paul Bohannon, ed., *Law and Warfare* (New York: Natural History Press, 1967).

2. The distinction is drawn from Thomas Grey, "Procedural Fairness and Substantive Rights," in J. R. Pennock and John Chapman, eds., *Nomos XVIII: Due Process* (New York: New York University Press, 1977), pp. 182–205.

3. The triad notion appears in Martin Shapiro, *Courts* (Chicago: University of Chicago Press, 1981), chap. 1; P. Gulliver, "Dispute Settlement Without Courts: The Ndendeuli of Southern Tanzania," in Laura Nader, ed., *Law in Culture and Society* (Chicago: Aldine, 1969), pp. 24–68.

Chapter VI: Procedures for Disputes

1. *Goss v. Lopez,* 419 U.S. 565, 581, 582 (1975).
2. Bernard Schwartz, *Administrative Law* (Boston: Little, Brown, 1984), sec. 5.1; Mauro Cappelletti, "Fundamental Guarantees of the Parties in Civil Litigation: Comparative Constitutional, International, and Social Trends," *Stanford Law Review* 25 (1973): 651–715; virtually the same text appears as "General Report" in Mauro Cappelletti and Denis Tallon, eds., *Fundamental Guarantees of the Parties in Civil Litigation* (Dobbs Ferry, N.Y.: Oceana, 1973). For specific examples, see the essays in the latter volume.
3. John Thibaut and Laurens Walker, *Procedural Justice* (Hillsdale, N.J.: L. Erlbaum, 1975), chap. 9; the dignitary position is taken in Richard Saphire, "Specifying Due Process Values: Toward a More Responsive Approach to Procedural Protections," *University of Pennsylvania Law Review* 127 (1978): 111–195; Frank Michelman, "Formal and Associational Aims in Procedural Due Process," in J. R. Pennock and John Chapman, eds., *Nomos XVIII: Due Process* (New York: New York University Press, 1977), pp. 126–171. The decisionist position is found in Thomas Grey, "Procedural Fairness and Substantive Rights," in Pennock and Chapman, eds., *Nomos XVIII,* pp. 182–205. The positions are discussed in, e.g., Robert Rabin, "Some Thoughts on the Relationship Between Fundamental Values and Procedural Safeguards," *San Diego Law Review* 16 (1979):301–312; Jerry Mashaw, *Bureaucratic Justice* (New Haven, Conn.: Yale 1983). Perhaps only John Thibaut and Laurens Walker, "A Theory of Procedure," *California Law Review* 66 (1978): 541–566, argues that an authoritarian, non-adversary procedure is more "accurate."
4. The phrase concerning school suspensions is from *Goss v. Lopez,* 419 U.S. at 581; the latter case is *Matthews v. Eldridge,* 424 U.S. 319, 335 (1976). It should be noted that, in that case, the chief issue was whether the hearing should be before or after suspension of the payment.
5. Laurence Tribe, "Structural Due Process," *Harvard Civil Rights— Civil Liberties Law Review* 10 (1975): 269–321; Mashaw, *Bureaucratic Justice,* p. 31.
6. *Califano v. Yamasaki,* 442 U.S. 682 (1979).
7. The phrase is from John Merryman, *Civil Law Tradition* (Palo Alto, Calif.: Stanford University Press, 1969), p. 126. The mechanical evaluation of witnesses is discussed also in Arthur Engelmann, *History of Continental Civil Procedure* (Boston: Lit-

tle, Brown, 1927), pp. 41–42. The formalism of the system is emphasized in R. C. VanCaenegem, "History of European Civil Procedure," *International Encyclopedia of Comparative Law* (New York: Oceana, 1971), vol. 16, chap 2.

8. John Langbein, *Torture and the Law of Proof* (Chicago: University of Chicago Press, 1977), pp. 4, 17. There is some controversy about how widespread the rule requiring confession was (Adhémar Esmein, *History of Continental Criminal Procedure* [Boston: Little, Brown, 1913], p. 626; Karl VonBar, *History of Continental Criminal Law* [Boston: Little, Brown, 1916], p. 157). The rule requiring confession for conviction is said to have prevailed also in ancient China (Ichisada Miyazaki, "Administration of Justice During the Sung Dynasty," in Jerome Cohen et al., *Essays on China's Legal Tradition* [Princeton, N.J.: Princeton University Press, 1980).

9. Max Weber, *Max Weber on Law in Economy and Society* (New York: Simon and Schuster, 1967), pp. 220–222, 231, chap. 11.

10. Mauro Cappelletti, *Procedure Orale et Procedure Ecrite* (New York: Oceana, 1971), p. 106.

11. The phrase concerning the Austrian code is from Adolf Homburger, "Functions of Orality in Austrian and American Civil Procedure," *Buffalo Law Review* 20 (1970): 24. For France, see "History of European Civil Procedure," pp. 2–65. For Germany, see Benjamin Kaplan, "Civil Procedure: Reflections on the Comparison of Systems," *Buffalo Law Review* 9 (1960): 409–432; William Fisch, "Recent Developments in West German Civil Procedure," *Hastings International and Comparative Law Review* 6 (1983): 221–282. See, generally, Cappelletti, *Procedure Orale;* Rudolf Schlesinger, *Comparative Law* (New York: Foundation, 1970), p. 305.

12. European Convention on Human Rights, art. 6(1); Jacques Velu, "La Convention Europeene des Droits de l'Homme et les Garanties Fondamentales . . . ," in Cappelletti and Tallon, eds., *Fundamental Guarantees,* pp. 245, 323.

13. *Pechter v. Lyons,* 441 F.Supp. 115 (S.D.N.Y. 1977) (deportation proceeding of alleged Nazi opened to press); Schwartz, *Administrative Law,* sec. 6.7.

14. *Fitzgerald v. Hampton,* 467 F.2d 755 (D.C. Cir. 1972); Ernest Fitzgerald, "Blowing the Whistle on the Pentagon," in Norman Dorsen and Stephen Gillers, eds., *None of Your Business* (New York: Viking, 1974), pp. 251–277.

15. Cappelletti, *Procedure Orale,* p. 106; Engelmann, *History of Continental Civil Procedure,* pp. 62–68.

16. Homburger, "Functions of Orality," p. 26.

17. *Goldberg v. Kelly,* 397 U.S. 254, 269 (1970).
18. For France, see VanCaenegem, "History of Europpean Civil Procedure," pp. 2–65; Peter Herzog, *Civil Procedure in France* (Hague: Nijhoff, 19677), pp. 282–286. The American case on the right to sum up in a criminal case is *Herring v. New York,* 422 U.S. 853 (1975).
19. Richard Canter, "Dispute Settlement and Dispute Processing in Zambia," in Laura Nader and Harry Todd, Jr., eds., *The Disputing Process: Law in Ten Societies* (New York: Columbia University Press, 1978), pp. 247–280. The "multiplex" concept is from Max Gluckman, *The Judicial Process Among the Barotse of Northern Rhodesia* (Manchester: University of Manchester Press, 1955), p. 16 and passim. Legal processes in underdeveloped societies are not always holistic and multiplex in Gluckman's sense; as in developed societies, there are degrees of the "legalistic" or the multiplex. See Lloyd Fallers, *Law Without Precedent* (Chicago: University of Chicago Press, 1969), pp. 326–332.
20. Edwin Hutchins, *Culture and Inference* (Cambridge, Mass.: Harvard University Press, 1980), pp. 64–66, 75–76, 116.
21. John Comaroff and Simon Roberts, "Invocation of Norms in Dispute Settlement: The Tswana Case," in Ian Hamnett, ed., *Social Anthropology and Law* (New York: Academic, 1977), pp. 77, 86. Similar analyses are used in Hutchins, *Culture and Inference,* and Gluckman, *Judicial Process.*
22. Henry Friendly, "Some Kind of Hearing," *University of Pennsylvania Law Review* 123 (1975): 1283. The Wigmore passage is quoted there.
23. Thibaut and Walker, *Procedural Justice,* chap. 8.
24. For the references to medieval French law, see Esmein, *History of Continental Criminal Procedure,* pp. 90–91, 106. For the European Convention, see art. 6(3)(d) thereof, and Velu, "La Convention Europeene," p. 327. For contemporary French law, see Françoise Grivart de Kerstat and William Crawford, *New Code of Civil Procedure in France* (Dobbs Ferry, N.Y.: Oceana, 1978), arts. 184–231. For German law, see Kaplan, "Civil Procedure." For U.S. law, see Federal Rules of Civil Procedure 37, 45; Administrative Procedure Act, 5 U.S.C. §§ 554, 556; Schwartz, *Administrative Law,* sec. 7.1. The U.S. constitutional position with respect to the right to call witnesses in an administrative proceeding is discussed in *Ponte v. Real—* U.S.—, 85 L.Ed.2d 553 (1985). For the civil-law view generally, Merryman, *Civil Law Tradition,* p. 124; Schlesinger, *Comparative Law,* 317.

25. Examples of questioning by parties as well as judges appear among the Ashanti (E. A. Hoebel, *Law of Primitive Man* [Cambridge, Mass.: Harvard University Press, 1954, p. 248), and the Soga (Fallers, *Law Without Precedent,* p. 22). For examples of cross-questioning generally, see note 26 following and Laura Nader, "Styles of Court Procedure: To Make the Balance," pp. 69–91 (Zapotec); J. Gibbs, "Law and Personality: Signposts for a New Direction," pp. 176–207 (Kpelle); and R. Verdier, "Ontology of the Judicial Thought of the Kabre of Northern Togo," 141–146, all in Laura Nader, ed., *Law in Culture and Society* (Chicago: Aldine, 1969).

26. Gluckman, *Judicial Process,* pp. 86–87. It is worth noting that the court tried the case in this way, relying almost entirely on defects in the councillor's story, because the testimony of the villagers was suspect; if Saywa was unpopular, his villagers might indeed "bind him with lies." Gluckman's cases, as well as others recorded by anthropologists describing other legal systems, reveal a special function for cross-questioning in tribal courts: It is a great time-saver. It is only when the judges cannot get at enough of the facts to resolve the case through cross-questioning the parties that they will say, "We need witnesses" (Gluckman, *Judicial Process,* p. 39). See Nader, "Styles of Court Procedure," for another example of the practice.

27. I don't want to take sides in the long-standing debate between common-law and civil-law jurists over which system, questioning by the judge or the lawyers, is more likely to get accurate answers. Blair Sheppard and Neil Vidmar, "Adversary Trial Procedures and Testimonial Evidence," *Journal of Personality and Social Psychology* 39 (1980): 320–332, lends some experimental support to the criticism by civil-law practitioners that the adversary "control" of witnesses tends to distort their testimony.

28. Elizabeth Loftus, *Eyewitness Testimony* (Cambridge, Mass.: Harvard University Press, 1979), p. 68 et passim.

29. Mark Galanter, "Reading the Landscape of Disputes: What We Know and Don't Know (and Think We Know) About Our Allegedly Contentious and Litigious Society," *UCLA Law Review* 31 (1983): 44.

Conclusion

1. A related set of ideas appears in Vincent Blasi, "Checking Value in First Amendment Theory," *American Bar Foundation Research Journal,* 1977, pp. 523–649.

2. J. Becker, "Reflections on the Formal Description of Behavior," in Danial Bobrow and Allan Collins, eds., *Representation and Understanding* (New York: Academic, 1975), p. 102.
3. Howard Gardner, *Frames of Mind: The Theory of Multiple Intelligences* (New York: Basic Books, 1983).
4. Jerry Fodor, *Modularity of Mind* (Cambridge, Mass.: MIT Press, 1983), p. 126.
5. See, e.g., Joseph Weizenbaum, *Computer Power and Human Reason* (San Francisco: Freeman, 1976); Morton Hunt, *Universe Within* (New York: Simon and Schuster, 1982), chap. 8.
6. Much study has been given, for example, to the Prisoner's Dilemma, in which two persons are isolated from one another and obliged to choose a course of action (e.g., whether to confess to a crime), when the result of the choice depends on the choice made by the other person. The special isolation of the participants in the dilemma is emphasized by its very name; but despite that isolation, the response of human participants is dependent upon their previous experience of the way other humans behave. In the iterated Prisoner's Dilemma, which is somewhat closer to the way people (and perhaps other creatures) actually make choices, the two individuals make a series of choices, relying on their experience of the results of the previous choice. The pattern of choices becomes interdependent in a primitive signalling system of communication through action (Robert Axelrod, *Evolution of Cooperation* [New York: Basic Books, 1984]).

Appendix I: Relativism

1. Maurice Mandelbaum, "Subjective, Objective, and Conceptual Relativisms," in Michael Krausz and Jack Meiland, eds., *Relativism: Cognitive and Moral* (Notre Dame, Ind.: University of Notre Dame Press, 1982), pp. 34–61.
2. Jack Meiland, "On the Paradox of Cognitive Relativism," *Metaphilosophy* 11 (1980): 115–126, makes a somewhat similar argument.

Appendix II: The Problem of Psychological Inquiry

1. J. P. Rushton, "Moral Cognition, Behaviorism, and Social Learning Theory," *Ethics* 92 (1982): 462. The description used here

applies most strongly to "radical" behaviorists, such as Watson and Skinner. Some others are, for example, merely "methodological" behaviorists, who accept the assumptions for purposes of experiment. See, e.g., E. P. Hilgard, "Behaviorism," in *Encyclopedia of Psychology* (New York: Herder and Herder, 1972).

2. B. F. Skinner, *Verbal Behavior* (New York: Appleton-Century, 1957), p. 5 et passim; Daniel Dennett, *Brainstorms* (Cambridge, Mass.: MIT Press, 1981), pp. 53–58; Michael Martin, "Are Cognitive Processes and Structure a Myth?" in Michael Martin, *Social Science and Philosophical Analysis* (Washington, D.C.: University Press of America, 1978).

3. Dennett, *Brainstorms*, pp. 54–58.

4. Noam Chomsky, review of Skinner, *Verbal Behavior, Language* 35 (1959): 26–59.

5. Jerry Fodor, Thomas Bever, and M. F. Garrett, *Psychology of Language* (New York: McGraw-Hill, 1974), pp. 1–22.

6. On the limitations of behaviorism from the point of view of cognitive psychology, see George Miller and P. N. Johnson-Laird, *Language and Perception* (Cambridge, Mass.: Harvard University Press, 1976), pp. 690–696; Chomsky, review of *Verbal Behavior*.

7. Skinner, *Verbal Behavior*, pp. 107–108.

8. Roger Shepard and Jacqueline Metzler, "Mental Rotation of Three-Dimensional Objects" *Science* 171 (1971): 701–703; critique in Dennett, *Brainstorms*, pp. 167–169.

9. Fodor, Bever, and Garrett, *Psychology of Language*, p. xi; P. W. Johnson-Laird and P. C. Wason, eds., *Thinking* (Cambridge, Eng.: Cambridge University Press, 1977), pp. 7–10.

Appendix III: False Consciousness, the Unconscious, and the Irrational

1. Sigmund Freud, *Interpretation of Dreams* (New York: Avon, 1965).

2. Jacques Lacan, "The Function and Field of Speech and Language in Psychoanalysis," in Jacques Lacan, *Ecrits: A Selection* (New York: Norton, 1977), pp. 30–113. Lacan distinguishes between speech and language, as does French structuralism, in a way of which I have not made use here.

3. Sigmund Freud, "The Unconscious," in Sigmund Freud, *General*

Psychological Theory (New York: Macmillan, 1963), p. 144 et passim.

4. Sigmund Freud, *Civilization and Its Discontents* (New York: Doubleday, n.d.), p. 40.'

5. Herbert Marcuse, *Eros and Civilization* (New York: Random House, 1962), and "Repressive Tolerance," in R. P. Wolff et al., *Critique of Pure Tolerance* (Boston: Beacon, 1965); see also the discussion in Russell Jacoby, *Social Amnesia* (Boston: Beacon, 1975). Cf. Peter Gabel, "The Phenomenology of Rights Consciousness and the Pact of the Withdrawn Selves," *Texas Law Review* 62 (1984): 1563–1599.

6. Jürgen Habermas, *Knowledge and Human Interests* (Boston: Beacon, 1971); Jessica Benjamin, "The Decline of the Oedipus Complex," in John Broughton, ed., *Critical Theories of Development* (New York: Plenum, in press); Joel Kovel, *Age of Desire* (New York: Pantheon, 1981).

INDEX

Abelson, R. P., 59–60, 178, 181
Access: to dialogue, 78, 122; need for, 15, 78, 122–125, 130; problems of, 123–148; right of, 78, 123–125
Accuracy, of dispute resolution, 157–158, 171
Ackerman, Bruce, 13, 212
Action: disciplines and, xiii; examples of, 102; problem-solving and, 18, 48, 175, 188; speech and, 100, 119. *See also* Communicative action; Decisions
Administrative agencies: processes of, 110, 120, 151–153; publicity and, 161
Adorno, Theodor, 221
Africa, media in, 134–135, 142
Agence France Presse. *See* News agencies
Allende, Salvador. *See* Chile
Alternatives, for decisions, 14, 69, 79, 82, 102, 106, 119, 125, 128, 158, 181
American Anthropological Association, 4
Analogy, linguistic, 54, 61

Analytic knowledge, 31–33
Anchoring heuristic, 61, 64–65, 69, 219
Anderson, Craig, 65
Andropov, Yuri, 10
Anglo-American. *See* Interpretation; Law; Rights
Answerable expression, 100–101, 105–106, 119–120
Argument: element of understanding, 65; procedural right, 163–165; speech and, 100–101
Artificial intelligence, 60, 181. *See also* Computer
Ash, Timothy Garton, 86
Attitude change, 65, 219
Audience, disputes and, 153
Aunt Julia and the Scriptwriter. See Vargas Llosa, Mario
Austrian Civil Code, 160, 162
Authority: government and, 17, 76, 77–78, 81, 114–119, 146, 182; in Poland, 86; trial process and, 124, 153
Availability heuristic, 61, 69
Ayer, A. J., 31–32, 33
Azande, 67, 115

Bakhtin, Mikhail, 46
Balance: of dialogue, problem of, 122, 127, 146; in media, 137–148
Baranczak, Stanislaw, 105
Barotse, 167–168, 170
Bay of Pigs. *See* Cuba
Behavior, social science concept of, 42, 179, 189–192
Benjamin, Jessica, 201
Betts, Richard, 97
Black Book of Polish Censorship, 104, 106
Bowerman, Melissa, 53
Brandeis, Louis (Justice), 100
Bransford, John, 59–60
Brennan, William (Justice), 124
British Broadcasting Company, 134–135, 138
Broadcasting, policy for, 134–140; in underdeveloped nations, 135, 145. *See also* Media; Radio; Television
Broughton, John, 57, 217

Canada, 141
Cappelletti, Mauro, 160
Carter Doctrine, 3
Castro, Fidel, 86–90, 97, 112
Catledge, Turner, 93, 96
Cavell, Stanley, 6
Censorship: of foreign ideas, 117, 142; generally, 103–110, 121; Nicaraguan, 103, 226; Polish, 85, 104–106; state intervention in media, 138–140, 145; the unconscious and, 198–199
Central Intelligence Agency (CIA), 91–93, 141, 143
Charismatic leader, 86–87, 116–117
Checks and balances, 175–176
Child, language and the, 53–56. *See also* Psychology; Understanding

Chile, 141, 143
Chomsky, Noam, 190, 213
Civil law, procedural system of, 158, 160, 165–167
Civilization and Its Discontents (Freud), 195–196, 199
Class interest, 9, 111, 117
Cognitive psychology. *See* Psychology
Collective: decisions, 181; needs and goods, 9, 12, 13, 79, 182. *See also* Planning
Collins, Allan, 63
Comaroff, John, 165
Committees for the Defense of the Revolution (Cuban), 88
Common law. *See* Procedure
Communications. *See* Media
Communicative action, 24, 54–56
Computer, models in psychology, 59–60, 177–181, 193
Confessions, 159–160
Confrontation, right of, 166, 170
Consequentialism, 17
Conservation, developmental concept, 55
Constitution, United States. *See* Argument; Due process of law; First Amendment; Law; Procedure; Supreme Court, U.S.
Contiguity, linguistic, 54, 61
Convention, as source of understanding, 37, 59
Cooperative principles (of communication), 209
Copy theory. *See* Correspondence theory
Corporation for Public Broadcasting (U.S.), 136–137
Correspondence theory, 29–34, 42, 45–47, 190
Council of Europe, 131, 166
Country Reports on Human Rights. *See* State Department
Courts, processes of, 151–153. *See also* Procedure
Creative, aspect of hermeneutics, 41, 48

Critical Legal Studies, 11, 76–77, 221–222
Critical theorists: hermeneutics and, 47; rationality and, 70–71; rights and, xii, 49–50. *See also* Critical Legal Studies; Marxism
Cross-examination, 166–168
Cuba: attempted invasion by U.S., 23, 81, 90–94, 102, 113, 176; Constitution, 9; generally, 15, 116; sugar harvest of 1970, 81–82, 86–90, 97, 102

Davidson, Donald, 37, 211–212
Decisionist, approach to procedure, 156–158
Decisions: aggregating individual, 182; group, 66, 112; limitations on, 48, 77, 101, 107, 110, 124, 148; methods, xiii, 13, 102, 152; modern rationality in, 17, 23, 97, 101, 148, 152; necessity for, 49, 51, 70, 107; political, 23, 40, 97, 102–103, 114, 115, 176; scenarios and, 97, 106. *See also* Disciplines; Interpretation; Prisoner's Dilemma; Problem-solving
Deconstruction, 76, 221–222
Democracy, free expression and, xii, 4, 7–8, 18, 75
Democracy in America (Tocqueville), 50
Derrida, Jacques, 221–222
Development, child. *See* Psychology
Devil's Advocate, 112–113
Dialogue: defined, 14; child development and, 54–56; differing media and, 140; free expression and, 14–17, 75, 78, 128; habits of, 55, 65; hermeneutic, 38–41; inquiry and, 48–51; Marxism and, 46–48; meaning and, xiii, 46, 101; media and, 125; modern rationality and, 68–69; natural science and, 45; political

institutions and, 151, 175–176; procedure and, 162, 164–168, 171; psychoanalysis and, 196; rights derived from, xiv, 48–49, 75, 77, 151, 159, 168, 180, 196; Solidarity and, 86; understanding and, 13, 14, 24–25, 82. *See also* Balance; Hermeneutics; Interpretation; Language; Meaning; Problem-solving; Understanding
Dignitary, approach to procedure, 156–158
Disciplines: censorship and, 107–108; criticism of, xiii, 50–51, 107; need for, xiii, 49, 107, 188. *See also* Decisions; Dialogue; Problem-solving
Dispute resolution: generally, 15, 152, 155–171; modern rational approach, 152. *See also* Procedure
Disturbance of the peace, legal concept, 109
Dominguez, Jorge, 90
Due process of law, 153, 155, 161

Effluent, chemical, as policy example, 40, 57, 63
Eighteenth Brumaire of Louis Bonaparte (Marx), 47
Einstein, Albert, 45, 64, 69
Elite. *See* Ruling group
Emancipatory discourse, 49, 76, 80, 195–196, 200
Emerson, Thomas, 13, 100
England. *See* Great Britain
Eskimos, 36
European Convention on Human Rights, 161, 166
Evans-Pritchard, Edward, 67, 115
Evidence, 168. *See also* Procedure
Experience and Future Discussion Group (Poland), 83, 85, 113
Expression. *See* Answerable expression; Free expression; Speech

244   Index

Fairness, 157–158, 161
Fairness doctrine (U.S.), 138
False consciousness, 47, 200–202
Family resemblance, concept for meaning, 35, 54
Federal Communications Commission, 138
First Amendment, 18, 161. *See also* Free expression; Law; Supreme Court, U.S.
Fitzgerald, Ernest, 161–162
Fodor, Jerry, 180
Foreign ideas, censorship of, 117, 142–143
Foreign policy. *See* United States
Formal operations, in psychology, 56, 58, 69
Formally rational. *See* Rationality
Forums, for discussion, 120, 133, 147
Frames, in psychology, 59, 218. *See also* Scenario; Schema; Script
France: broadcasting in, 134–137; freedom of information in, 131; procedure in, 160, 163, 167
Frankfurt School. *See* Critical theorists
Franks, Jeffrey, 59–60
Free expression: accepted arguments for, 4, 12, 75, 140, 147; democracy and, 4, 7–8, 18, 75; dialogic argument for, 51, 75, 78, 99–122, 128; free trade in ideas, 4, 5–8; Freud and, 199; language and, xii, 13–15, 78; Marxism and, 10–12, 200; media governing boards and, 133–139, 146; minimum program, 143–148; political effects of, 101, 176; procedure, relation to, xiii, 175; socialism and, xii; underdeveloped countries and, 12, 122, 140–147. *See also* First Amendment; Free inquiry; Individualism; Obligation of government
Free inquiry: hermeneutics and, 48–51; modern rationality and, 69

Free market, ideology of, 143
Free trade in ideas, xii, 4, 5–8
Freedom of association, aspect of dialogue rights, 78
Freedom of information: right of, 129–132, 147; statutes, 129, 131
Freud, Sigmund, 195–202
Friendly, Henry, 166

Gadamer, Hans-Georg, 38–40, 72
Gardner, Howard, 180
Gelb, Leslie, 94, 96, 97
Germany, West: broadcasting, 134–138; procedure in, 160, 166
Ghana, 134
Gierek, Edward, 83–84, 112
Gilligan, Carol, 58, 216
Gluckman, Max, 164, 167, 171
Goldberg v. Kelly (U.S. Supreme Court), 162
Gomulka, Wladyslaw, 83–84, 115
Goodale, James, 125
Government. *See* State
Governing boards for media. *See* Free expression
Great Britain: freedom of information in, 131; media, 134–137
Grice, H. P., 36, 38, 209
Guatemala, 91, 231

Habermas, Jürgen, 67, 201
Hanson, Norwood, 45
Hearing, 15, 153, 155–160, 162. *See also* Procedure
Hearsay, evidence concept, 170
Helsinki Accords, 3, 12
Henkin, Louis, 3
Hermeneutics: censorship and, 105; critical, 24, 41, 47, 48, 168; disputes and, 158–163, 168; double hermeneutic, 43, 196, 210; free inquiry and, 48–51; generally, 37–42; political institutions

and, 176; psychology and, 71–72, 168, 193, 198, 200. *See also* Computer; Dialogue; Marxism; Natural science; Social science
Heuristics, 25, 72, 102, 181; natural, 60–66, 68–69. *See also* Anchoring heuristic; Availability heuristic; Representativeness heuristic
History: computers and, 181; and hermeneutics, 41
Holmes, Oliver Wendell (Justice), 5, 7
Hughes, Thomas, 95, 114
Human rights, 16; political issue of, xii, 3–4. *See also* Helsinki Accords; United Nations

Independent Broadcasting Authority (Great Britain), 138
India, 133
Individualism: free expression and, xii, 4–5, 8, 18, 75; relation to dialogue rights, 17, 18, 76, 99, 177, 181; rights and, 177. *See also* Rights, Anglo-American tradition of
Intelligence Oversight Committees (Congressional), 95
Intention, 36, 40, 56, 59
International Program for Development of Communications (UNESCO project), 144
Interpretation: Anglo-American theory, 36, 38, 41; censorship and, 106; citizens' attitude toward, 115; dialogue for, xii, 25, 101; dispute-resolution and, 152–153, 158; interdependent, 24–25, 40, 72; limitations of, xiii, 48, 72, 120; methods, 14, 36, 152, 177; simulation of, 177–178; social practice and, 35. *See also* Decisions; Hermeneutics; Meaning; Problem-solving; Psychology; Thinking; Understanding

Irrational: contrast with rational, 78, 81–98; effects of censorship, 106; in psychology, 195–202

Johnson, Lyndon Baines, 94
Judgment. *See* Heuristics; Interpretation
Judicial Process Among the Barotse of Northern Rhodesia (Gluckman), 167
Jury, as problem-solvers, 62, 69

Kahnemann, David, 62–63
Kalecki, Michael, 85
Katz, Elihu, 135
Kaunda, Kenneth, 12
Kennedy, John, 23, 96, 114; administration of, 90–94, 113
Kenya, 134
Knowledge: language and, 35, 40, 46, 55–56; Marxist approach, 47; relativism, 187–188; scientific, 44–46. *See also* Hermeneutics; Interpretation; Understanding
Kohlberg, Lawrence, 25, 52, 57–59, 216–217
Kovel, Joel, 201

Lacan, Jacques, 196–197
Lakatos, Imre, 45–46
Language: behaviorist theory of, 191–192; child development and, 53–56; computers and, 178; idiosyncratic nature of, 56, 72, 177; language-game, 34; philosophy of, 14, 27–42, 71–72; psychoanalysis and, 196–198; public nature of, 27, 34, 46, 56, 71, 177. *See also* Dialogue; Hermeneutics; Interpretation; Meaning; Problem-solving; Understanding

Language and Cognition (Schaff), 47
Latin America, 142, 158
Law: American constitutional, 109, 133, 153, 163, 166; contrast with fact, 163; free expression and, 119–122, 128, 136, 147, 230; hermeneutics and, 40–41. *See also* Dispute-resolution; Free expression; Procedure; Supreme Court, U.S.; *names of specific doctrines*
Leading, evidence concept, 169
Legitimacy. *See* Authority
Lenje, 164
Liberalism. *See* Rights
Limitations: on participants in discussion, 77, 110–114; on subjects of discussion, 77, 102–110. *See also* Decisions; Disciplines; Interpretation
Lindblom, Charles, 126
Littering, legal concept, 109
Locke, John, 29
Loftus, Elizabeth, 168–169, 218
Logic, 29, 56, 69
Logical empiricism, 31, 33

Magic: dispute resolution and, 152, 159; language and, 15, 17. *See also* Myth
Mail rates, special, 134
Marcuse, Herbert, 71, 221
Marketplace of ideas. *See* Free trade in ideas
Marx, Karl: free expression for, 12; knowledge for, 47. *See also* Marxism
Marxism: dialogue rights and, 13, 195; free expression and, 10–12, 200; hermeneutics and, 46–48
Meaning: categories for problem-solving, 61; child's methods for, 53–56; generally, 6, 28, 35; indeterminacy of, xii–xiii, 24, 187; invariant, 47, 210, 214; J. S. Mill's use of, 6, 207; uncon-

scious, 197. *See also* Correspondence theory; Dialogue; Hermeneutics; Interpretation; Language; Understanding
Media: dominance by West, 140–146; popular, 125–126; power of, 94; state intervention in, 132–140. *See also* Free expression; Newspapers; Radio; Television
Meiklejohn, Alexander, xii, 7, 17
Memory, 168, 217
Mercurio, El. See Chile
Metaphor, 54
Method: behaviorist, 189–192; language and, 14, 25, 38, 60, 72; problem-solving, 14, 60, 181; rights of, 16, 175, 183; scientific, 69. *See also* Decisions; Dialogue; Hermeneutics; Interpretation
Metzler, Jacqueline, 192
Mill, J. S., 5–7, 8, 17, 207
Mind: models of, 193; nature of, 60; rejection by behaviorists, 190
Modern, 67, 78
Modern rationality, 14, 25, 67–70, 78, 115, 152, 220
Modern state, 82, 101, 115
Moral development, 25, 57, 216–217
Multiplex disputes, 164, 171
Murrow, Edward R., 94
Myth, as interpretive framework, 67–68, 115, 116–117, 152, 220. *See also* Magic

Narrative: in cognition, 59, 61; prose, 63
Natural science: hermeneutics and, 44–46; problem-solving in, 64, 69
New World Information and Communication Order (NWICO), 142–143
New York Times, 93, 229

News agencies, international, 141–142, 144, 146
Newspapers, 156, 184; in Africa, 134
Newsprint, as instrument of control, 133, 146
Nicaragua, 103, 226, 231
Non-Aligned News Pool, 144
Notice, procedural right to, 155–158
Nyerere, Julius, 12

Obligation of government, 15, 17, 75–76, 99–102
Oil prices, 127
Ombudsman, 129, 131
On Liberty (J. S. Mill), 5, 107
Open-world, concept in cognitive science, 63–64, 66, 181
Orality, in procedure, 160, 163, 170
Ordeal, trial by, 152, 159
Overinclusive, legal concept, 109, 120

Painting, problem-solving in, 63–64
Pentagon Papers, 94, 96, 130
Peru, 145
Piaget, Jean, 25, 55, 56–58, 66, 69, 215
Planning: Cuban, 89–90; contrast with market, 98; economic, in Poland, 83–86
Poder Popular (Cuban), 89–90
Poland, 15, 81–86, 97, 102, 106, 112, 115, 117; Solidarity in, 81, 82, 84–86, 117
Policy. *See* Decisions
Polish League for Independence, 117
Political speech, special category, 108–109, 119
Politics and Markets. See Lindblom, Charles
Pollis, Adamantia, 12

Pornography, 109
Prejudgments, 38–40, 48–49
Prisoner's Dilemma, 238
Problem-solving: citizens' attitude toward, 115; computers and, 180; language and, xii, 14, 17, 24, 60–66, 99, 148, 151, 175, 181. *See also* Decisions; Hermeneutics; Heuristics; Interpretation
Procedure: adversary, 165–166, 237; Anglo-American, 160, 162, 163, 166–167, 171; medieval, 159; rights of, xiii, 15, 153–154, 168, 175. *See also* Civil law; Courts; Cross-examination; Disciplines; Due process of law; Hearing; Witnesses
Programme Complaints Commission (Great Britain), 138
Psychology: behaviorist, 189–192; cognitive, 14, 24, 52, 151, 168–169, 192; developmental, 53–59; psychoanalytic, 195–202. *See also* Moral development; Thinking
Publicity, of proceedings, 161–162, 164, 170

Quine, Willard, 32–33, 35, 37, 38, 42, 55, 211–212

Radio, 145–146. *See also* Broadcasting; Media; Television
Rationality: bounded, 63; defined, 15, 66–67; formal, 14, 25, 170–177; relation to natural heuristics, 61–62, 72; repressive, 70–71. *See also* Irrational; Modern rationality
Rawls, John, 99
Regularities, in language, 53, 208
Relativism, 51, 187
Representativeness heuristic, 61, 69
Reston, James, 94

Reuters. *See* News agencies
Ricoeur, Paul, 39
Rights: Anglo-American tradition
   of, xii, 4, 8, 11, 16, 18, 99,
   147, 177; civil, 16, 154, 176;
   indeterminacy and, xiii, 76–77;
   natural, 16; universalist argu-
   ment for, xiii, 16. *See also* Access;
   Dialogue; Free expression; Hu-
   man rights; Obligation of gov-
   ernment; Procedure; Socialism
Roberts, Simon, 165
Rule, in language, 208
Ruling group, 111, 113, 115, 118
Rushton, J. P., 189
Russell, Bertrand, 29–30, 36
Russia, rights arguments in, 9, 117

Sandel, Michael, 8
Scanlon, Thomas, 5, 8, 99–100
Scenario, 83, 105, 188. *See* Frames;
   Schema; Script
Schaff, Adam, 47
Schank, Roger, 59–60, 178, 180,
   181
Schema, xiii, 13, 59, 105, 168. *See
   also* Frames; Scenario; Script
Schlesinger, Arthur, Jr., 93, 113
Schwab, Peter, 12
Science. *See* Natural science; Social
   science
Script, 59, 63, 168, 178. *See also*
   Frames; Scenario; Schema
Script Applier Mechanism (SAM),
   59–60, 181
Shepard, Roger, 192
Simon, Herbert, 63
Skinner, B. F., 191–192
Slavery, effect on free thought, 103
Social Contract theory, 99
Social science, hermeneutics and,
   42–44
Socialism: human rights and, 3; ar-
   guments abut free expression,
   xii, 9–12; legal system of, 158.
   See also Marxism
Solidarity. *See* Poland

Sorensen, Theodore, 91
Soviet. *See* Russia
Sparer, Edward, 10–11
Speech: defined for right of expres-
   sion, 100–102, 119; by the
   state, 122, 132–140. *See also*
   Answerable expression; Dialogue;
   Language
State, intervention in communica-
   tions, 132–140. *See also* Authori-
   ty; Modern state
State Department, United States:
   Country Reports on Human
   Rights Practices, 4; Vietnam
   and, 95
Stereotypes, xiii, 59, 66, 68. *See
   also* Heuristics; Scenario; Schema;
   Script
Structuralism, 196
Styles. *See* Disciplines
Supernatural. *See* Magic
Supreme Court, United States: ac-
   cess and, 123–125, 131; public
   media rights and, 136; school
   suspension and, 155; social se-
   curity and welfare and, 157,
   159, 162. *See also* Law; *names of
   specific doctrines*
Sweden, 131
Synthetic knowledge, 31
Szulc, Tad, 93

Tanzania, 132–133
Tarski, Alfred, 211–212
Tax exemption, 132, 146
Television, cable, 126, 229; foreign
   programming, 141; generally
   126; underdeveloped nations
   and, 141. *See also* Broadcasting;
   Media
Texts, understanding, 39
Thibaut, John, 156, 158, 166
Thinking, 178–181. *See also* Prob-
   lem-solving; Psychology
Third world. *See* Underdeveloped
   nations
Tocqueville, Alexis de, 51

Toleration, 121
Totalitarianism, myths of, 116–117
Tractatus Logico-Philosophicus (Wittgenstein), 19–31, 33, 35
Traditional society. *See* Myth
Translation: example of interpretation, 50–51; Quine's usage, 33, 35, 55
Triad, in disputes, 153
Trial: as search for truth, 124; in tribal societies, 154, 164. *See also* Procedure
Trobriand Islands, 164–165, 170
Truth: hermeneutics and, 39–40, 49; J. S. Mill and, 6–7; in natural science, 46; Tarski's theory of, 211; toleration and, 121; trial and, 124. *See also* Correspondence theory
Tswana, 165
Tversky, Amos, 62–63
Two Dogmas of Empiricism (Quine), 32–33

Unconscious, 195–202
Unconscious, The (Freud), 198
UNESCO, 140–146, 233
Underdeveloped nations, free expression and, 12, 122, 140–147
Understanding: child's, 56; contextual, 34, 48, 59; dialogic, 13, 14, 15, 24, 38, 65, 79, 99, 118, 151; generally, 23, 24, 60–62, 177; holistic nature of, 33, 56, 59; implicit, 35, 38, 40, 43, 49; objective, problem of, 47, 51. *See also* Argument; Dialogue; Hermeneutics; Interpretation; Meaning
United Nations, 8; Declaration of Human Rights, 3, 4, 12. *See also* UNESCO
United Press. *See* News agencies
United States: communications policy, 134–138, 145; dominance in media, 141–143; foreign policy, 94–96, 112, 176; human rights policy, 3. *See also* Cuba; Procedure; State Department; Supreme Court, U.S.
Universalist argument. *See* Rights
Universalizable, moral development and, 58, 217
Universals, contrast with relativism, 51. *See also* Meaning

Vagueness, of laws, 109, 120
Vargas Llosa, Mario, 145
Verificationism, 31, 35
Vietnam, 94–95, 114, 176
Volosinov, V. N., 46
Voting, 43–44

Walker, Laurens, 156, 158, 166
War Powers Resolution (U.S.), 95
Watson, John, 189
Weber, Max, 86, 160, 170, 223
Wedell, George, 135
Whitney v. California (U.S. Supreme Court), 100
Wigmore, John, 166
Wildavsky, Aaron, 127
Winograd, Terry, 60, 180
Wire services. *See* News agencies
Witnesses, 166–170. *See also* Cross-examination; Procedure
Wittgenstein, Ludwig, 27, 29–31, 33, 35, 42, 43, 211

Yugoslavia, 10

Zambia, 134, 164
Zimbabwe, Mass Media Trust, 134–135, 145